# Play the Alekhine

## Valentin Bogdanov

*Translated by Serge Marudov*

First published in the UK by Gambit Publications Ltd 2009

ISBN-13: 978-1-906454-15-9
ISBN-10: 1-906454-15-9

DISTRIBUTION:
Worldwide (except USA): Central Books Ltd, 99 Wallis Rd, London E9 5LN, England.
Tel +44 (0)20 8986 4854 Fax +44 (0)20 8533 5821. E-mail: orders@Centralbooks.com

Gambit Publications Ltd, 99 Wallis Rd, London E9 5LN, England.
E-mail: info@gambitbooks.com
Website (regularly updated): www.gambitbooks.com

Edited by Graham Burgess
Typeset by John Nunn
Cover image by Wolff Morrow
Printed in Great Britain by Cromwell Press Group, Trowbridge, Wilts.

10 9 8 7 6 5 4 3 2 1

**Gambit Publications Ltd**
*Managing Director:* Murray Chandler GM
*Chess Director:* Dr John Nunn GM
*Editorial Director:* Graham Burgess FM
*German Editor:* Petra Nunn WFM
*Webmaster:* Dr Helen Milligan WFM

# Contents

# Symbols

| | |
|---|---|
| x | capture |
| + | check |
| ++ | double check |
| # | checkmate |
| !! | brilliant move |
| ! | good move |
| !? | interesting move |
| ?! | dubious move |
| ? | bad move |
| ?? | blunder |
| Ch | championship |
| (n) | nth match game |
| (D) | see next diagram |

## Translator's note

I would like to thank Dr Jorge Chávez for his kind assistance.

*Serge Marudov*

## Editor's note

As author of the books *The Complete Alekhine* and *New Ideas in the Alekhine Defence*, and the Alekhine material in *Nunn's Chess Openings*, I clearly have a close personal connection with the opening covered by Valentin Bogdanov in this book. It was therefore a pleasure to incorporate additional material and games that appeared after the manuscript was submitted for translation, together with some extra references and corrections to standard theory from my own sources.

*Graham Burgess*

# Introduction

This book is devoted to the opening that bears the name of the fourth world champion, Alexander Alekhine. During the period of the reformation of the classical laws of the opening by the 'Hypermoderns', he was the first to use this defence in professional competitions.

The initial position of the Alekhine Defence occurs after 1 e4 ♘f6 *(D)*.

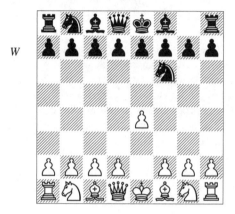

The move looks blatantly provocative; however, it is in full accordance with the innovations of that time when the role of the pawn-centre was being revised. Black invites his opponent to advance with the gain of a tempo, seizing space and building a pawn-centre to suit White's taste – ranging in size from modest to maximal. Black figures that it will be insufficiently supported and that the larger the centre White erects, the more vulnerable it will be.

During the almost century-long history of this provocative defence, numerous attempts have been made at direct refutation, which has suited the defence's proponents just fine – strong action induces counteraction of the same strength. Another White strategy is less comfortable for them psychologically – to be satisfied with a small but lasting advantage, limiting Black's counterplay to the minimum. Nevertheless, the defence lives on, even though it retains the reputation of a difficult and strategically

risky opening. It has been seen in world championship matches and continues to supplement the arsenal of many outstanding players, usually as a reserve choice, or as a surprise weapon. Few high-level players employ it as their main reply to 1 e4. Of these we shall mention grandmasters Lev Alburt and Vladimir Bagirov, and of those active today, Alexander Baburin, while Alexander Shabalov has used it on many occasions. Of the world elite, its more notable 'occasional' users are Nigel Short, Michael Adams, Vasily Ivanchuk, Peter Svidler, Hikaru Nakamura and Magnus Carlsen.

This book is not an encyclopedia of the Alekhine Defence. Instead, the aim is to explain the main ideas behind the opening, in particular in its currently most popular lines and any that have undergone extensive development in recent years. It is also a concise guide to the theory of the most important lines for the reader to know and will help orientate the reader in further study of this fascinating opening. It is highly recommended that the book is used in conjunction with an up-to-date database and a good analytical engine. Of course, the choice of games and variations to feature is a rather subjective matter, but the references used here are largely from the practice of recent years and should give a good feel for the modern Alekhine.

The book is structured as follows:

Chapter 1 examines systems where White refrains from crossing the demarcation line immediately by playing 2 e5. These lines tend to lack a distinctive Alekhine flavour, and in many cases can transpose to other openings. On the other hand, they are not the most critical replies – this is immediately evident when we consider that the most important of them, 2 ♘c3, can be met by 2...e5, reaching a Vienna Game, which is not considered the most testing follow-up to 1 e4 e5.

The Chase Variation, 2 e5 ♘d5 3 c4 ♘b6 4 c5 ♘d5, is the subject of the second chapter.

Here the e- and c-pawns take full advantage of the opportunity to chase the enemy knight. This leads to positions of a unique and sharp type, where White is truly burning his boats.

In Chapter 3 we investigate the most combative set-up, the Four Pawns Attack: 2 e5 ♘d5 3 d4 d6 4 c4 ♘b6 5 f4 (D).

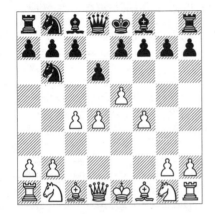

White erects a large pawn-centre in the hope that it will provide cover for an speedy attack, while Black strives to prove that this edifice is insufficiently secure.

The next two chapters are devoted to White's most popular reply to the Alekhine, by which he combines a moderate seizure of space with piece development, normally starting with 2 e5 ♘d5 3 d4 d6 4 ♘f3 (D), which is sometimes called the Modern Variation.

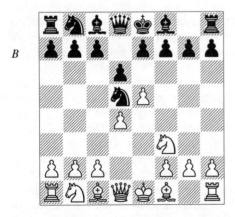

Chapter 4 deals with the traditional main line 4...♗g4, while Chapter 5 examines Black's

4th-move alternatives, most notably 4...dxe5 5 ♘xe5 c6 (D), which can nowadays be regarded as the main line of the whole opening.

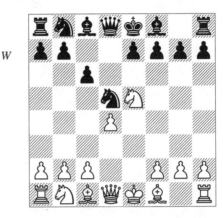

It is very popular in current practice, and its theory is being elaborated at a rapid pace. In this chapter we also take a brief look at White's other piece-developing options on move 4, the most important of which is 4 ♗c4.

The Exchange Variation is the subject of Chapter 6. Here White makes the exchange on d6 himself, considerably limiting both sides' aggressive options and seeking a small but enduring advantage. This line has enjoyed a great deal of popularity in the last decade, particularly due to some sophisticated piece set-ups that seek to stifle Black's counterplay.

Finally, the short seventh chapter deals with all other replies to 2 e5 ♘d5, except 3 d4 and 3 c4; the most important of these is 3 ♘c3 (D).

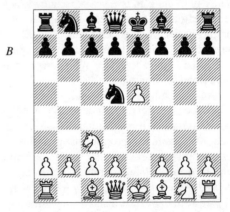

# 1 White Does Not Play 2 e5

It is not easy to explain the reasons that make White reject the obvious 2 e5. Normally when White adopts a sideline, it is based on a desire to reduce the need for opening preparation. However, in the case of 2 ♘c3 (by far the main alternative to 2 e5), White is inviting transpositions to a variety of other major openings, all requiring a certain amount of additional preparation, unless they happen to fit exactly with his existing repertoire. Meanwhile, in the main lines following 2 e5, the choice of variation lies primarily with White, and in many of them the volume of data is smaller than in the lines of this chapter. Nevertheless, in about a quarter of the games played in this opening, the e-pawn isn't tempted into invading the enemy territory.

Building an opening repertoire is a personal matter, and the inclusion of this or that system can be the result of similarity of its ideas to preferred systems in other openings. Conversely,

the motivation can be a desire to deny the opponent the possibility of reaching his favourite positions. In the case of 2 ♘c3, one motivation may be that some Alekhine players tend to react over-aggressively to this quiet move, and get themselves into trouble without White having to take any great risks himself. One should bear this in mind when deciding how to meet this move!

Game 1 (Renner-Konopka) is devoted to the rather dull 2 d3. The rest of the games feature 2 ♘c3 d5, which some sources call the Scandinavian Variation. In Game 2 (J.Fries Nielsen-Sandström) the likeness to the Scandinavian Defence is most apparent, as White exchanges pawns on d5. In Games 3 (Zezulkin-Seils), 4 (Predojević-Mrkonjić) and 5 (Petr-M.Grünberg) White instead plays 3 e5, and Black's reaction (3...d4, 3...♘e4 and 3...♘fd7 respectively) defines three distinct main lines.

## Game 1
## Christoph Renner – Michal Konopka
### *Austrian Team Ch 2003/4*

**1 e4 ♘f6 2 d3** *(D)*

If the pawn is not to advance, it has to be defended. Out of the multitude of possible defences, only two are more or less in accordance with the principles of opening play (the other being 2 ♘c3, covered in Games 2-5). Such play does not aim at refuting Black's opening move. White voluntarily blocks the bishop's diagonal and intends to steer the game into quiet systems of other openings.

We cannot recommend 2 ♗c4?!. This is not a pawn sacrifice as the pawn is promptly regained after 2...♘xe4 3 ♗xf7+ ♔xf7 4 ♕h5+ g6 (4...♔g8 is good as well) 5 ♕d5+, but Black's pawn preponderance in the centre and advantage in development are more significant factors than

his loss of castling rights. In the coming struggle, Black will be the more active side.

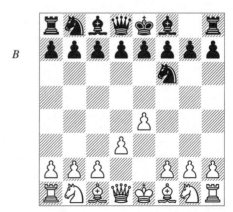

**2...e5**

Those who wish to transpose into acceptable lines of the Sicilian or Pirc Defence can do so with 2...c5, 2...g6 or 2...d6, but the main alternative to the text-move is 2...d5.

Then White can seek the same set-as in the main game by playing 3 ᐞd2. Often Black agrees to that and chooses 3...e5 or 3...ᐞc6, but there is also the option of carrying out ...c5 and ...ᐞc6 first, and then choosing a set-up depending on White's actions: this can be a subsequent ...e6 with transposition into a closed form of the French Defence or else, should a knight appear on f3, posting the potentially 'bad' bishop to g4 while the diagonal is still open.

French themes are also evident in the case of the pawn advancing: 3 e5 ᐞfd7 (D).

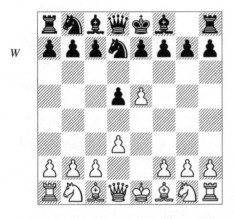

*W*

Now it has to be supported by one of its neighbours. 4 f4 initiates the more original play; then White has several options in setting up the queenside pawns – c4+d3, c3+d3 or nevertheless d4. We should mention the dark side of this decision: if the foot-soldier on f4 ends up blockaded or stuck in some other way, it will annoy the dark-squared bishop; moreover, in such 'French' set-ups this square is often useful for knight manoeuvres. If 4 d4 is chosen, Black can consider himself a tempo up because the pawn has spent two moves on this advance, but in closed positions that is not so important. Here too, the c8-bishop's diagonal remains potentially open, although at the moment it is blocked by a knight that may have trouble finding gainful employment should it be transferred to b6.

**3 ᐞf3**

Now White has a reversed Philidor Defence. This position can also arise from the Petroff, if White plays the insipid 3 d3 (after 1 e4 e5 2 ᐞf3 ᐞf6).

In similar positions Philidor himself, a great proponent of pawn play, recommended 3 f4 (D).

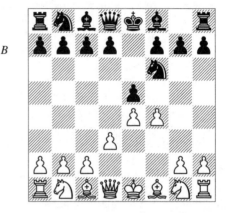

*B*

This move is topical to this day. It is based on a plausible idea – exchanging a flank pawn for a central one. However, pawn advances in the opening can often be detrimental to development; in this case the king's cover is weakened as well. Black can go for the pawn sacrifice played by Alekhine: 3...ᐞc6 4 ᐞf3 d5 (this might be dubious, with 4...exf4 followed by ...d5 deserving preference) 5 exd5 (better than 5 fxe5 dxe4, when Black is at least equal) 5...ᐞxd5 6 fxe5 ♗g4 7 ♗e2. Now Black can regain the pawn immediately with 7...♗xf3 8 ♗xf3 ♕h4+ 9 g3 ♕d4 10 c3 ♕xe5+ 11 ♕e2, leaving White with the hope of some advantage due to the bishop-pair, or, in order to intensify the threat, play 7...♗c5 first. Also not bad is 3...exf4 4 ♗xf4 ᐞc6, leaving ...d5 in reserve for a little while.

**3...ᐞc6**

The main difference between the positions of the two armies lies in the fact that White has played d3 (which postpones the light-squared bishop's aggressive ambitions to a distant future) while Black has played ...ᐞc6. According to opening principles, this difference benefits Black, and even though it is White's turn to move, it is logical to suppose that his claim to an opening advantage has been sharply reduced.

**4 c3** (D)

The fianchetto of the king's bishop is not an uncommon sight either. This universal method of development for White is popular, for example, in the Closed Sicilian, but the difference lies in the black army's disposition. Here there is a black pawn on e5, and his development is extremely rapid; the rest of the black forces can be deployed in schemes including either ...d6 or ...d5. As one example we shall give the opening of Lukin-Makarychev, Pavlodar 1987: 4 g3 d5 5 exd5 ♘xd5 6 ♗g2 ♘de7 7 0-0 g6 8 ♘bd2 ♗g7 9 ♖e1 0-0 10 ♘c4 f6 11 b3 ♖e8 12 ♗b2 ♘f5 13 c3 ♘d6 14 d4 ♘xc4 15 bxc4 ♘a5 16 ♕a4 c5 17 dxe5 ♗d7 and Black seized the initiative.

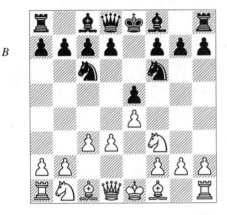

B

This position is more commonly reached via a different move-order, and can be classified as belonging to the Ponziani Opening (1 e4 e5 2 ♘f3 ♘c6 3 c3). The classical set-up implies a series of moves consisting of c3, ♗e2, 0-0 and ♘bd2 in some order.

**4...d5**

White's modest treatment of the opening leaves Black an ample choice of replies, but that does not mean that he can easily seize the initiative. White plans to carry out d4, when Black must constantly calculate a variety of scenarios that the events in the centre may follow. If Black is content with that, he can choose 4...♗e7 or 4...g6. With the text-move, Black above all is the first to determine the pawn-structure, without waiting for White to prepare d4. The most likely subsequent scenario involves an exchange on e4. It would be naïve to hope for White to take on d5 too soon, granting Black the greater freedom in deploying his

forces; meanwhile, as the pieces develop, Black will find it harder and harder to coordinate the simultaneous defence of both the d5- and the e5-pawns.

**5 ♘bd2 a5**

The bishop's post on c5 has to be secured first; otherwise the white b-pawn's sprint, with tempo, to b5 would have tragic consequences for its black counterpart on e5.

**6 ♗e2 ♗c5 7 0-0 dxe4**

This move is playable but far from forced, as it activates the e2-bishop and relinquishes control of c4. To complete his development, White usually brings his queen's bishop out to b2, and waiting until he does so before contemplating concrete action is an attractive idea; for example, 7...0-0 8 b3 ♖e8 9 a3 b6 10 ♗b2 ♗b7 11 b4 ♗d6 12 ♖e1 ♘e7 13 ♗f1 ♘g6 14 ♕c2 c5 15 bxa5 ♖xa5 16 exd5 ♘xd5 17 ♘c4 ♖a8 18 d4 ♘df4 with lively play, Jovanović-Brenjo, Serbian Team Ch, Zlatibor 2007. It is possible that Black wanted to avoid the simplifications after 7...0-0 8 ♘xe5 ♘xe5 9 d4 ♗b6 10 dxe5 ♘xe4.

**8 dxe4 0-0** *(D)*

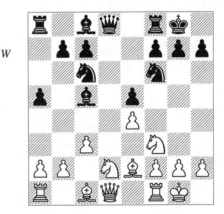

W

**9 a3**

White is not afraid of the blockading 9...a4 because he has 10 ♗b5, so he prepares to push the pawn to b4 in one move.

White has comfortable development with 9 ♕c2, when the knight will start eyeing, after ♘c4-e3, the d5- and f5-squares. Black has no particular problems, and at first sight his pieces appear to be the more active, but it is not as easy for him as for his opponent to find an obvious plan of concrete immediate action, while excessive placidity and planless play have ruined many a game.

**9...♕e7 10 ♖b1 ♗g4 (D)**

Black has no shortage of good squares, and he is not cramped, so he has no reason to strive for simplifications. This raid by the bishop aims not for an exchange but to provoke h3, which, considering the planned transfer of a knight to f4, would be good for Black. 10...♖d8 11 ♕c2 a4 looks even more tempting, as now in reply to 12 ♗b5 there is already 12...♘g4 threatening 13...♗xf2+.

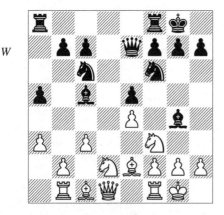

**11 b4 axb4 12 axb4 ♗a7**

After 12...♗b6, the bishop will in a move or two come under attack by ♘c4.

**13 h3 ♗d7**

13...♗h5 deserves attention, as 14 ♘h4 can be countered with 14...♘xe4; however, Black leaves this square empty for a different manoeuvre.

**14 ♗b2**

As has already been mentioned, the standard regrouping in such positions is typically initiated by the queen's move to c2, which relieves the knight from the defence of the e4-pawn and prepares its transfer along the c4-e3 route. The bishop's development to b2 looks logical as well: the queenside pawns' further advance cannot be prevented, while control of the d4-square is retained.

**14...♘h5 (D)**

White takes aim at the e5-pawn. 14...♘e8?! in order to prepare ...f6 is too passive: after 15 b5 the other knight will have to retreat to the back rank as well, as 15...♘a5? runs into the unpleasant 16 c4 f6 17 ♗c3. The indirect defence by

14...♖fd8 15 b5 ♘a5 16 c4 ♗e8 (or 16...♗e6), counterattacking e4, is possible, but Black preferred to go for a tempting pawn sacrifice.

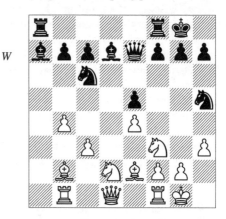

**15 b5**

The immediate capture is bad (15 ♘xe5? ♘xe5 16 ♗xh5 ♗a4), but White might consider 15 ♖a1.

**15...♘a5 16 ♘xe5 ♘g3**

Alternatively, 16...♕xe5 17 ♗xh5 was worth considering, when Black can force a draw by 17...♗xh3 18 gxh3 ♕g3+, or aim for more by 17...♖fd8, with complex play.

**17 ♘xd7 ♕xd7 18 ♖e1 (D)**

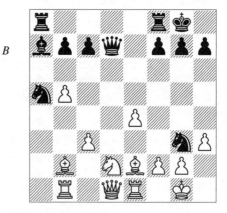

**18...♖ad8?!**

This may be a case of 'the wrong rook', because after 18...♖fd8 19 ♘f3 ♘xe4 20 ♘d4 ♘xc3 21 ♗xc3 ♖xd4, the a8-rook turns out to be performing the useful function of defending the otherwise loose knight on a5. The game would then be roughly balanced.

**19 ♗c1?!**

White would have done better to return the extra pawn with 19 ♘f3 ♘xe4 20 ♘d4. Now 20...♘xc3?! is dubious in view of 21 ♗xc3 ♗xd4 22 ♗xa5 ♗xf2+ 23 ♔xf2 ♕f5+ 24 ♔g1, when White gets too much material for the queen, whereas after 20...c5 21 bxc6 ♘xc6 22 ♗g4 ♕d5 23 ♕f3 White's bishop-pair secures him a modest advantage.

**19...♕d6** *(D)*

**20 ♖a1??**

A terrible move. Tempted by the prospect of winning a piece, White fails to see a textbook mate. There is approximate equality after 20 ♗f1, clearing the road to f3 for the queen; in that case Black can force an immediate draw by 20...♗xf2+ 21 ♔xf2 f5 22 exf5 (22 e5 ♘e4+) 22...♖xf5+ 23 ♔g1 ♕c5+ 24 ♔h2 ♕d6 25 ♔g1. Playing 20 ♗g4?! with the same goal is not as good because of 20...h5.

**20...♕b6 21 ♔h2 ♕xf2 22 ♖xa5**

It is clear that after 22 ♖f1 ♘xf1+ 23 ♕xf1 ♕xf1 24 ♘xf1 ♗b6 Black should have no great

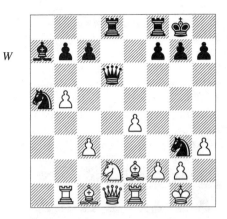

W

trouble bringing the a5-knight back into play, and his extra exchange will secure him the victory.

**22...♗b6 23 ♖a2 ♕f4**

There is no defence against the smothered mate.

**24 ♘f3 ♘f1++ 25 ♔h1 ♕h2+ 26 ♘xh2 ♘g3# (0-1)**

## Game 2
# Jens Ove Fries Nielsen – Ludvig Sandström
### *Stockholm 2002*

**1 e4 ♘f6 2 ♘c3** *(D)*

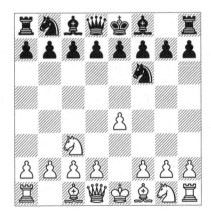

B

This is the main and most natural way of refraining from the immediate advance of the e-pawn. White deprives the enemy knight of the d5-square, and so the threat of e5 gains in strength. Black's reply must take this into account.

**2...d5**

2...e5 (Vienna) and 2...d6 (Pirc) transpose to openings that lie outside our scope, and the position after 2...e6 3 e5 (3 d4 again leads to other openings, most likely a French) 3...♘d5 will be briefly examined in Game 25, via the move-order 2 e5 ♘d5 3 ♘c3 e6.

Let's have a look at the continuation 2...♘c6 3 d4 d5 4 e5 ♘d7. Now 5 ♘xd5 ♘db8 6 ♘e3 ♕xd4 7 ♕xd4 ♘xd4 promises White a more pleasant middlegame, as the transfer of the knight from g8 to b8, in addition to the loss of time, has somewhat cramped Black's queenside. White can also hope for an advantage after 5 ♘f3: the position is similar to a French Defence line that doesn't enjoy a particularly good reputation; moreover, the difference in the position of the queen's knight (on c3 instead of d2) can only improve White's mood. Black has some consolation in the fact that the c8-h3 diagonal is still open and the light-squared bishop can be brought out after 5...♘b6, but the price is a further loss of time and the knight's ineffective posting.

**3 exd5**

This transposes to a line that can also be claimed by the Scandinavian Defence (1 e4 d5 2 exd5 ♘f6 3 ♘c3), but according to the standard opening classification it belongs to our opening. For 3 e5, see Games 3-5.

**3...♘xd5** *(D)*

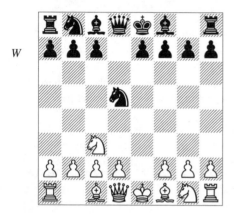

**4 ♗c4**

An obvious move, creating concrete threats. 4 d4 and 4 ♘f3 leave Black with a wider choice of replies.

**4...♘b6**

Let's consider the alternatives in increasing order of popularity:

a) 4...♗e6 is a pretentious move that may cause White to search for an immediate refutation, and this can result in him wasting time to little effect. It is more sensible to settle for a small but clear and stable edge after 5 ♕f3 c6 6 ♘ge2 ♘c7 7 ♗xe6 ♘xe6. Then White has the better development, and in reply to an attempt to bring out the bishop to g7, queenside castling followed by a kingside pawn-storm looks good.

b) 4...♘xc3 is fully playable. The most accurate continuation for White is considered to be 5 ♕f3 e6 6 ♕xc3: he has provoked ...e6, which blocks the c8-bishop, and kept his pawn-chain intact. However, the queen's position on c3, in front of its own infantry, is not without its drawbacks. The pawn-structure after the more straightforward 5 bxc3 can be seen in many openings, and the doubled pawns are compensated by the appearance of a half-open b-file. In both cases, White enjoys a little more freedom,

and Black must carefully watch that this freedom doesn't transform into a vigorous attack on the black king.

c) After 4...e6 the play will usually transpose to lines considered via 4...♘xc3 or 4...♘b6. White can try to grab a pawn by 5 ♗xd5?! exd5 6 ♕e2+, but this is a highly dubious venture; e.g., 6...♗e6 7 ♕b5+ ♘c6 8 ♕xb7 ♘b4 9 ♕b5+ (or 9 ♘b5 ♖c8 10 ♘d4 c6 11 ♕xa7 ♗d7!) 9...c6! 10 ♕a4 ♗d7!.

d) 4...c6 *(D)*.

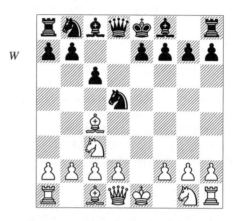

Together with the text-move, this continuation is the one seen most often today. One reason for this decision is immediately obvious: it bolsters the knight without blocking the light-squared bishop's diagonal. However, White can throw yet another unit into the attack on d5 by 5 ♕f3, when Black must either move the knight or acquiesce to moving the e-pawn after all. If the knight beats the retreat by 5...♘f6, the c8-bishop will be hobbled by 6 h3, leaving it to face the same problems. Usually Black is satisfied with provoking the enemy queen's sortie to f3, depriving its own knight of its best post, and strengthens the central position of his stallion by 5...e6. The position of the c6-pawn is not final, and it hopes to advance, freeing the passive bishop, and in some cases it can support a diversionary operation on the queenside; for example, 6 ♘ge2 ♘d7 7 d4 ♘7f6 8 ♗d2 ♗e7 9 0-0-0 ♕c7 10 g4 b5 11 ♗d3 ♗b7 12 g5 ♘xc3 13 ♘xc3 c5 14 ♗xb5+ ♔f8 15 ♕h3 ♘d5 with sharp play, Nanu-Abdelnabbi, Tanta 2003.

**5 ♗b3 ♘c6**

The main rival to the text-move is the preliminary 5...c5 *(D)*.

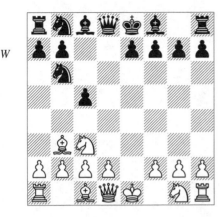

W

This move stakes out control of d4, and there is also a blatant threat of ...c4, against which there are two defences. 6 ♕h5 is a tactical one, with the same goal of forcing 6...e6, when White will subsequently strive to exchange the dark-squared bishops after 7 d3, and should Black allow it by 7...♘c6 8 ♗g5 ♗e7, the weakness of the d6-square and the c5-pawn becomes perceptible. However, Black can play 7...♗e7 first, avoiding the exchange. Besides that, there is the tempting pawn sacrifice 6...c4 7 ♗xc4 ♘xc4 8 ♕b5+ and now 8...♘c6 9 ♕xc4 e5 or 8...♗d7 9 ♕xc4 ♗c6.

The second defence is 6 d3. If Black plays ...♘d4 and White exchanges it off, then the c-file will be open and the pawn-structure will favour Black. In reply, White will seek chances in a kingside attack.

**6 ♘f3 (D)**

Here too, White can restrict Black's queen's bishop by 6 ♕f3, controlling f5, but after 6...e6 the white bishop on b3 cannot be called active either.

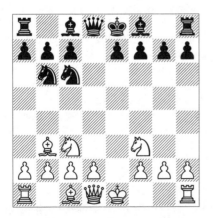

B

**6...♗f5**

The g4-square is mined: 6...♗g4?? is met with the standard blow on f7, but this more modest development is OK for Black.

We should mention 6...g6 as deserving attention; for example, the knight thrust 7 ♘g5 brings no dividends: 7...e6 8 d3 ♗g7 9 h4 h6 10 ♘f3 e5, N.Rogers-Shabalov, US Open, Cherry Hill 2007. Black has harmonious development and the better control of the centre.

6...e5?! is another attempt to secure control over d4, but it is risky, as it opens a diagonal for the b3-bishop. After 7 d3, 7...♗g4?! 8 h3 ♗h5? 9 ♘xe5!! gives White a successful version of Legall's trap, while 7...♗e7 can be met with the standard 8 ♘g5.

**7 d4**

White has to make a resolution on two points: what to do with the d-pawn and whether he should plan to advance the a-pawn in the immediate future. The purpose of this raid is not so much to chase the enemy knight about or to weaken his pawn-structure – Black cannot allow the pawn to reach a6 – as to secure the bishop's retreat in case of ...♘a5. Whether White should safeguard this bishop against exchange is a matter of taste, considering that this exchange costs Black time and opens the a-file for White. As development nears completion, the motivation to keep the bishop-pair will grow stronger, and all the same White will have to decide whether to prevent the exchange after all, and if so, when. 7 a4 can be played already, when 7...a5 is the most natural reaction. As for the d-pawn, the modest advance to d3 lays no claim to an advantage, while on d4 the pawn itself will become the centrepiece of the conflict.

**7...e6 8 a4**

White decides to determine the position of the a-pawns at a moment when this change in the pawn-structure somewhat loosens the b4- and b5-squares.

**8...a5 (D)**

Now the security of the d4-pawn has to be provided for. The events in the centre may develop as follows: for the assault on the pawn Black can bring out the bishop to f6 and try to liquidate one of its defenders, the f3-knight. Ideally, White would like to cement the centre with c3, but the c3-knight has no convenient square to move to at the moment: after ♘e2, the

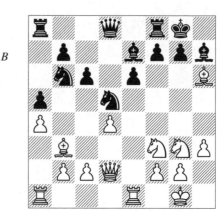

move ...♗g4 would gain in strength, so any re-arrangement of the forces has to be combined with prophylaxis. Of course, the problem can be solved radically with the advance to d5, but the ensuing simplifications lead to equality; only if White succeeds in parrying Black's threat while keeping an active pawn in the centre can he hope for any advantage.

**9 0-0 ♗e7 10 h3?!**

Not mandatory at the moment. 10 ♗f4 seems better, when 10...♗f6 can be met by 11 ♘b5, when after 11...♖c8, in order to expel the knight from b5 Black will have to regain control over d6. That's why in the game Fedorov-Varga, Romanian Team Ch, Timisu de Sus 1998, Black abandoned the idea of pressurizing the d4-pawn and chose the same transfer as in this game of the knight to d5: 10...♘b4 11 ♖e1 0-0 12 ♘e4 ♘4d5 13 ♗g3.

**10...0-0 11 ♗f4 ♘b4 12 ♖e1 c6?!**

Black in his turn misses the opportunity to simplify the position and force White to determine the position of his pieces with 12...♘4d5.

**13 ♘e4 h6**

Now this move provokes a sacrifice that is unclear but dangerous.

**14 ♘g3 ♗h7 15 ♕d2 ♘4d5 16 ♗xh6** *(D)*

Calculating all the variations at the board is hardly possible; while the black king has a lot of defenders, White already has two pawns for the piece, and attacking is usually more fun than defending.

**16...gxh6 17 ♕xh6 ♖e8**

White was threatening ♘h5. Besides the text-move, there are two other continuations: 17...♗f6?! can hardly be recommended since 18 ♘h5 ♗g6 19 c4 gives White a dangerous attack

after both 19...♗xh5 20 cxd5 ♗g6 (20...♗xf3 21 ♗c2) 21 dxe6 ♘d5 22 exf7+ ♔xf7 23 ♘e5+ and 19...♘b4 20 ♖xe6 fxe6 (or 20...♗xh5 21 ♖xf6 ♗g6 22 ♖f4) 21 ♕xg6+ ♔h8 22 ♕h6+ ♔g8 23 ♖e1. Perhaps the strongest move is 17...♔h8, vacating the g8-square for the rook.

**18 ♖e5 ♗f8**

Black could also try 18...♗g6!?, meeting 19 ♖xe6 by 19...♗f6.

**19 ♖g5+ ♔h8 20 ♘e5 ♖e7 21 ♕h4 ♘d7?**

This is a mistake. Control of f6 should have been secured by 21...♖c7, which also relocates the rook to a safer post, when the line 22 c4 ♘b4 23 ♘h5 ♗h6 24 ♘f6 ♕xf6 25 ♖g8+ ♔xg8 26 ♕xf6 ♗g7 would hardly scare Black. Given that Black is somewhat tied up, White can perhaps play more slowly, with moves like 22 c3 (threatening ♗c2) 22...♗g7 23 ♖e1 ♔g8 24 ♕g4.

**22 ♖h5?**

It is hard to explain this move: White simply presents Black with the gift of two tempi and allows him to rearrange his forces. There were several enticing continuations: while 22 ♗xd5 ♘xe5 (or 22...exd5 23 ♖h5 f6 24 ♘g6+ ♔g8 25 ♘xe7+ ♕xe7 26 ♕g4+) 23 ♖h5?! (White should prefer 23 dxe5 exd5 24 ♖h5 f6 25 exf6 ♖f7, when Black is trying to hang on by his fingertips) 23...♘g6 (23...f6 and 23...f5 are both met by 24 ♗xe6) 24 ♖xh7+ ♔g8 25 ♘e4 ♗g7 26 ♖xg7+ ♔xg7 27 ♕f6+ leaves Black with some defensive chances, 22 ♘e4! appears decisive.

**22...♘5f6!**

It looks like White only considered the move by the other knight, i.e. 22...♘7f6?, when 23 ♗xd5 wins. Now he has to beat a retreat, giving

Black the task of finding a way of taking advantage of this gift.

**23 ♖g5 ♗g7 24 c3**

White can try 24 ♗c4!? with similar ideas, though Black can then reply 24...♕f8 25 ♘xd7 ♖xd7, given that the loose d4-pawn is significant in the line 26 ♘h5 ♘xh5 (or 26...♖xd4!?) 27 ♖xh5 ♖xd4.

**24...♕f8?!** *(D)*

Not the best decision. Redeployment with 24...♘f8 25 ♗c2 ♖c7 looks the most convincing, while 24...♔g8 also gives Black winning chances. The attempt to gain counterplay by 24...♕b6 is unconvincing after the cold-blooded 25 ♖a3.

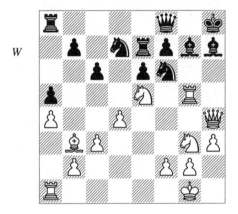

W

**25 ♘xd7 ♖xd7?**

The second and final losing move. After the correct 25...♘xd7 26 ♖e1 ♖ee8 it is hard to see a plan to strengthen the position of either side. If White plays ♗c2, this takes the pressure off the e6-pawn and allows ...f5, while playing ♘h5 denies the rook that square and makes ...♗h6 possible. On the other hand, Black can place on f6 neither bishop, because of ♗c2, nor the knight, which is met, as in the game, with ♘h5, while preparing ...c5 makes little sense, as it runs into d5, and Black cannot afford to give up the f5-square.

**26 ♘h5!**

Decisive. Now 26...♘e8 is met with 27 ♖xg7 ♘xg7 28 ♘f6.

**26...♘xh5 27 ♖xh5 ♕g8 28 ♖e1**

White outlines the following plan of attack: the second rook goes to g3, immobilizing the enemy queen and bishops, ♗c2 forces the reply ...f5, the rook goes from g3 to g5 and no defence against the capture on h7 is apparent. White gets a queen and two pawns, and his opponent two rooks and a 'bad' king. There is little Black can do to prevent this.

**28...♗f8 29 ♖g5 ♗g7 30 ♖e3 ♕d8**

Not wishing to wait for White to demonstrate the winning plan, Black ends the game at once, rather than prolong his suffering during the technical stage.

**31 ♗c2 f5 32 ♖xe6 ♗f6 33 ♖xf6 ♕xf6 34 ♖g8+ ♔xg8 35 ♕xf6 1-0**

## Game 3
# Yuri Zezulkin – Joerg Seils
## *2nd Bundesliga 2003/4*

**1 e4 ♘f6 2 ♘c3 d5 3 e5** *(D)*

A more ambitious continuation than the capture on d5: White crosses no man's land and lays claim to a space advantage. Several paths are available to Black: the first (3...♘e4 – Game 4) leads forward, and the second (3...♘fd7 – Game 5) back.

**3...d4**

And the third is based on a counterattack. Similar lines can be found in other openings as well, such as the Flohr-Mikenas Attack in the English Opening.

**4 exf6**

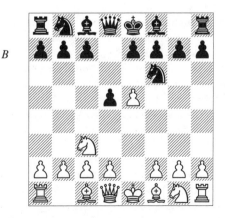

B

4 ♘ce2 *(D)* is another option.

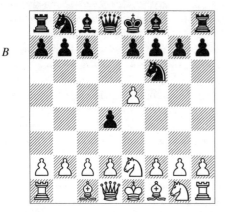

B

Taking advantage of the fact that the d5-square is not available to the knight due to the loss of a pawn and that 4...♘fd7 allows 5 e6, White allows Black just three options. We shall examine 4...♘e4 in the notes to the next game, which leaves us just one knight move, 4...♘g4, to consider here. After the obligatory reply 5 f4, Black usually doesn't mind spending a tempo on 5...h5 to secure a decent future for the knight, which would risk finding itself out on the rim should White have enough time to carry out h3 and g4. After 6 ♘f3 c5 we get a diagonally symmetrical pawn-formation. White will find it difficult to claim an advantage; for example, 7 h3 ♘h6 8 ♘g3 ♘f5 9 ♗b5+ ♘c6 10 ♘xf5 ♗xf5 11 ♗xc6+ bxc6 12 ♘h4 g6 13 d3 ♕d5, Krstić-Khaetsky, Croatian Team Ch, Šibenik 2007.

The third option is the pawn sacrifice 4...d3, hampering White's development. Its acceptance suits Black just fine, while 5 exf6 dxe2 is less pleasant. Now 6 ♕xe2 forces 6...gxf6, but even with other captures on e2, recapturing with the g-pawn leads to a more interesting game than the passive 6...exf6, as there is no reason why the resulting positions should be worse for Black than the similar lines in the French or the Caro-Kann. We should also mention the alternative 5 ♘f4 dxc2 6 ♕f3, depriving the f6-knight of the d5-square. Black has to choose between 6...♘fd7 7 e6 ♘e5 (or 7...♘f6) or the even sharper 6...g5. The resulting positions have rarely been seen in practice, and haven't earned a final evaluation and deserve further testing.

**4...dxc3 5 fxg7**

Now 5 bxc3 exf6 promises little for White. The typical drawback to this type of pawn-formation with doubled f-/c-pawns is that the opponent has an extra pawn on the opposite flank, which can prove a potent asset in an endgame. There is such a pawn in this case too, but in a devalued form, as turning it into a passed pawn is beset with problems, while the slight superiority in the centre is offset by the increased solidity of Black's kingside. Those who are after a greater asymmetry may prefer 5...gxf6. Quite insipid is 5 fxe7.

**5...cxd2+** *(D)*

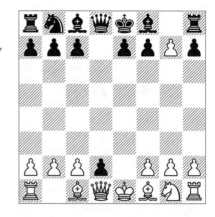

W

White's minimal advantage is due to his better pawn-structure, since Black has more pawn-islands and may find it risky to castle kingside. In the case of the queen exchange 6 ♕xd2 ♕xd2+ 7 ♗xd2 ♗xg7 8 0-0-0 White manages to defend b2 by natural means, but the vulnerability of Black's kingside is less pronounced, there are no 'bad' pieces on the board, and Black's defensive resources secure this line a high drawing probability. There is more than one sensible plan of development; we shall give the opening of the game Shabanov-Rozentalis, Ashdod 2003 as an example: 8...♘c6 9 ♘f3 ♗g4 10 ♗e2 0-0-0 11 ♖he1 ♗f6 12 h3 ♗e6. This treatment of the opening is in accordance with the principle "less is more, as long as the opponent has no counterplay" and this approach has an increasing number of followers in today's chess. Those who prefer a sharper struggle will choose to keep the queens on the board.

**6 ♗xd2 ♗xg7 7 ♕f3**

White must be willing to sacrifice a pawn, as 7 c3 is too sluggish and weakens important squares and diagonals. The natural developing moves 7 ♗d3, 7 ♗c4 and 7 ♘f3 have been tested, but it is two queen thrusts that are the most popular.

7 ♕h5 is outwardly more aggressive than the text-move, but allows 7...♕d4 in reply. This is not as much a desire to exchange the queens at any cost as an attempt to hamper White's smooth development. For instance, after 8 c3, Black does not intend 8...♕e5+?!, when White will earn an extra tempo attacking the bishop when it comes to e5, but rather 8...♕e4+. The sacrifice of the b2-pawn (and perhaps of its neighbour on c2) after 8 ♘f3 looks tempting but is double-edged. Refusing the gift is risky: 8...♕e4+?! 9 ♗e2 and 9...♗g4? is bad because of 10 ♕xf7+.

We now return to 7 ♕f3 *(D)*:

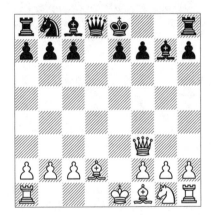

This move looks more modest, but the queen enjoys greater freedom and is more effective here.

**7...♕d6**

If Black goes for the critical pawn capture 7...♗xb2, then after the obvious 8 ♖d1 he needs to take precautions against discovered attacks such as ♗c1. Covering the queen by placing a piece on d7 is too cramping, so the queen must come out. The sortie can be initiated with 8...♕d4, for the moment not allowing White's light-squared bishop to develop to c4 and threatening the leap of Black's own bishop to g4. Alternatively, Black can pick 8...♕d6, with a possible transfer to g6. In either case, White has ample compensation for the pawn.

Even if Black decides not to get too greedy, he still has to prepare for the coming opposition of the white rook and his queen. The latter has to come out, if only to clear the way for castling queenside. The threat is still one move away, and Black sometimes uses this respite to play 7...♘c6, hoping that he will gradually consolidate his position in the line 8 0-0-0 ♕d6 9 ♗c3 ♕h6+. We should make a note of 8 ♗b5 ♕d6 9 ♗c3 (if Black succeeds in keeping the bishop-pair, he is ready to enter the endgame even with his queenside pawn-structure spoiled as well, so it is desirable both to break up the pawns and to exchange the bishops off) 9...0-0 10 ♗xc6 ♗xc3+ 11 ♕xc3 bxc6 12 ♘e2 ♗a6 13 ♖d1 ♕e6 14 ♕e3 ♕xe3 15 fxe3 ♖fd8 16 ♖xd8+ ♖xd8 17 ♖f1, planning a rook-lift to the fourth rank in order to probe the weaknesses, Hector-Kengis, Haninge 1992.

We now return to 7...♕d6 *(D)*:

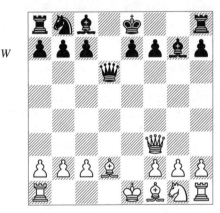

Moving the queen immediately gives Black a greater freedom of action.

**8 ♗c3**

In reply to 8 0-0-0, Black can pester the enemy queen with offers to exchange, starting with 8...♕f6, which the text-move prevents. We should also mention 8 ♗c4, when Black usually chooses 8...0-0 as the least of the evils.

**8...♗xc3+**

Even though it looks overly optimistic, 8...e5 deserves some testing. It seems that the knight can make it to d4 in time, which blocks the d-file and should give Black some counterplay.

**9 ♕xc3 ♖g8 10 ♗d3 ♕c6**

This is the move Black, persistent in his desire to exchange the queens, was counting on.

**11 ♕d2** *(D)*

Given White's development advantage, he could now have sought to profit from an exchange of queens by 11 ♘e2!? ♕xc3+ 12 ♘xc3. Then Black's worries about meeting the threat to the c7-pawn may permit White to exchange his unit on g2 for the enemy's counterpart on h7, and in the resulting situation the newly-passed h-pawn could prove dangerous.

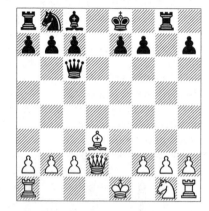

**11...♕xg2**

Consistent but not mandatory. Black can instead complete his development harmoniously by 11...♗e6!?. If White goes in for the win of a pawn by 12 f3?! ♘d7 (or 12...♘a6!?) 13 ♗xh7 ♖h8 14 ♗e4 ♕b6 15 0-0-0 0-0-0, then the development advantage now swings to Black, and threats like ...♘c5, ...♘f6 and ...♗xa2 promise him full compensation.

**12 0-0-0 ♘c6 13 ♘e2 ♕g5?!**

A fundamentally incorrect decision. In positions where you cannot calculate all the variations, pawns should be taken if you cannot see a definite refutation. After 13...♕xf2 14 ♖hg1 ♖xg1 15 ♖xg1 e5 the black king doesn't mind a walk all the way up to c5; it will be difficult for the two remaining white pieces to maintain simultaneous control of both the d- and the g-files.

**14 f4 ♕c5?** *(D)*

This seems to be the decisive mistake. The queen should have stayed on the kingside by 14...♕h5 in order to make the black king's life easier, as he has the prospect of taking part in the struggle for the g-file with ...♔f8, or else choose the tempo-gaining 14...♕a5, although in both cases the advantage is with White.

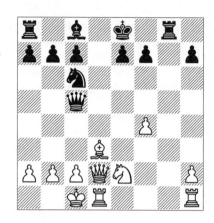

**15 ♖hg1 ♖f8?!**

If Black had seen how little time he had left, he would have probably preferred to seek some chances after 15...♖xg1 16 ♖xg1 f5.

**16 ♖g5 f5**

No better is 16...♕d6 17 ♘c3 with the threats of 18 ♖d5 and 18 ♘b5; for example, 17...♘b4 18 ♘b5 ♘xd3+ 19 ♕xd3 ♕xf4+ 20 ♔b1 ♗e6 21 ♕e4 and c7 cannot be defended.

**17 ♗e4** *(D)*

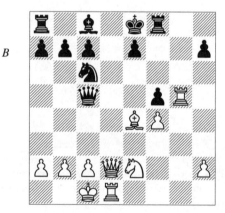

Bringing up the last reserves. The bishop not only attacks the defender on c6 but also gets ready to work the weakened diagonal from h5.

**17...h6?**

Black now loses nice and quickly, but even 17...♗e6 18 ♗f3 fails to consolidate his position. The d8-square is inaccessible to the rook because of the check on c6, while after 18...♖f6 19 ♘c3 White has a multitude of threats: ♘b5, ♘e4, ♕g2, ♖dg1 and one of them will prove decisive.

**18 ♗xc6+ ♕xc6**

18...bxc6 19 ♖g6 loses as well, but not in such a forced manner.

**19 ♕d8+**

The subsequent operation is not difficult to calculate, as the variation does not branch out and every move is obvious.

**19...♔f7 20 ♖g7+ ♔xg7 21 ♕xe7+ ♖f7 22 ♖g1+ ♕g6 23 ♕e5+ ♔h7 24 ♖xg6 ♔xg6 25 ♕e8**

The last moments of the nominal material parity. The following knight manoeuvre cannot be prevented. White wins the exchange and a couple of pawns, while preventing Black from developing his queenside and stifling any attempt at building even a semblance of a fortress.

**25...♔g7 26 ♘g3 b6 27 ♘h5+ ♔g6 28 ♕g8+ ♔xh5 29 ♕xf7+ ♔h4 30 ♕f6+ 1-0**

## Game 4
# Borki Predojević – Nenad Mrkonjić
### *Bizovac 2005*

**1 e4 ♘f6 2 ♘c3 d5 3 e5 ♘e4** *(D)*

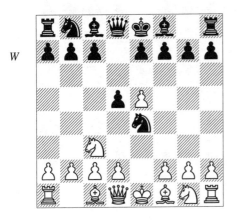

This ambitious move leads to play of a unique and difficult nature, and so is popular among die-hard Alekhine enthusiasts. However, it is also risky, and may objectively be a little dubious.

**4 ♘ce2**

At first sight this is an odd move that is detrimental to White's development, but he has good reason to expect to earn a healthy dividend on the lost tempo by attacking the black knight, which has infiltrated his ranks and now may have difficulty finding a convenient retreat. Alternatives:

a) 4 ♘xe4 dxe4 doesn't promise White much at all. The e5-pawn is more vulnerable than its counterpart on e4, so 5 d4 is mandatory, when Black has to choose whether to exchange on d3 or hang on to the e4 'splinter', denying the white pieces their best squares for a while.

After 5...exd3 White can exchange queens with 6 ♕xd3 ♕xd3 7 ♗xd3 (in order to prevent the enemy queen from taking part in the attack on the e5-pawn), when Black has some problems with his light-squared bishop, but they are certainly not insoluble, while the e5-pawn may make a nice target – indeed, Black has scored well from this position in practice. If Black decides to keep the e4-pawn, it is logical to bring out the bishop first by 5...♗f5, as the immediate 5...e6 transposes to a line of the French Defence that has the reputation of being difficult for Black.

b) On the other hand, after 4 d4 ♘xc3 5 bxc3 c5 the comparison of the resulting position with variations of the French is much more favourable for Black: the defects in White's pawn-structure promise Black standard counterplay without having to pay for it with the light-squared bishop's passivity. This position is discussed in further detail in the notes to Game 25, via the move-order 2 e5 ♘d5 3 ♘c3 ♘xc3 4 bxc3 d5 5 d4 c5.

c) 4 ♕f3 is the best-founded alternative to the move in the game. After 4...♘xc3 5 dxc3 *(D)* a formation that we shall see again later arises.

The recapture with the d-pawn does not create organic defects in the white pawn-chain; moreover, it facilitates rapid and comfortable development. If the black pawn hadn't made it to d5 already, Black could have hoped to exchange it for its opponent on e5 and in the future capitalize on the numerical advantage on the kingside. On the other hand, Black hasn't

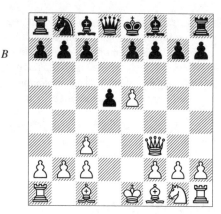

done anything suspect and if White castles queenside, Black's counterattack may prove dangerous, as in the following game: 5...c6 6 ♗f4 ♗f5 7 0-0-0 e6 8 ♕g3 h6 9 h4 ♕a5 10 ♔b1 b5 11 ♘f3 c5 12 h5 ♘a6 13 ♘h4 ♗h7 (here 13...♗e4 has been recommended, in order to provoke f3 and so prevent the king's rook from operating along the third rank after ♖h3) 14 ♕g4 b4 15 ♗d2 c4 (with the terrible threat of ...b3) 16 ♘g6 with great complications, Adams-Agdestein, Oslo Challenge (2) 1994.

We now return to 4 ♘ce2 *(D)*:

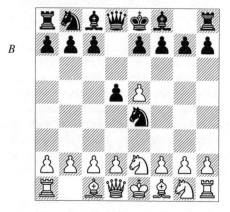

With the possibility of an exchange on c3 ruled out, Black must constantly have at the ready an evacuation plan for the e4-knight.

**4...♘c5**

Addressing the problem of the knight's security at once. 4...d4 is more popular. The main merit of this move is that the d4-square is denied to the enemy pawn, and its main drawback is that the invasion of the hostile territory is not yet supported by any reserves. There are two

ways to attack the bridgehead. The first, 5 ♘f3, is relatively little studied and sometimes gives rise to lines of a rather sharp character. It is obvious that 5...c5??, taking away the knight's last retreat-square, is out of the question, while the situation after 5...d3 6 cxd3 is clearly worse for Black in comparison to the similar idea from the previous game: instead of settling down in the cosy stable on d5, the knight has to keep looking for an acceptable post. There remain 5...♘c6 and 5...♗g4. Here are some possible continuations:

a) 5...♗g4?! 6 c3 *(D)* (6 ♘exd4 ♕xd4 7 ♘xd4 ♗xd1 8 f3 is good for White) and now:

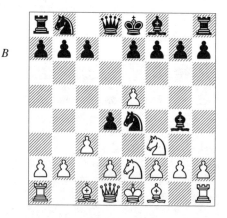

a1) 6...♘c6 transposes to line 'b1' just below.

a2) 6...dxc3 7 ♕a4+!? ♘d7 8 ♕xe4? (8 ♘xc3!) 8...♘c5, regaining the sacrificed piece after 9...♘d3+ and ...cxb2.

a3) 6...♗xf3 7 gxf3 ♘g5 8 ♗g2 ♘e6 9 ♕a4+ (9 f4!?) 9...c6 10 cxd4 and the white pawn cluster in the centre evokes associations with the battle formation of the Teutonic knights.

b) 5...♘c6 6 c3 and then:

b1) 6...♗g4?! is strongly met by 7 ♘exd4! ♘xe5 8 ♕e2 ♕d5 9 ♘b5! (J.Graf) 9...0-0-0 10 c4 ♕e6 11 d4 with a large advantage (e.g., 11...♘g6? 12 d5 ♕f5 13 ♘bd4 and White wins).

b2) 6...dxc3 7 bxc3 ♗g4 8 d4 e6 should, it seems, be acknowledged as the most playable continuation, and the one most in accordance with the spirit of our opening, although White's chances appear to be preferable.

The second and the main way is to play 5 c3 *(D)* at once.

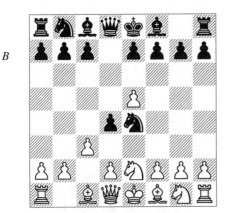

In reply to the apparently impossible capture 5...dxc3, 6 ♕a4+ is met by 6...♘d7, when it is once again imprudent to take on e4, but 7 ♘xc3 promises a healthy superiority in the centre. The natural 6 bxc3 ♘c5 7 d4 ♘ca6 seems to reduce Black's play *ad absurdum* – what a concept, to drive the knight from f6 to a6! However, all is not that simple, as the white knight is spinning aimlessly, whereas Black has a clear plan of embarking on the occupation of the strong point on d5 after ...c5 with a subsequent exchange of the pawns.

The pawn sacrifice 5...♘c6 is the main continuation. The capture 6 cxd4 may lead to original play after 6...♘g5 7 f4 ♘e6 8 ♘f3 ♘exd4 9 ♘exd4 ♘xd4 10 ♕a4+ ♘c6 11 ♗b5 ♗d7 12 e6?! ♗xe6 13 ♘e5 ♕d6 (or 13...♕d5!? 14 ♘xc6 ♗d7!, as indicated by Burgess) 14 ♘xc6 bxc6 15 ♗xc6+ ♗d7, when Black is not worse in any way. White can hang on to the pawn with 7 ♕a4, but his pieces are cramped and Black has opportunities for creating counterplay. The other way to accept the sacrifice, 6 ♘xd4 ♘xd4 7 ♕a4+ c6 8 ♕xd4 ♕xd4 9 cxd4 *(D)*, is more critical.

Clearly Black enjoys at least some compensation due to the d5-square and the extra pawn's reduced value, but in practice Black's position has proved tricky to handle. His main problem is not so much the missing pawn as the lack of counterplay; passive defence is a cheerless occupation, while attempts at taking active measures more often than not lead to the creation of additional weaknesses, as in the following example: 9...♘g5 10 ♗c4 (10 ♗d3!?) 10...b5?! (too incautious, as the lack of targets in Black's position is its main strength, and any loosening

needs a specific justification; the normal plan is 10...♘e6 intending ...♘c7, ...♗e6-d5 and ...e6) 11 ♗b3 ♗e6 12 d3 ♗xb3 13 axb3, and despite the white pawn-formation being broken in two places, in the subsequent struggle Black's weakness on the a-file decided the game, Jobava-Nalbandian, Batumi 2003.

The other retreat path – via the kingside – is prepared with 4...f6. After 5 d3 ♘g5 White either plays 6 f4, driving the knight to f7 and hoping to capitalize on the space advantage, or seeks to utilize his superior pawn-structure after 6 ♗xg5 fxg5 7 h4 g4. Both continuations lead to non-standard positions, but White ought to have the better chances. After the latter, play might continue 8 d4 c5 9 dxc5 ♘c6 10 ♘f4, when 10...g6 transposes to the 8 ♘f4 line, while 10...d4 has been used by Almeida; or 8 ♘f4 g6 9 d4 c5 (9...♗h6 is an alternative) 10 dxc5, when *NCO* gives 10...♘c6 11 ♕xd5 ♕a5+ 12 c3 ♗h6 13 ♘ge2 ♗f5 14 b4 ♕a3 15 ♕b3 ♕xb3 16 axb3 ♘xe5 17 ♖d1 0-0 as unclear.

**5 d4 ♘e6** *(D)*

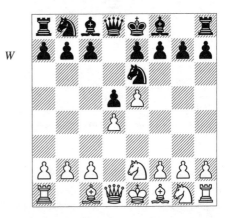

A closed pawn-formation has appeared, akin to French set-ups. The unusual position of the knight on e6 is not bad *per se*, although it obstructs both bishops. The g7-square, where it is headed, outwardly looks like a poor place to post the knight and may well turn out to be so later, but in the fight to blockade White's kingside pawn advance it may prove to be functional enough. For the moment, the c8-bishop hasn't lost the hope of active development outside the pawn-chain. Counting the time lost by the contestants on the piece transfers is not so important here, as in a closed position the value of a tempo is decreased.

**6 f4**

In classical French variations, this move is not made without thinking first. The f4-pawn cements the central wedge, of course, but usually doesn't force the weakening ...g6 and limits the scope of the white pieces. Here the real threat of a further advance obliges the g-pawn to step forward, so the case for the f-pawn's advance is stronger. However, there are other natural continuations, such as 6 ♘f3, 6 g3 and the most common and possibly strongest move 6 ♗e3!?, which temporarily halts ...c5.

**6...c5 (D)**

The situation in the centre is usually clarified at a later stage, with the question of the c8-bishop's future taking priority: 6...g6 7 ♘f3 ♗g7 8 h3 h5 9 g3 ♗f5 10 ♗e3 ♗e4 11 ♗g2 ♘f5 12 ♗f2 e6, Videki-M.Grünberg, Pecs 1997.

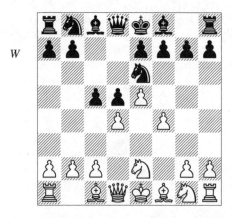

**7 c3 cxd4**

Perhaps Black was tempting White into the line 8 f5 ♘c7 9 ♘xd4 g6 10 e6 with sharp play.

**8 cxd4 g6 9 ♗e3**

An attempt at deployment without letting Black's light-squared bishop out.

**9...♘c6 10 ♘c3 ♗g7 11 ♗f2**

A useful prophylactic retreat, inviting Black to decide whether he should continue to prepare to bring out the c8-bishop, when ♕b3 has to be taken into account.

**11...e6 (D)**

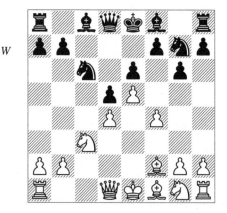

Black does not persist and leaves the bishop in the trenches, guided by the standard plan for such set-ups: to give White a weakness on the queenside and determine the pattern of counterplay based on that.

**12 ♘f3 ♗e7 13 ♗d3 0-0 14 0-0 ♗d7**

Both sides have completed their development and must decide what to do next. White would like to exchange the dark-squared bishops, but that is not easy to combine with the defence of the d4-pawn; playing g4 is not enough to prepare the f5 advance. Besides, it creates weaknesses in the white camp as well, which Black can expose with a counter-advance of his f-pawn.

**15 ♖c1 ♕a5 16 a3 ♖fc8 17 ♕d2 ♕d8 18 b4 a6 19 ♔h1 ♘a7**

Black is ready for wholesale exchanges: first two pairs of minor pieces are to leave the battlefield via b5 (the possible doubling of pawns is not a concern); then it will be the turn of the major pieces along the c-file; avoiding the exchange would mean ceding the file. Following that, White will himself offer the exchange of his potentially 'bad' dark-squared bishop via h4. However, the resulting queen and knight endgame promises him no advantage; a knight vs knight ending might offer some slight chances, but Black can agree to a queen exchange on either c6 or c4, thus improving his pawn-structure. The other plan of counterplay involves 19...b5 with the subsequent exploitation of the c4 outpost.

**20 f5!?** *(D)*

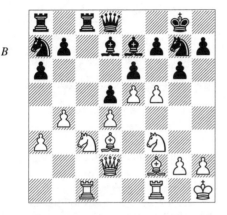

The larger part of the black army is concentrated on the queenside, so, taking advantage of the insufficient protection of d5, White sacrifices a pawn and breaks open the enemy king's cover.

**20...♘xf5 21 ♗xf5 gxf5**

Capturing with the other pawn, on both the previous move and now, is hopeless: White takes on d5, and Black's misfortune lies not in the fact that he has given up the extra pawn, but that he will have to acquiesce to the exchange of the e7-bishop. Then an attack on the dark-square holes in the black camp will decide the game.

**22 g4 fxg4?**

Too optimistic; now White's attack takes on a textbook character. 22...f4 is more natural, as it keeps the position as closed as possible. This leads to unclear play, as after 23 ♕xf4 ♘b5 the white pieces are not ready to create real threats; the f7-pawn is easily defended, and it is a long way to h7. A rapid transfer of a knight to h5 could be dangerous, but 23 ♘e2?! is well met with 23...♗b5.

**23 ♖g1 f5**

Black has no time to set up even a makeshift defence after 23...h5 24 ♕h6 ♗e8 with the idea of 25 ♕xh5 f5 because of 25 ♖xg4+ hxg4 26 ♖g1 with mate.

**24 exf6 ♗xf6 25 ♖xg4+ ♔h8 26 ♘h4**

The simplest. The only defender is exchanged off, and Black has no time to bring up the reserves.

**26...♕e7 27 ♗xf6+ ♕xf6 28 ♘e5 ♗e8 29 ♖cg1 ♗h5 30 ♖f4 ♕h6 31 ♕e3 ♖g8 32 ♘f7+ ♗xf7 33 ♕e5+ ♖g7 34 ♖xf7 ♖ag8 35 ♖gxg7 1-0**

# Game 5
## Martin Petr – Mihai Grünberg
### *Plzen 2004*

**1 e4 ♘f6 2 ♘c3 d5 3 e5 ♘fd7** *(D)*

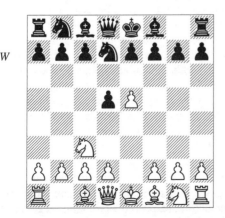

The most solid continuation, although in most games it leads to a transposition into another opening. It is easy to see that after 4 d4 e6 the initial position of a popular variation in the French Defence appears on the board, a variation that has a decent reputation... but let's leave it for the appropriate books to cover that system and examine the continuations that are unique to this particular move-order and give the position an original character, although it must be said that the choice of the pattern of the subsequent struggle remains with White.

After 4 f4 too, there is hardly any independent play: the game is liable to transpose into the 4 d4 c5 5 f4 line (see below), or some variation of the French, or else lines without d4 that can also be reached from the f4 Sicilian; e.g., 4...e6 5 ♘f3 c5 6 g3 ♘c6 7 ♗g2 ♗e7 8 0-0 0-0 – a line that dates back to Nimzowitsch-Alekhine, Semmering 1926. After 9 d3, Black is advised to play 9...f6, giving himself some breathing room at the cost of a slight weakening.

First let's have a look at the exchange in the centre: 4 ♘xd5 ♘xe5 (D).

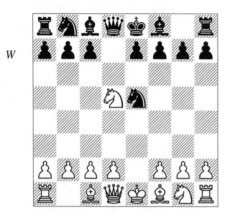

W

White's claim to an opening advantage is hard to justify – he has no development advantage, and Black has better prospects of establishing control of the centre. White usually goes for a set-up in the spirit of the Réti Opening based on piece pressure in the centre, with the queen's bishop typically developed to b2: 5 ♘e3 c5 (both 5...♘ec6 aiming for ...e5 and the developing 5...♘bc6 are good as well) 6 ♘f3 ♘xf3+ 7 ♕xf3 ♘c6 8 ♗c4 e6 9 ♕g3 ♕d6 10 b3 ♗d7 11 ♗b2 f6 12 0-0-0 0-0-0, Pilgaard-Gausel, Gausdal 2003.

There remains the cramping pawn sacrifice, which in fact occurred in our game via a different move-order. White can carry it out at once by 4 e6 fxe6 (D).

The justification for this sacrifice is evident: Black has problems with development, and his king's pawn-cover is weakened. On the other hand, classical wisdom teaches us that if the opponent sacrifices a centre pawn and you see no forced win for him, you should take the pawn. This type of offer occurs in other openings as well; there is also a thematically similar sacrifice of the d-pawn, although it is not as common. If White aims to play this way, it is most logical to do it on the fourth move. Although

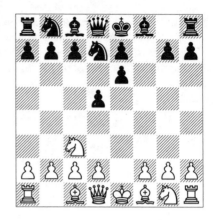

W

after 5 d4 Black is not obliged to reply with 5...c5 (transposing to the main game), it is not clear that he has a better continuation at his disposal. 5...g6 looks risky due to 6 h4 (planning to wreck Black's kingside) meeting 6...♘f6?! by 7 h5, when 7...♘xh5? loses to 8 ♖xh5 gxh5 9 ♕xh5+ ♔d7 10 ♘f3 ♗g7 11 ♗h6 ♗f6 12 ♘xd5 exd5 13 ♕xd5+ ♔e8 14 ♕h5+ ♔d7 15 ♘e5+ with a rout. However, 6...♗g7 7 h5 ♘f8 is a much tougher defence (e.g., 8 ♗f4 c5 9 ♘b5 ♘a6 {9...cxd4!? Davies} 10 ♘f3 ♗d7 11 ♘e5 ♕a5+ 12 ♕d2 ♕xd2+ 13 ♔xd2 gxh5!?). It is hard for Black to rule out White's kingside threats, since playing 5...♘f6 first means giving White a head-start in the fight for the important blockading square e5.

**4 d4**

With this move-order, Black, as has already been mentioned, can switch to the French Defence by playing 4...e6.

**4...c5**

With this move, Black avoids an immediate transposition to main lines of the French, though that opening is always in the background.

**5 e6**

This is the main continuation. Other moves:

a) White can play 5 dxc5 e6 6 ♘f3 transposing to another popular, though less complex, French line.

b) White doesn't have sufficient compensation for the piece after 5 ♘xd5?! cxd4 6 ♕xd4? (6 e6 ♕a5+) 6...♘b6 7 c4 e6 8 ♗g5 ♗b4+ 9 ♔e2 ♕d7.

c) After 5 f4 Black can take advantage of the fact that the c8-bishop's path is not yet blocked by playing 5...cxd4 6 ♘b5 (the capture by the queen has been played as well, although Black can consider it as a concession on White's part) 6...♘c6 7 ♘f3 ♘db8 (7...♕a5+ 8 ♕d2 ♕b6 is interesting, although rarely played) 8 ♘bxd4 ♗g4.

**5...fxe6** (D)

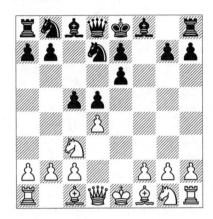

**6 ♘f3**

The struggle over the blockade of Black's central pawn-formation will be at the centre stage of the upcoming conflict, and the move in the game appears to be the most logical choice. Let's consider two alternatives:

a) 6 ♗d3 creates a blunt threat that Black can meet in two ways. One way is 6...g6, but after 7 dxc5 followed by h4-h5 the d3-bishop can be considered to be placed relatively well. Nevertheless, it seems that in the coming blockade the bishop would prove to be more useful on b5. 6...♘f6 is preferable, even though it weakens Black's control of the e5-square. Securing the bishop's position with 7 dxc5 allows the immediate 7...e5, while after the blockading 7 ♘f3 White must be ready to move the bishop yet again, at once or a move later.

b) 6 dxc5 is a consistent move, as the discovered attack on the d5-pawn is another means to keep its neighbour immobilized, and maintaining the pawn tension favours Black. After 6...♘c6 7 ♘f3 this merely comes down to a transposition of moves, while independent play with 7 ♗e3 is hardly to be recommended, since after 7...♘f6 White cannot prevent the ...e5 advance.

**6...♘c6 7 ♗b5** (D)

This move, too, often trades places with the next one. One advantage to bringing out the bishop first is that if White plays 7 dxc5 then he has to take into account the prophylactic 7...a6,

preserving both knights for the struggle for the centre squares. Black could also try 7...g6 8 h4 ♗g7 9 h5 ♘xc5, for instance.

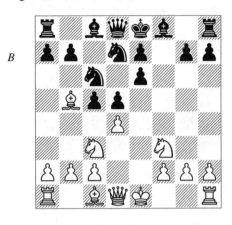

**7...g6**

Bagirov's recommendation 7...e5?! has attracted few followers, as the following miniature proved convincing: 8 dxe5 e6 9 ♘g5 ♘d4?! (Black should probably try 9...♘dxe5, but his position is far from easy) 10 ♕g4 ♕e7 11 ♘xh7 ♘xc2+ 12 ♔d1 ♘xa1 13 ♘xd5 exd5 14 ♗g5 ♕xe5 15 ♕h5+ 1-0 Hector-Konopka, 2nd Bundesliga 1996/7.

**8 dxc5 ♗g7 9 ♗e3**

White already must take into account the advance of the d-pawn, followed by the e-pawn, so it is too late for a raid with the h-pawn. Actually, by developing the bishop to b5, White announces his intention to play for the blockade of d4 and e5. For the time being Black controls the latter, though he cannot occupy it as the d5-pawn would be *en prise*. Neither can White reconquer this point with the support of the bishop from f4 or d4, as that runs into ...e5 with tempo. A rook must be brought up to e1 as a reserve, and only then will ♗d4 become possible. Black has to search for a way to counter this.

**9...♕a5** (D)

In order to force the bishop to declare its intentions. White does not mind exchanging it on c6 in principle, but that strengthens d5, in which case White must be ready to blockade the centre, so as not to allow ...e5.

**10 ♗d2?!**

This move fails to impress if only because with his next move White showed that he is

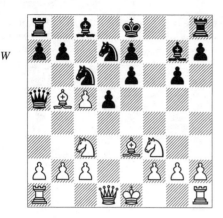

willing to acquiesce to the repetition of moves, which is a concession on his part according to the opening canons.

Dubious is 10 ♗xc6?! bxc6 11 0-0, when the immediate 11...e5? is bad because of the sacrifice 12 ♘xd5 with the following sample line: 12...cxd5 13 ♕xd5 ♖b8 14 ♘g5 ♖f8 15 ♘e6 ♗f6 16 ♗d2. However, the preliminary 11...♖b8! forces White to solve difficult problems.

10 a4 is somewhat more acceptable. White does not begrudge giving up another pawn after 10...♗xc3+ 11 bxc3 ♕xc3+ 12 ♔f1 since Black's kingside is weak, the blockade remains and the loss of castling rights is of no consequence, as the king's rook is placed quite well on h1 to support the raid by the h-pawn. In Becker-Rabiega, Berlin 2003, Black preferred 10...a6 11 ♗e2 ♕b4 (with a double threat of capturing on b2 or d4) 12 ♗d2 ♕xc5 13 0-0 0-0 14 a5 ♕d6 15 ♖a4 (indirectly defending against 15...e5 because of 16 ♘xd5), when the position was complex but Black's chances were preferable.

The best reply seems to be 10 0-0, as played in Hector-Vl.Sergeev, Berlin 1995. There followed 10...0-0 11 ♖b1 a6 12 ♗xc6 bxc6 13 ♖e1 ♕c7 14 ♘g5 ♘e5 15 ♗d4 ♖f5 16 ♘h3 ♘f7 17 ♗xg7 ♔xg7 18 ♘a4 e5 19 ♘b6 ♖b8 20 c4. Although Black has managed to advance in the centre, White also has his share of achievements: he has exchanged off Black's active minor pieces, leaving the passive pieces on the board, and prepares a new blockading set-up to contain Black's centre pawns.

**10...♕c7 11 ♗e3 0-0**

Black turns down the threefold repetition and takes up the challenge of fighting for more.

**12 0-0** (D)

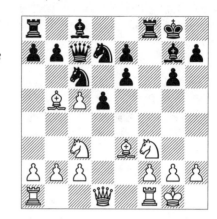

White has pretty much completed his development (which cannot be said about his opponent) and for the moment restrains the enemy centre. Whether it can be set in motion is the main theme of the coming struggle. The half-open f-file adds to the position's complexity with the constant threat of eliminating an important blockader – the f3-knight – with an exchange sacrifice.

**12...a6**

For now 12...♖xf3?! promises little in view of 13 ♕xf3 d4 14 ♗f4 ♘ce5 15 ♕e2 dxc3 16 ♗xd7 ♗xd7 17 ♖fe1 cxb2 18 ♖ab1, so the choice lies between 12...♘de5 and the text-move.

**13 ♗a4 ♘f6** (D)

Here too, 13...♘de5 is good, but Black decided to get the knight to g4 without immobilizing the e6-pawn.

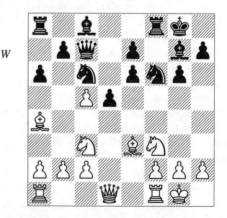

**14 ♗xc6**

White at last decides to occupy the blockade squares. The prophylactic 14 h3!? looks good, when it is wrong to play 14...d4? because of 15 ♘xd4 ♘xd4 (if 15...♖d8 at once, then White eliminates one of the attackers by 16 ♗xc6 bxc6 and unpins the queen with, for instance, 17 ♕f3) 16 ♗xd4 ♖d8 17 ♗e5.

**14...bxc6**

An interesting alternative is the immediate 14...♘g4 15 ♗d4 ♖xf3 16 g3 ♗xd4 17 ♕xd4 (17 ♕xf3 ♘e5) and now 17...bxc6 18 ♕xg4 ♖f7 or 17...♘e5 and the white queen is uncomfortable.

**15 ♗d4 ♘g4 16 ♗xg7 ♔xg7?!**

After the stronger 16...♖xf3 17 g3 ♖f7 18 ♕xg4 ♔xg7, White cannot stop ...e5, and will have to try to prevent a further advance with f3, but Black has ways to strengthen his position further.

**17 ♖e1?!** *(D)*

White allows the exchange sacrifice, and that's unjustified optimism. At first sight, Black does not have many dangerous pieces involved in the attack, but White failed to appreciate his ability to bring up the reserves. Also bad is 17 g3? e5, but after 17 h3 ♖xf3 18 hxg4 ♖f4 19 g3 ♖f7 20 ♘a4 the defensive resources are far from being exhausted, although the advantage is, of course, with Black.

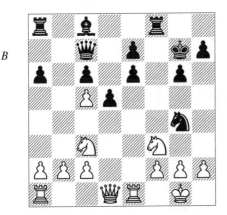

**17...♖xf3 18 ♕xf3 ♕xh2+ 19 ♔f1 a5**

One move to activate both inactive pieces. The other obvious continuation, 19...e5, also looks enticing.

**20 ♔e2 ♗a6+ 21 ♔d1**

After 21 ♔d2 ♕h6+ 22 ♔d1, besides the opportunity to transpose back into the game, there is the still more convincing 22...♖f8 23 ♕xg4 ♖f4.

**21...♕h4 22 g3 ♕h5 23 ♘e2 e5** *(D)*

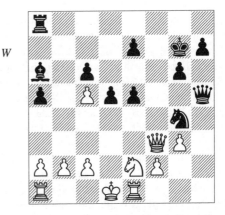

With material approximately equal, the black pieces dominate the board. There remains one task – to pick out of the multitude of winning continuations one that is sufficiently accurate.

**24 ♘d4 exd4 25 ♖xe7+ ♔h8 26 ♔e1 ♕h3 27 ♔d2 ♕h6+ 28 ♔e1 ♖f8 29 ♕xg4 ♕h1+ 30 ♔d2 ♖xf2+ 31 ♖e2 ♖xe2+ 32 ♕xe2 ♕h6+ 0-1**

Let's sum up the results of the chapter. Sidelines are rarely critical in the evaluation of any opening, and this is also the case here. While 2 d3 only requires Black to be familiar with a couple of the set-ups available to White, after 2 ♘c3 not all roads lead to Rome. The exchange on d5 does not give Black any particular reason for concern, but the lines from Games 3 and 4 contain a significant amount of strategic (as well as tactical) risk, and 3...♘fd7 should be recognized as the most solid continuation. However, solidity is not the normal reason our opening is played. We should add that the Vienna Game and the French and the Scandinavian lines that can be reached from 2 ♘c3 all enjoy the reputation of being quite correct for Black, with the Vienna option (2...e5) quite likely to take a lot of 1 e4 players outside their main repertoire preferences.

# 2 The Chase Variation

In all systems of our opening, except those of the previous chapter, the pawn advances by 2 e5 and invites the knight on a journey along a strictly defined route after 2...♘d5 (we shall not waste time searching for the most rational way to obtain an advantage after 2...♘e4?!, as it is clear even in the most obvious line 3 d3 ♘c5 4 d4 ♘e6 5 d5 ♘c5, although 3 d4 is perhaps a more clinical attempt at refutation). Now the hand all but stretches out to continue chasing the mustang, and White often gives in to the impulse with 3 c4, when the obvious reply is 3...♘b6. If the "attack while you can" strategy is to be followed further, then after 4 c5 ♘d5 *(D)* we have the system examined in this chapter.

What is so attractive about this position for White? Significant space has been seized without sacrificing development; however, to seize does not mean to keep. The pawns have advanced far ahead of the main forces and it is not feasible to keep them as a bridgehead, so they will have to be exchanged – one or both – or sacrificed while converting their value into other pluses, such as a kingside initiative. This system is not considered particularly dangerous,

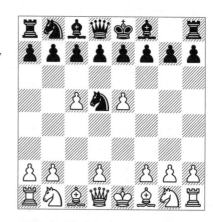

W

but its tactical content is attractive to attacking players.

With his next move, White normally continues harassing the knight, but now with a piece. Game 6 (Sveshnikov-Beletsky) examines the first method of the attack: 5 ♘c3. If the first step is made by the bishop, viz. 5 ♗c4, the subsequent play may take on a gambit-like character, as in Game 7 (Mirallès – Santo-Roman), or material parity may be maintained, as in Game 8 (Potkin-Mamedyarov).

## Game 6
## Evgeny Sveshnikov – Alexei Beletsky
*Russian Team Ch, Togliatti 2003*

**1 e4 ♘f6 2 e5 ♘d5 3 c4**

This move serves as an introduction to several major systems. White takes advantage of the enemy knight's kind offer and enthusiastically grabs the space.

**3...♘b6 4 c5**

The main alternative is 4 d4 d6, which leads to the Exchange Variation (Chapter 6) in the case of 5 exd6, and the Four Pawns Attack (Chapter 3) after 5 f4. In these cases it does not matter much whether White advances his c-pawn or d-pawn first.

We should also mention a couple of rare continuations unique to this move-order, whose main goal is to obtain original positions with novel content.

Let's start with 4 a4. Besides the threat to win the knight, White presents the a1-rook with the opportunity to come into play first; e.g., after 4...a5 5 ♖a3 (White can also switch to the Exchange Variation, where the a-pawns' moves can make quite a difference in some lines, especially if White seeks to play a quick c5 advance), such an early appearance of the rook on the third rank provides for some non-standard play. The more natural 4...d6 5 a5 ♘6d7 also leaves White with a variety of options, including 6 e6 fxe6 7 d4 ♘f6 8 g4.

With 4 b3, White takes advantage of the fact that one of Black's kingside defenders has galloped far away and aims his bishop there, eyeing the g7-pawn. Opposing the bishop along the long diagonal with 4...g6 allows White to embark on unclear play by 5 ♕f3 (with the threat of c5) 5...c5 6 ♗b2 ♗g7 7 a4 (in reply to 7 e6 Black can play either 7...0-0 or 7...f6) 7...a5 8 d4 (or even 8 b4). The main continuation is considered to be 4...d6 5 exd6 exd6 6 ♗b2 ♘c6 7 ♘f3 d5, when the black king's bishop is for the moment confined to f8, so Black will develop the queenside first and may follow up with castling queenside.

**4...♘d5 (D)**

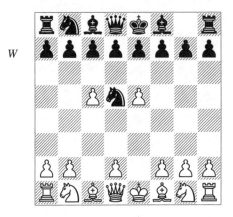

**5 ♘c3**

White forced the enemy knight to return to the centre in order to develop while attacking it. We shall examine using the bishop for this purpose by 5 ♗c4 in the following games. 5 d4 is not particularly popular; after 5...d6 6 cxd6 cxd6 the game transposes into a well-known c3 Sicilian variation, although Black also has 6...exd6, with good squares to develop his pieces to.

**5...e6**

Black must either exchange the knight or defend it. First let's consider 5...♘xc3. Now 6 bxc3 doesn't present Black with any difficulties, as after 6...d6 a favourable version of a well-known type of position appears. The main continuation is the non-traditional capture away from the centre by 6 dxc3 (D).

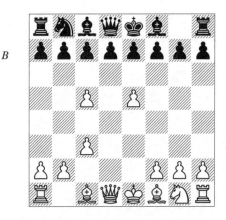

This opens not only the bishop's diagonal but also the queen's file, which hinders exchanges in the centre. Here 6...b6, based on the tempting idea of removing the c5-pawn without spending a centre pawn on it, is not practical, as White can saddle Black with development problems after 7 ♕f3 or 7 ♗g5. Instead, Black has three main continuations:

a) 6...d6 seeks to exchange White's overactive pawns. White fights for an advantage with 7 cxd6 exd6 8 ♗f4 aiming to create a weakness on d6, and after 8...d5 9 ♘f3 he hopes that his extra pawn on the kingside will prove to be more valuable than Black's on the queenside. Instead, 7 ♗c4 allows, among other replies, 7...d5 8 ♕xd5 ♕xd5 9 ♗xd5 e6 and 10...♗xc5 with good prospects of equalizing.

b) 6...e6 attacks the c5-pawn. However, White has a more than adequate counter-threat in the attack on the g7-pawn by 7 ♕g4, when Black already has to take into account the bishop's move to g5. Black can parry the direct threats, for instance with 7...h6, but the initiative and the freedom of choice is on White's side.

c) 6...♘c6 makes a preliminary attack on the e5-pawn, provoking 7 ♘f3 in order to block the queen's diagonal, and only now does Black target c5 by 7...e6. This version offers Black better chances than in the previous line. You can only marvel at the intricate manoeuvres of his pieces in the game Djurhuus-Gausel, Norwegian Ch, Alta 1996: 8 ♗e3 (8 b4 should probably be met by 8...b6, as played by Almeida, rather than 8...d6 9 ♗g5!?) 8...♗e7 (8...b6 is possible here too, and was Bagirov's preference) 9 ♗d3 b6 10 cxb6 axb6 11 ♕e2 ♗b7 12

♗f4 ♖a4 13 ♗g3 ♕a8 14 a3 ♘b8 15 ♖d1 h5 16 h4 ♖g4 17 ♖d2 ♗a6 18 ♕d1 ♖h6 *(D)*.

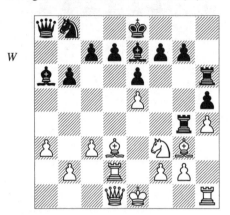

The centre pawns remain in their places while the pieces enter the fray via the flanks.

If Black prefers to maintain the knight in the centre, it has to be defended with a pawn. In addition to the text-move, let's consider 5...c6 *(D)*. Then:

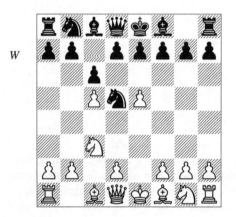

a) The position after 6 ♗c4 is more often reached via a different order of White's last two moves, which we shall examine later.

b) 6 ♘xd5 cxd5 7 d4 can obviously transpose to the equivalent 5...e6 variation, while experience with 7...♘c6 8 ♘f3 b6 is limited.

c) The other natural continuation is 6 d4. Black's wish to take full advantage of the far-advanced enemy pawns suggests the plan of exchanging them for his flank pawns, in order to keep his own central pawns for the subsequent struggle. This reason partly explains the choice of 5...c6. Strategically this is correct,

but it leads Black to fall behind in development. For example, Lenderman-Shabalov, New York rapid 2005: 6...b6 7 ♘xd5 cxd5 8 cxb6 ♕xb6 9 ♘e2 ♘c6 10 ♕b3 e6 11 ♕xb6 axb6 12 ♗d2 ♗e7 13 ♗c3 b5 14 b3 f6; here White didn't play actively enough and Black achieved a promising position. Clarifying the situation in the centre with 6...d6 is more solid, but on the other hand this offers fewer chances of unbalancing the game. 7 cxd6 exd6 8 ♘f3 may offer White the more pleasant position, though 8...dxe5 9 ♘xe5 ♗e6 looks very solid.

**6 d4**

Once again we shall defer the discussion of the bishop's move to c4 to the next game, which leaves us only one alternative to consider here: the immediate exchange of the knights by 6 ♘xd5 exd5, which precludes a later capture on c3. The main position arises after 7 d4 d6 (as always, 7...b6 is an alternative, and here it transposes to our main game) 8 cxd6 cxd6 9 ♘f3 ♘c6 *(D)*.

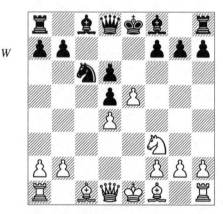

We should note that the diagram position can also be reached from the 5...c6 line, and also the Alapin (1 e4 c5 2 c3) and even the Rubinstein (1 e4 c5 2 ♘f3 ♘f6) variations of the Sicilian. A fairly large body of practical experience of this position has been accumulated, most of it quite benign from Black's viewpoint. White must first of all decide where to put the king's bishop. 10 ♗e2 allows Black to occupy f5 (though 10...dxe5 followed by 11...♗b4+ has been the most common reply in practice), while 10 ♗d3, allowing the pin by ...♗g4, looks aggressive, although here too, Black's position has great reserves of solidity.

We now return to 6 d4 *(D)*:

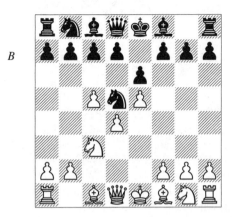

**6...b6**

As already mentioned, 6...d6 is the more traditional way to undermine the centre. Then after 7 cxd6 cxd6 8 ♘f3 we again find ourselves on a visit to our more affluent relatives – this position arises much more frequently in the c3 Sicilian. The most common line runs 8...♘xc3 9 bxc3 ♕c7 10 ♗d2 ♘d7, and it is considered very satisfactory for Black. Often 'hanging pawns' arise after a capture by White on d6.

There is another option as well: exchanging at once by 6...♘xc3. White has only one recapture, 7 bxc3, and now it must be decided which side to undermine the c5-pawn from. If 7...b6, then 8 cxb6 is somewhat of a concession; more principled is 8 ♕g4 bxc5 9 ♗g5 ♗e7 10 ♗xe7 ♕xe7 11 ♕xg7 ♖f8 12 ♘f3 cxd4 *(D)*.

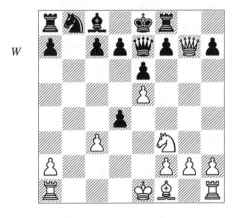

Black is dismantling White's centre, but his king is not particularly secure. 13 ♗e2 f5 14 ♕h6 led to a sharp and very unclear struggle in

Sveshnikov-Solozhenkin, Russian Ch, St Petersburg 1998.

After 7...d6 8 cxd6 cxd6, we again have a position that arises more often from a c3 Sicilian. 9 ♘f3 transposes to the line we mentioned at the start of the note, but White can also make use of the fact that he hasn't yet deployed this knight, and support his e-pawn with 9 f4.

**7 ♘xd5**

The exchange on b6 now or on the next move promises little; e.g., 7 cxb6 axb6 8 ♘xd5 exd5 9 ♘f3 ♗e7 10 ♗d3 ♗a6 11 0-0 c6 12 ♘e1 0-0 13 f4 f5 14 ♘f3 ♗xd3 15 ♕xd3 ♘a6 and the knight is headed for an excellent post on e6, while both sides' pawn-structures have their pluses and minuses, Frolov-Abrashkin, Russia Cup, Samara 2002.

**7...exd5 8 ♗e3** *(D)*

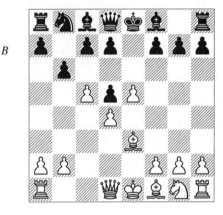

It is precisely on this move, which aims to preserve the c5-pawn that cramps the enemy, that White bases his hopes for an advantage.

**8...bxc5**

It is evident that ...b6 and ...d6 don't blend well; it's not just a loss of a tempo but also a hole on c6. Black may choose not to hurry with the exchange on c5; then it is more logical to play at once 8...♗a6 9 ♗xa6 ♘xa6 10 ♕a4 ♕c8 11 b4 c6, when the remaining pieces can be put to good use.

**9 dxc5 c6 10 ♕a4**

Black's queenside pieces have only one path of deployment left, via the a6-square, but White is unable to block it. After 10 ♗d3 Black can choose between the forcing line 10...♘a6 11 ♖c1 ♕a5+ 12 ♗d2 ♕xa2 13 ♖a1 ♕xb2 14 ♗xa6 ♗xa6 15 ♖xa6 ♕xe5+ 16 ♘e2 ♗xc5 with unclear compensation for the piece, and seeking equality by exchanging with 10...♕a5+.

The text-move is another attempt at hampering Black's development. In a later game Sveshnikov preferred 10 ♕d2 ♗e7 11 ♘f3 0-0 12 ♗d3 ♗a6 13 0-0 ♗xd3 14 ♕xd3 a5 15 ♖ac1 ♘a6 16 ♗d4 ♘c7, although here too, it seems that Black is OK, Sveshnikov-Shabalov, Liepaja rapid 2004.

**10...a5 11 ♘f3 ♗a6 12 ♖c1** *(D)*

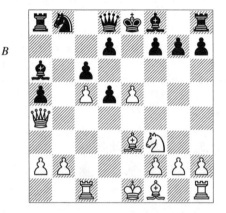

A conflict is brewing over the c5-pawn, which Black can attack three times. Therefore a third defender will be required; this can be the queen on a3 with the subsequent regrouping ♗d4 and ♕e3. Here White had to decide which concession would prove the less serious – helping Black to develop or losing the right to castle. Counting the tempi produces approximately the same result, but White's actual choice requires a subsequent g3, which weakens the light squares and the knight's position; this encourages Black to consider the possibility of opening the f-file in the future.

**12...♗xf1 13 ♔xf1 ♘a6 14 g3**

Perhaps the best plan against Black's counterplay along the b-file was the b4 advance, which had to be begun now and prepared step by step: 14 a3!? ♖b8 15 b3 (if 15 b4 ♕c8 16 ♕xa5 at once then 16...♘xb4 leads to complications that are not unfavourable to Black) 15...♖b5 16 b4; it is useful to lure the rook to b5 where it will come under attack.

**14...♖b8 15 ♕c2**

If 15 ♕a3 ♗e7 16 ♔g2 0-0 17 ♗d4 then, as mentioned earlier, 17...f6 looks good.

**15...♖b5** *(D)*

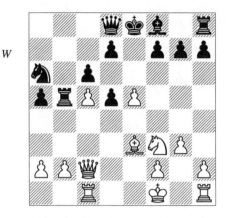

**16 ♔g2?!**

Now this is risky. 16 a4 creates mutual weaknesses, but the game remains in the balance, whereas now Black gets the upper hand.

**16...♗xc5 17 a4**

There was another version of the sacrifice: 17 ♗xc5 ♖xc5 18 ♕d3. In both cases White has partial compensation for the pawn, based on his chances on the kingside, where Black has few defenders. White's actual choice is based on the fact that a pawn on b5 will add an extra sharp twist to the position.

**17...♗xe3 18 axb5 ♘b4** *(D)*

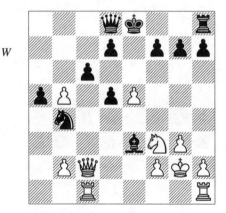

**19 ♕f5?!**

19 ♕a4 is objectively stronger, with good chances to restore the material parity, but sacrifices are usually not made with the aim of starting to regain the material immediately.

**19...♗xc1 20 ♖xc1 g6 21 ♕h3 0-0 22 ♕h6 f6 23 e6?!**

By refusing to switch to playing for a draw with 23 bxc6 dxc6 24 ♕e3, White continues to court complications, somewhat comforted by the fact that the f-file remains closed.

**23...dxe6 24 ♘d4 ♛d6 25 bxc6 ♖c8 26 h4**

The last reserve, and one that unexpectedly turns out most effective.

**26...e5 27 ♘b5 ♛b8?? (D)**

The queen should remain in touch with the f-pawn; after 27...♛e7, for instance, Black has real winning chances, although it still would have demanded a certain care with regard to the enemy passed pawn.

How easy it is to turn the evaluation of a position upside down. Black thought he was gaining a tempo by attacking the white knight, but the grim reality was that he left his king without protection for a moment – and it's game over.

**28 h5! ♖xc6 29 hxg6 ♛b7 30 ♘d6 ♛g7 31 gxh7+**

Simpler is 31 ♛xg7+ ♔xg7 32 ♘f5+, winning the rook.

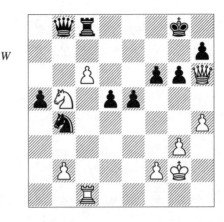

*W*

**31...♛xh7 32 ♛xf6**

White chooses to sacrifice his rook, with the final attack carried out by the joint efforts of the queen and the knight.

**32...♖xc1 33 ♛d8+ ♔g7 34 ♛e7+ ♔g6 35 ♛e6+ ♔h5 36 ♛xe5+ ♔g6 37 ♛f5+ ♔h6 38 ♛f6+ ♔h5 39 ♘f5 ♘d3 40 ♘g7+ 1-0**

## Game 7
# Gilles Mirallès – Marc Santo-Roman
### *Montpellier 2003*

**1 e4 ♘f6 2 e5 ♘d5 3 c4 ♘b6 4 c5 ♘d5 5 ♗c4 (D)**

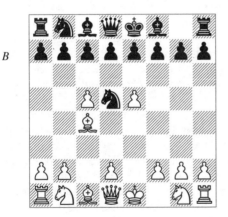

*B*

This attack presents Black with fewer options – one of the pawns has to protect the knight.

**5...e6**

5...c6 is covered in Game 8.

**6 ♘c3**

If White is not tempted by the lines involving a possible sacrifice of the c5-pawn, he has 6 d4. The main set of tools for playing such positions was presented in the previous games, but any small change may introduce significant differences. The two ways to undermine White's pawn-centre are both viable options here:

a) With 6...d6 7 cxd6 cxd6 we are once again on a visit to the same c3 Sicilian system. We should remark that this particular variety is considered quite acceptable for Black.

b) 6...b6 (D) leads to play unique to the Alekhine.

Here too it is possible for White to play to maintain the pawn outpost on c5. The difference is that it is the bishop that is exchanged on d5, while its black counterpart, potentially 'bad' because of the resulting pawn-structure, is deprived of the rival for whom it could seek to be exchanged, and it has trouble finding adequate work: 7 ♗xd5 exd5 8 ♘f3 ♗a6 9 ♘c3 c6 10 b4 ♗c4 11 ♘d2 ♗d3 12 ♛f3 ♗g6 13

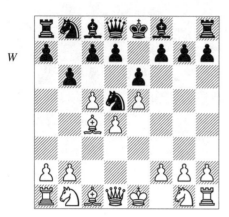

0-0, Yakovenko-Piven, Internet 2004. The other plan begins with the exchange of the pawns by 7 cxb6 axb6; while acquiescing to Black having the better pawn-structure, White seeks compensation in the form of an initiative in the centre and on the kingside; e.g., 8 ♘e2 d6 9 0-0 ♗b7 10 ♕b3 dxe5 11 dxe5 ♘d7 12 ♕g3 ♘e7 13 ♘d4 c5 14 ♘xe6 with a double-edged struggle, Potkin-Neverov, St Petersburg 2000.

**6...♘xc3**

Other moves:

a) The trappy 6...♘f4?! (based on 7 ♕g4? ♕h4!) only succeeds in transferring the knight to g6 (after 7 ♕f3 or 7 g3), where it doesn't look particularly impressive.

b) Bolstering the knight's position with 6...c6 followed by ...b6 is also possible; the hole on d6 is of a temporary nature and gives Black no cause for alarm; we shall discuss this in the notes to the next game via the move-order 5...c6 6 ♘c3 e6.

c) Those who love to defend can try the immediate 6...♗xc5. Regaining the pawn by taking on d5 promises no advantage, while 7 ♕g4 can be met with 7...0-0 8 d4 f5, but the most principled continuation is the immediate 7 d4, when Black has to conduct a defence after 7...♗b4 8 ♗xd5 exd5 9 ♕g4 ♔f8, while extreme optimists may also play 7...♘xc3 8 bxc3 ♗e7 (or 8...♔f8) 9 ♕g4 g6 10 ♗h6.

d) The thematic 6...d6?! in this particular situation has disappeared from practice thanks to a line that involves a piece sacrifice: 7 ♘xd5 exd5 8 ♗xd5 c6 (in reply to 8...dxe5 White has 9 ♕f3 or 9 ♕b3 with a double assault on b7 and f7; therefore Black tries to drive the bishop away first) 9 ♗xf7+ ♔xf7 10 cxd6, obtaining

three pawns for the piece. For a while the line was considered problematic, but today few players are willing to go in for this position as Black.

**7 dxc3** *(D)*

7 bxc3 is also seen. Then 7...♗xc5 8 d4 returns us to the position discussed in the previous note via 6...♗xc5 7 d4 ♘xc3 8 bxc3; the normal continuation, leading to standard play, is 7...d6 (or 7...d5) 8 cxd6 cxd6.

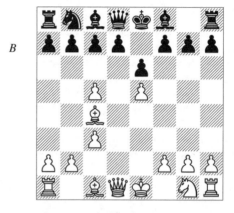

With the text-move (7 dxc3), White sacrifices a pawn, hoping for compensation in the form of an attack on g7.

**7...♘c6**

The immediate capture, 7...♗xc5, is very rarely played. After 8 ♕g4 Black is faced with a depressing choice between 8...g6, 8...♔f8 and 8...♖g8. However, the principal argument against this move is a logical one: if Black wishes to play ...♗xc5, there is not a single obvious reason why ...♘c6 should not be played first.

There is also the tempo-gaining 7...♕h4!?, taking control of the g4-square. Now 8 ♕d4 defends everything, but with the queens off the board it is Black who will be fighting for the advantage. Therefore White will have to give up the pawn after all by 8 ♕e2 ♗xc5 and try to take advantage of the enemy queen's early sortie with 9 g3 ♕e7 10 ♕g4 or 9 ♘h3. Black has scored well with 7...♕h4, but this is based on too few games to consider it a truly ringing endorsement.

**8 ♗f4**

8 ♘f3 blocks the queen's diagonal, while 8 f4? fails to protect the pawn as Black plays 8...♘xe5 all the same.

**8...♝xc5**

If Black plans to counterattack with the g-pawn anyway, it seems to make sense to do so at once, while he still controls the square: 8...g5. However, White can reply 9 ♝g3 and the absence of his queen from g4 takes the sting out of ...h5, while the holes in Black's kingside remain.

Another form of diversion, 8...♛h4 (which also threatens ...♞xe5), appears to be better justified. The idea is to provoke 9 g3, when after 9...♛e7 White has no time for 10 b4 because after 10...g5 the more valuable pawn on e5 is lost. Thus White sacrifices the pawn by 10 ♞f3 ♛xc5, with quite sufficient compensation.

**9 ♛g4 g5 (D)**

This counter-sacrifice keeps the variation alive. Other replies, such as 9...g6, 9...♝f8 and 9...♚f8, don't lose by force (and have in fact scored quite well in the small sample of games with each), but those willing to choose them are hard to find.

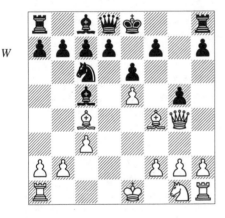

**10 ♝xg5**

The endgame arising after 10 ♛xg5?! ♛xg5 11 ♝xg5 ♞xe5 12 ♝f6 ♞xc4 (Black may grab a third pawn as well by 12...♝xf2+ 13 ♚e2 ♞xc4 14 ♝xh8 ♝xg1, even though it helps White's development) 13 ♝xh8 ♞xb2 is clearly more pleasant for Black.

**10...♜g8**

This is the point of the previous move. Black either forces the exchange of queens, when his broken kingside is less of a liability, or entices White into more substantial sacrifices. Naturally, 10...♞xe5? fails to 11 ♛h5.

**11 ♝xd8**

There is little point in inserting 11 h4 h6 or 11 f4 h6 (11...♞xe5 is also good), and 11 ♞f3? loses to 11...♞xe5, so the only real alternative – and one that is most dangerous – is 11 ♞h3! (D).

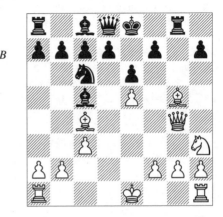

Now 11...♞xe5? is again bad because of 12 ♛h5. 11...h6?! is possible, but after 12 ♝xd8 ♜xg4 13 ♝e2, if Black plays 13...♜xg2 14 ♝xc7, then in comparison to the main game White has managed to get in a useful move for free, which gives him an advantage both objectively and psychologically. Those who like playing with a non-standard material balance may try 13...♚xd8 14 ♝xg4 ♞xe5. A pawn for the exchange is a bit short of full compensation, but the balance is somewhat improved by the fact that the black pawns control the centre, and the centre remains important even with the queens off the board.

The main continuation is 11...♝e7!. Again the exchange of queens promises little: after 12 ♝xe7 ♜xg4 13 ♝xd8 ♚xd8 14 f4 ♜xg2 15 0-0-0 ♚e7 White is active enough to regain his pawn, but that's all. 12 f4 is the most unpleasant reply for Black:

a) After 12...h6 the capture on g4 will not attack c4 and White keeps his pluses without giving up a pawn.

b) In the line 12...♝xg5 13 fxg5 ♞xe5 14 ♛e4 Black's weak squares and lagging development are more than ample compensation for the pawn.

c) After the main continuation 12...♞xe5 13 fxe5 ♝xg5 14 ♛h5 ♜g7 15 0-0 ♛e7, no completely reliable path to equality has been demonstrated (for either side!) either. That fact, together with the highly concrete nature of the play making sharp prepared surprises more likely, has led to this traditional main line of the Chase Variation falling from favour, and players are tending to prefer one of the many earlier deviations, from move 5 onwards. After 16 ♗d3, Black has scored well with 16...b6 (though there is scope for further exploration here), while a critical line runs 16 ♖f3 b6 17 ♖g3 h6 18 ♘f2 ♕c5 19 ♕e2 d6 20 h4! ♗f6! 21 ♖e3! ♗b7 (21...dxe5 22 ♕f3 ♗xh4 is also possible, but 21...♗xe5? loses to 22 b4) 22 b4 ♖xg2+ 23 ♔f1 ♕xe3 24 ♗b5+ ♔f8 25 ♕xe3 ♗xe5, when Rybka insists that Black's attack is sufficient for a draw, but you will no doubt want to check this very carefully before giving up your queen in an actual game!

**11...♖xg4 12 ♗e2 ♖xg2 13 ♗xc7** (D)

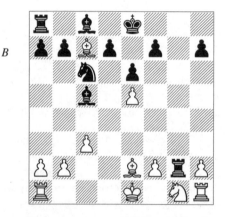

Despite the exchange of queens, Black still has some cause for concern: he is behind in development, his king is not secure and, given the dark-square weaknesses in the centre, is liable to be boxed in.

**13...b5**

It is risky to part with the dark-squared bishop to win a pawn after 13...♗xf2+ 14 ♔f1. The main continuation used to be the developing 13...b6 and in the sample variation 14 ♘h3 ♗b7 15 ♗f3 ♖g8 16 0-0-0 ♖c8 (16...♘a5 may be even more comfortable) 17 ♗d6 ♗xd6 18 exd6 things are tolerable for Black. However, when White started to force the capture on f2 by means of 14 b4, Black found himself with much more tricky and concrete problems to solve, though after 14...♗xf2+ 15 ♔f1 ♖xg1+ 16 ♔xf2 ♖g6 17 ♖hg1 ♗b7 18 ♗h5 ♘e7 19

♗xg6 hxg6 he may well have enough compensation for the exchange.

The text-move keeps the option of retreating to b6 open, and after 14 ♗xb5 ♖xf2 the tempo spent on capturing the pawn imbues Black's counterplay with more strength.

**14 ♘h3 ♗b7** (D)

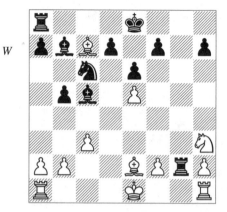

**15 ♗f3**

A more principled continuation would be to question the extent of Black's compensation for the pawn after 15 ♗xb5!?. White's actual choice steers the game into a level field.

**15...♖g8 16 ♔e2 ♖c8 17 ♗d6 ♗xd6 18 exd6**

The d6-pawn has inherited some of the functions of the departed bishop, but is itself a target of attack. Hence White has to hurry.

**18...♘a5 19 ♖ag1 ♗xf3+ 20 ♔xf3** (D)

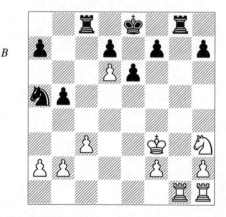

**20...♖g6**

The idea is to lure the knight to f4. If at once 20...♖xg1 21 ♖xg1 ♔f8, Black has to take 22 ♘g5 into account.

21 ♘f4 ♖xg1 22 ♖xg1 ♔f8 23 ♖g5

In order to prepare the invasion by the rook, the fifth rank has to be blocked. The immediate 23 ♘h5 is met with 23...♖c5, and White cannot play 24 ♘f6 because of the check on f5.

**23...a6 24 a4**

Here too, it is too early for 24 ♘h5, since Black has 24...h6.

**24...f5 25 axb5 axb5 26 ♘h5 ♖c6 27 ♖g7 ♖xd6 28 ♖xh7 ♘c4 ½-½**

## Game 8
# Vladimir Potkin – Shakhriyar Mamedyarov
### Abu Dhabi 2005

1 e4 ♘f6 2 e5 ♘d5 3 c4 ♘b6 4 c5 ♘d5 5 ♗c4 c6 *(D)*

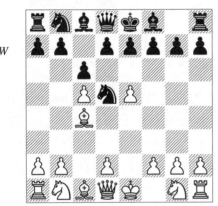

W

Outwardly this looks less useful than supporting the knight with the e-pawn. It does not assist Black's development (and even deprives the b8-knight of its best square), as it has only opened a diagonal for the queen, which Black will not normally seek to develop early in the game. However, there are pluses as well – the d5-knight is defended economically, without wasting the potential of the centre pawns or permanently obstructing the c8-bishop's diagonal. In essence, this is a more ambitious strategy for Black, as he retains many options for eliminating White's pawns in ways that will grant Black a central majority, and also makes it hard for White to find concrete targets.

**6 ♕e2**

The idea of this move is to restrict Black's options in the centre. 6 d4 allows the traditional undermining by 6...b6 or 6...d6, when the struggle takes on a familiar look.

The main continuation, 6 ♘c3, offers a choice of three plans:

a) Black can exchange by 6...♘xc3 7 dxc3. The sole difference from the previous game is that the pawn is on c6 instead of e6. This gives Black the opportunity to go for 7...d5 8 cxd6 exd6 9 ♘f3 d5 10 ♗d3; this pawn-formation was mentioned in Game 6. This seems a better option than weakening the dark squares by 7...b6 8 ♘f3 e6, which led to trouble in the following example: 9 ♗g5 ♗e7 10 ♗xe7 ♕xe7 11 ♕d6 bxc5 12 0-0-0 ♕xd6 13 exd6! *(D)*.

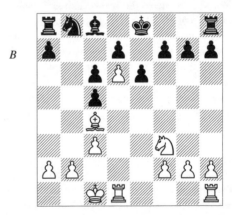

B

The b8-knight's stable door has been locked, Donev-Bruns, Dornbirn 1990.

b) Black can defend the knight with the other pawn: 6...e6. Black plans to solve the problem of the c8-bishop by bringing it out to a6 after ...b6. The immediate attempt to latch onto the weakened dark squares by 7 ♘e4 b6 8 ♘d6+ (after 8 d4 bxc5 9 dxc5 Black can also reply with 9...♗xc5) 8...♗xd6 9 cxd6 can lead to the centre pawns becoming a burden as Black will attack them from the rear. White's hopes for an advantage are based on his larger space, better development and, accordingly, greater freedom of choice, as for example in the following game: 7 d4 b6 8 cxb6 axb6 9 ②f3 ♗e7 10 0-0 ♗a6 11 ♕e2 0-0 12 ♗d2 f5 13 ♗xa6 ♖xa6 14 ②xd5 cxd5 15 a4, Nurkić-Runić, Tuzla 2006.

c) The main line is 6...d6 *(D)*, immediately undermining the centre pawns. Then:

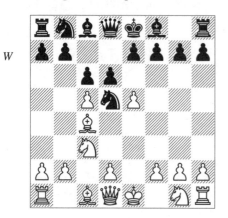

c1) There are no reasons to count on an advantage after 7 ②xd5?! cxd5 8 ♗xd5 e6 and, depending on where the bishop retreats, Black takes on c5 or e5. The sacrifice by analogy with the previous game (note 'd' to Black's 6th move), where White's chances associated with his three-pawn centre wedge were improved by Black's loss of the right to castle, 9 ♗xe6 ♗xe6 10 cxd6, clearly loses here. Thus we see a major motivation for choosing 5...c6 over 5...e6, as White must instead choose something less direct.

c2) 7 cxd6 exd6 leads to relatively quiet play: 8 ②xd5 (or 8 ②f3, when 8...dxe5 9 ②xe5 ♗d6 led to equality in Sveshnikov-Kengis, Latvian Ch, Riga 2006: 10 d4 0-0 11 0-0 ♗e6 12 ♕b3 ♗xe5 13 dxe5 ②xc3 14 bxc3 ♗xc4 15 ♕xc4 ②d7 16 e6 ½-½) 8...cxd5 9 ♗xd5 dxe5 10 ♕b3 ♕c7 (a line that dates back to 1946!).

c3) 7 ♕f3?! has the same idea as line 'c4', but is worse, as after 7...②d7 the capture on e5 will occur with gain of tempo.

c4) 7 ♕b3 is the ambitious move. Black then has two sharp lines:

c41) 7...②d7 8 ②xd5 ②xc5 (bad is 8...cxd5? 9 ♗xd5 e6 10 ♗xe6 fxe6 11 ♕xe6+ ♕e7 12 ♕xe7+ with four pawns for the piece) 9 ②c7+ ♔d7 10 ♕e3 ♔xc7. After 11 d4 White's compensation isn't wholly convincing after either 11...d5 12 dxc5 dxc4 13 ♗d2 ♕d3 or 11...♗e6 12 ♗e2 ②d7 13 ②f3 ♗d5 14 0-0 e6, so 11

♗xf7 is probably a better idea, with complications that are hard to assess after either 11...♗f5 12 d4 ②d3+ 13 ♔f1 or 11...♕d7 12 d4 ♕f5 13 ♗c4 ♗e6 14 ♗e2 ②d7.

c42) 7...dxe5 8 ②xd5 cxd5 9 ♗xd5 e6 10 ♗xb7 ♗xb7 11 ♕xb7 ♕d5. After the exchange of the queens the extra pawn cannot be kept, while in the case of 12 ♕c8+ ♔e7 13 ♕c7+ ♔f6 14 d4 ②c6 15 ②f3 it is not clear whether White can take advantage of the black king's 'centralization'.

**6...e6**

With ...d6 forestalled, ...b6 is a natural alternative. Why not 6...b6 at once? White doesn't mind sacrificing the c5-pawn and if Black takes it with the b-pawn, White gets an advantage in development, while it is still hard for Black to advance in the centre. Therefore in reply to 7 ②c3 it is wise not to accept the sacrifice with 7...②xc3 8 dxc3 bxc5 but to play 7...e6 instead, which in the game Black does at once, prompting d4. The other attempt to snatch the c5-pawn – 6...♕a5 – doesn't spoil Black's pawn-structure, but the queen's sortie is time-consuming and by showing disdain for material with 7 ②f3 ♕xc5 8 d4, White gets a noticeable lead in mobilization of his army.

**7 d4 b6**

Now the capture on c5 is a real threat, so White exchanges first.

**8 cxb6 axb6** *(D)*

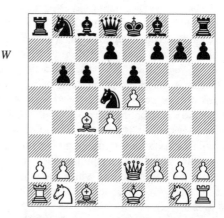

We have a position typical of the whole system. Black has managed to fulfil a part of his program: he has disposed of the enemy pawn on c5 in an efficient way, without compromising the c8-bishop's prospects, whose appearance on a6 cannot be prevented. In return, Black has conceded space to White, but that often happens in our opening and is the norm rather than the exception.

**9 ♘h3?!** *(D)*

9 ♘f3 looks more natural. Besides the exchange of the light-squared bishops (though neither side will rush into actually making the exchange, as this eases the opponent's deployment) Black also has plans involving ...f5, with a view to exchanging yet another white centre pawn for one of his flank pawns, or else obtaining more space and security on the kingside. For example, 9...♗a6 10 b3 (10 ♘c3 ♗e7 11 0-0 0-0 and here 12 ♘e4 can be met by 12...f5, as in Scotto-Shabalov, St Martin 1993) 10...♗e7 11 0-0 0-0 12 ♘bd2?! f5?! (12...b5!? is already an idea) 13 exf6 ♘xf6 14 ♖e1 ♔h8 15 ♘e5 ♕e8 16 a4 ♕h5 and here the careless 17 ♕d3?? led to material losses after 17...b5! in Dannevig-Burgess, Gausdal 1990.

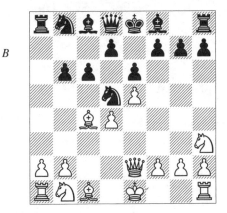

White's motivation for the text-move is not generally so he can follow up by advancing the f-pawn, as in such positions this advance is more often than not anti-positional. The main virtue of 9 ♘h3 is leaving the queen's path to g4 open, which is the main obstacle to the development of the f8-bishop. As for its drawbacks, we shall not list them, as they are self-evident.

**9...d6**

A new plan. Earlier ...♗a6 in combination with ...♗b4+ used to be played, in order to gain time for castling, or the diversionary sortie 9...♕h4. Black wants to see what kind of advantage he can extract from his control of the c5-square; perhaps the c8-bishop deserves a

better fate than an exchange and may become the master of the a6-f1 diagonal.

**10 0-0**

Naturally, White does not wish to make the exchange of pawns himself on d6.

**10...dxe5 11 dxe5 ♘d7** *(D)*

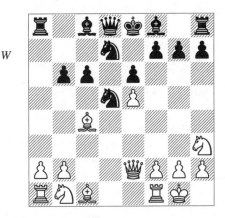

**12 ♖e1**

The overprotection of the e5-pawn is not redundant, as the h3-knight is out of the picture, while the queen would prefer that this task didn't restrict her mobility.

**12...b5**

Not really a sacrifice, as after 13 ♗xd5 cxd5 14 ♕xb5 ♗a6 Black can regain his material at once, but it is even more interesting not to waste time on this but, for starters, to try to secure an advantage in development.

**13 ♗b3 ♘c5 14 ♗g5**

Black has created a concrete threat, and if White continues to retreat the bishop by 14 ♗c2, it is likely to be further harassed with 14...♘b4. Defending the bishop by 14 ♘d2 shuts the c1-bishop in. Hence the text-move, seeking to gain a tempo.

**14...♘f4!** *(D)*

With this far from obvious tactical blow, Black effectively solves his main opening task – from striving to equalize he goes to full equality at least. White's reply is forced.

**15 ♘xf4 ♕xg5 16 ♘h3**

This is not the only move to parry both threats; 16 ♕f3 looks more natural than returning the knight to the edge of the board.

**16...♕h4 17 ♘d2 ♗e7 18 ♕e3**

Over the past few moves, Black has solved some of his problems, but the c8-bishop remains

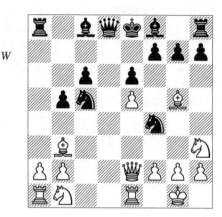

passive. White could have picked another plan, such as preserving his remaining bishop. However, the attempt to set up a blockade on c5 is an obvious continuation and looks absolutely logical.

**18...0-0 19 ℤec1**

Of course, White would have liked to move the other rook here, but the a2-pawn needs protection.

**19...♘xb3 20 ♘xb3 ℤd8**

Indirectly protecting c6 due to the threat of a counterblow on a2. 20...ℤa4 was the alternative, preventing the idea that now follows.

**21 ♘f4 (D)**

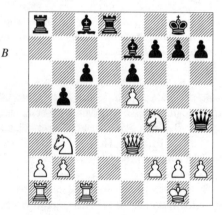

The other knight is bound for c5.

**21...♗g5?!**

A committal decision. Black goes into a sharp endgame with mutual weaknesses, but his c8-bishop is for the moment out of play. It would be interesting to leave the queens on the board, considering that White's kingside pawns still have to move one way or another, creating

weaknesses. For example, 21...♗b7 is possible, when 22 ♘d3?! is dubious in view of 22...♗g5 23 f4 ℤxd3 24 ♕xd3 ♗xf4 25 g3 ♕g5 with a strong initiative.

**22 g3 ♗xf4 (D)**

Keeping the queens on with 22...♕g4?! is risky. In the line 23 f3 ♕f5 24 ♘d4 ♗xf4 25 gxf4 ♕g6+ 26 ♔h1 ♗b7 27 ℤg1 ♕h6 28 ♘b3 the activity of the white pieces more than makes up for the defects in his pawn-structure. Black could have tried to provoke the advance of the h-pawn to h4 first by 22...♕h6, and after 23 ♘c5 to begin to open the position with 23...f6.

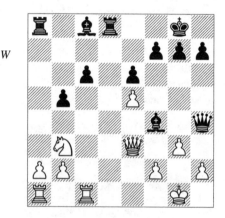

**23 ♕xf4 ♕xf4**

And now 23...♕h5 deserved attention. The possible threat to the e5-pawn (after ...ℤd5) then demands that White spend some time on prophylactic measures.

**24 gxf4 ℤa4**

In the line 24...♗d7!? 25 ℤd1 ♗e8 26 ℤd6 the bishop is not much to look at, but for the moment it defends the flank, while securing the weaknesses on a2 and f4 along with a long-term blockade of the black pawns is harder.

**25 ℤxc6 ℤxf4 26 ♘c5**

Another way to immobilize the bishop – 26 ℤc7! – looks much more attractive, and only after 26...ℤc4 (ℤac1 was threatened) play 27 ♘c5, when it is hard to see how Black is to defend against the advance of the a-pawn. An important nuance is that Black cannot exchange the b-pawns – the other rook will invade down the newly opened file, which spells fewer chances to hold the endgame where the bishop will have to be given up for the a-pawn.

**26...h5**

This opens an escape hatch for the king as well as being a broad step forward by the potential passed pawn. However, 26...f6 is more promising, making a short step in order to clear the c8-h3 diagonal for the bishop and obtaining counterchances along the f-file. After ...fxe5 the outpost on d4 will be handy.

**27 Ξc1 b4 28 b3?** (D)

After 28 a4 sooner or later the bishop will have to be given up for this pawn. Black will then need to seek counterplay on the kingside to save the game.

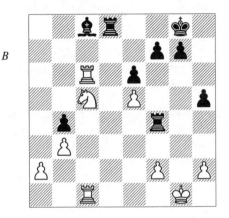

White's actual move is hard to understand; was Ξc4 the idea?

**28...Ξg4+ 29 Φf1**

The move in the opposite direction keeps the bishop in its place, but leaves the king further from the centre, while the c1-rook must stay on the back rank.

**29...Φd7 30 ⵡxd7**

White has to exchange – any grounds for White's advantage disappear along with the bishop.

**30...Ξxd7 31 Ξ1c4?!**

However, White does not seem to want to reconcile himself to equality. An easier way to draw is to go into a single rook endgame after 31 Ξ6c4. In lines like 31...Ξd2 32 Ξxg4 hxg4 33 Ξc4 Ξxa2 34 Ξxg4 Ξa5 or 31...Ξgd4 32 Ξxd4 Ξxd4 33 Ξc4 Ξd2 34 Ξxb4 Ξxa2 a symbolic advantage remains on Black's side. In the game, Black could have forced similar play with 31...Ξd2, but there are plenty of drawish tendencies in rook endgames. White's actual choice gives Black the extra option of going

into a double-rook endgame where the struggle flares up again.

**31...Ξd1+ 32 Φe2 Ξgg1**

32...Ξd5!? is more interesting and promising.

**33 Ξxb4 Ξge1+ 34 Φf3 Ξxe5** (D)

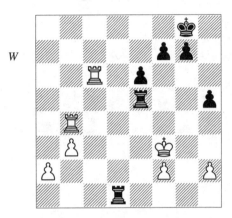

The game has taken on a sharp character. White has a pair of passed pawns, while on the other hand, Black may profit from the white king getting in the way of his own pieces.

**35 Ξc2 g5 36 Ξe4 Ξed5 37 a4 g4+ 38 Φe2?**

The wrong way. On g2 the king risks finding himself in a mating-net, but 38 Φg2 was nevertheless correct, since after the text-move the black h-pawn proves to be faster than its rivals.

**38...Ξh1 39 Ξd2 Ξf5 40 Φd3?**

The final loss of time. The only attempt at resistance consisted of trying to set up a race of the passed pawns, with 40 h4!? a reasonable way to delay Black's kingside progress.

**40...Ξxh2 41 Ξee2 h4 42 b4 h3 43 b5 Ξh1 44 Ξe4 Ξg5 45 Ξde2 h2 0-1**

In the system examined in this chapter, White's board-wide play provides for a high level of tension from the very first moves. However, the committal nature of his set-up gives Black targets for counterplay, and it is mostly Black who picks the outlines of the subsequent struggle – from the classical approach, where his primary task is reaching equality (and in the main lines he has every reason to expect to do so), to sharp play with winning chances for both sides. True fans of our opening usually don't find the prospect of playing against this system at all depressing.

# 3 The Four Pawns Attack

In this system, White again accepts the knight's kind offer and builds an imposing central formation: 1 e4 ♘f6 2 e5 ♘d5 3 d4 d6 4 c4 ♘b6 5 f4 (D).

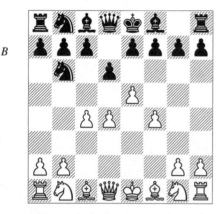

White adopts a maximalist approach: he throws into combat as many pawns as possible while maintaining their mobility. In order to remain strong, any pawn-centre needs to be flexible and capable of fulfilling several functions, including the ability to advance and preferably in a number of different ways. Generally speaking, White is seeking to use his pawns as cover for an attack that will be launched as soon as Black has determined the location of his king, but the pawns' mobility comes into play in many lines in an intricate battle resulting from Black's attempts to dismantle the phalanx.

We should note that White has not had to pay for this imposing pawn-mass with a delay in development (as he does, for instance, in the King's Indian line of the same name), as Black's only achievement while White has been moving his pawns has been to reposition his knight from f6 to b6. More pertinent is the fact that the centre is somewhat loose, and in order to destroy it (after a preliminary exchange ...dxe5 and fxe5) it is enough to play ...c5 while keeping d5 under control. This is not easy to carry out, of course, but the goal has been defined. There is also the secondary plan of undermining the centre with ...f6, when after exf6 and ...♗xf6 the weakness on e6 is balanced by the pressure on d4.

The immediate thrust ...c5, allowing the advance of the d4-pawn in hopes of demonstrating the weakness of the resulting centre, is examined in Game 9 (Movsesian-Luther). In the rest of our games in this chapter, Black seeks to restrain the pawn-centre, at least for a few moves, before attacking it. Then the main decision is whether to play an early ...♘c6. While its advantages are unquestionable, this posting also has one flaw – it blocks ...c5, so the d5 advance will be harder to force – on Black's terms, at any rate. Lines where Black decides to develop other pieces first are the subject of Game 10 (Olivier-Yanev). Variations where Black develops the knight to c6 but does not allow the d-pawn to advance (either by increasing his guard on the d5-square or by undermining the piece support for the pawn's advance) are examined in Game 11 (Nakamura-Benjamin). And finally, the most combative and chaotic line, where White seizes the initiative by advancing with d5, is presented in Game 12 (L.Dominguez-Almeida).

## Game 9
## Sergei Movsesian – Thomas Luther
### *European Ch, Istanbul 2003*

**1 e4 ♘f6 2 e5 ♘d5 3 d4 d6 4 c4 ♘b6 5 f4 dxe5**

This exchange exposes the d4-pawn to attack and weakens the e5-pawn's protection. Black intends, either immediately or later, to knock away its other support by ...c5.

Sometimes Black refrains from exchanging and plays 5...♗f5 *(D)* at once.

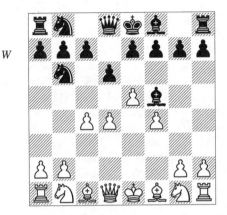

This may come down to a mere transposition of moves (compared to 5...dxe5 6 fxe5 ♗f5 or 5...dxe5 6 fxe5 ♘c6 7 ♗e3 ♗f5), but there are independent ideas in which the d6-pawn is used in other operations, primarily as preparation for ...c5 in the line 6 ♘c3 e6 7 ♘f3 ♘a6. Black threatens to destroy White's centre as well as ...♘b4, and White must determine how to transform the position's current set of pluses into another. A reliable continuation is 8 a3 c5 9 dxc5 dxc5 10 ♗e3, but it involves the exchange of queens, and thus any advantage for White will be minimal. The exchange of bishops by 8 ♗d3 sharpens the play; e.g., 8...♗xd3 9 ♕xd3 c5 10 dxc5?! (10 d5 is interesting; e.g., 10...exd5 11 cxd5 dxe5 12 0-0!?) 10...♘xc5 11 ♕e2 dxe5 12 ♘xe5 f6 13 ♕h5+ g6 14 ♘xg6 hxg6 15 ♕xh8 ♕d4 with strong counterplay, Djurhuus-Agdestein, Norwegian Ch playoff (2), Asker 2000.

Sometimes the d6-pawn is given a different mission – 7...♗e7 (instead of 7...♘a6) 8 ♗e3 0-0 9 ♗d3 d5 (the preliminary exchange of the bishops is also played). This method of counterattacking the centre is in itself typical of this opening, but Black's light-squared bishop is usually exchanged for the f3-knight; here it leaves the board together with its opposing number while the knight remains, which in a closed position favours White.

The joint offspring of the Pirc Defence – 5...g6 – has a birth defect, as the knight has

galloped too far from the defence of the king-side. White can try to profit from this at once by 6 ♘c3 ♗g7 7 ♗e3, when 7...♗e6 is met by 8 d5!, and 7...0-0 8 c5 ♘6d7 9 ♘f3 (the brutal advance 9 h4 looks good too) 9...b6 10 cxd6 cxd6 11 ♗c4! gives White excellent play. Exchanging queens also promises Black no joy: 7...dxe5 8 dxe5 ♕xd1+ 9 ♖xd1 ♗e6 10 b3 f6 11 c5! ♘6d7 12 ♘b5 ♘a6 13 c6! bxc6 14 ♘d4, Cheparinov-M.Grünberg, European Ch, Antalya 2004.

5...c5?! 6 dxc5 ♘6d7 7 cxd6 exd6 8 exd6 ♘f6 9 ♕e2+ ♗e6 10 ♘c3 g6 11 ♗e3 ♗g7 12 0-0-0 0-0 13 ♘f3 ♘c6 14 ♕d2 ♕a5 15 ♘d4 left Black a pawn down for very little in Smeets-Wohl, Zwolle 2001.

5...g5?! is a notorious move that has never become respected, but has never been completely refuted either. After 6 exd6 ♕xd6 7 ♘c3! ♗g7 8 ♗e2 c5 9 ♘b5 ♕d8 10 dxc5 ♘6d7 11 fxg5 ♘c6 12 ♘f3 a6 13 ♘c3 ♕a5 14 0-0 White has a significant advantage, although in Gerigk-Teske, Bundesliga 2009/10 he failed to follow up vigorously enough and ended up losing.

**6 fxe5 c5**

White's centre invites exactly this type of undermining thrust, but normally it is carried out only after some preparation, generally with the aim of preventing the advance to d5 and so forcing an exchange of pawns. The immediate attack forces White to advance, and has generally enjoyed no more than a semi-correct reputation. It gained some popularity in the last quarter of the 20th century and leads to very sharp play.

**7 d5 *(D)***

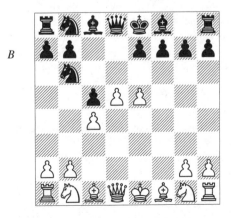

**7...e6**

An interesting alternative is to fianchetto the king's bishop before continuing the assault on White's pawn-centre. This idea has scored well in practice for Black, but theoretically there are some unanswered questions, which is not too surprising given that White is also granted time to support his centre, and has several possible ways to do so. After 7...g6!? 8 ♘c3 ♗g7 9 ♗f4 (both 9 ♘f3?! ♗g4 and 9 ♗e3?! 0-0 10 ♗xc5 ♘8d7 show Black's plans working nicely) 9...0-0 10 ♕d2 (10 ♘f3 ♗g4 11 ♕e2 e6 12 0-0-0 exd5 13 ♘xd5 ♘xd5 14 ♖xd5 ♕a5 was OK for Black in Y.Vovk-Khvorostinin, Ukrainian Team Ch, Alushta 2007) 10...e6 (D), White has two main options:

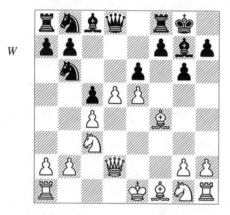

a) 11 0-0-0 exd5 (11...f6 12 ♘f3 has scored well for White in practice) 12 cxd5 and here:

a1) 12...♗g4 13 ♖e1 c4 14 h3 ♗f5 15 g4 ♗d3 16 ♗xd3 cxd3 17 ♕xd3 ♘a6 18 d6 ♖c8 19 ♔b1 ♘c5 (19...♘b4 20 ♕d1 ♘c4 21 ♖h2 led to a win for White in Movsesian-Z.Varga, Czech League 2004/5, but the position isn't exactly clear at this point; 19...♘c4!? is perhaps also best met by 20 ♖h2!?, since 20 ♘d5 ♕a5 21 ♘f3 ♘xb2! 22 ♕b3 ♖c5 23 ♗d2 ♕a4 24 ♘e7+ ♔h8 25 ♖e3 ♖b5 26 ♕xa4 ♘xa4+ 27 ♖b3 is an unclear ending) 20 ♕e2 ♘e6 21 ♗g3 ♘c4 22 ♘f3 ♕a5 23 ♖c1 ♗h6 24 g5 ♗xg5 25 ♘xg5 ♘xg5 26 ♖hd1 is messy but should probably favour White, Ilinčić-Marinković, Vrnjačka Banja 1989.

a2) 12...♖e8 13 ♖e1 (this leads to an entertaining example, but 13 ♗g5 looks like the most testing move: 13...f6 {13...♕c7!?} 14 exf6 ♗xf6 15 ♘f3 and now Black should probably try

15...♗f5 since 15...♗g4? loses to 16 ♕f4, B.Cox-St Jean, corr. 2002) 13...♘a6 14 ♘f3 ♘b4 15 ♗g5 f6 16 ♗h4 ♗f5 17 ♗b5? a6! 18 exf6 (18 ♗xe8 loses to 18...♘d3+ 19 ♔d1 ♘c4) 18...♖xe1+ (missing 18...axb5!! 19 f7+ ♔xf7 20 ♗xd8 ♖exd8 with an overwhelming attack) 19 ♖xe1 ♗xf6 20 ♖e8+ ♕xe8 21 ♗xe8 ♘c4 22 ♗f7+ ♔xf7 23 ♕h6 ♘d3+ 24 ♔d1 ♗g7 25 ♘g5+ ♔f8 26 ♘xh7+?! (26 ♕xh7) 26...♔g8 27 ♘f6+ ♔f7 28 ♕g5 ♖h8 29 ♘fe4 ♖e8 30 d6 ♘dxb2+ 31 ♔c2? (31 ♔c1) 31...♘xd6 32 ♕xf5+ and 0-1 B.Smith-Shabalov, King of Prussia 2007.

b) 11 d6 ♘c6 12 ♘f3 ♘d7 13 ♕e3 f6 (13...♘d4 is another idea) and then:

b1) 14 0-0-0 fxe5 (14...♘dxe5!?) 15 ♗h6 (15 ♗g5!?) 15...♘d4 16 ♗xg7 ♔xg7 17 ♘xe5 ♘f5 18 ♕e1 ♕g5+ 19 ♖d2 ♘d4 (19...♕e3 20 ♕xe3 ♘xe3 21 ♘f3 favoured White in Klinger-Bischoff, Zug 1985) 20 ♘d3 followed by h4-h5 leaves White with the initiative.

b2) 14 exf6 ♘xf6 (14...♕xf6?! 15 ♗g5 ♕f7 16 0-0-0 ♘d4 17 ♗d3 ♘f5 18 ♗xf5 exf5 19 ♘d5 led to a White win in Jansen-Marcinkiewicz, corr. 2002) 15 ♕xc5 ♘e4 16 ♘xe4 ♖xf4 might be OK for Black; e.g., 17 ♕e3 (17 ♗d3 ♕b6) 17...♕a5+ 18 ♘c3 ♗d7 19 0-0-0 ♖af8.

We now return to 7...e6 (D):

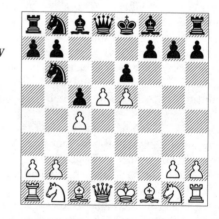

**8 ♘c3**

It is clear that 8 d6? is bad due to 8...♕h4+, as the attempt to trap the queen may succeed after 9 g3 ♕e4+ 10 ♕e2 ♕xh1 11 ♘f3 ♘c6 but will cost White dearly.

**8...exd5**

Black can try 8...♕h4+ here too, but after 9 g3 ♕d4 White can choose 10 ♕xd4 cxd4 11

♘b5 ♘a6 12 d6 f6 13 ♘f3 ♗d7 14 ♘bxd4 fxe5 15 ♘xe5 ♗xd6, when he can count on a small advantage, or he can seek larger rewards by gambit play with 10 ♗d2! ♕xe5+ 11 ♗e2, aiming to exploit White's development advantage resulting from Black's queen moves.

The exchange in the game sets the enemy e5-pawn free again, but Black's c5-pawn can also advance and, most significantly of all, an important diagonal is opened.

**9 cxd5 c4** (D)

Another version of the queen sortie, 9...♕h4+ 10 g3 ♕d4, is sometimes seen here, but it is regarded as very dubious, as White gets a strong initiative with a pawn sacrifice: 11 ♗b5+ (less generous players may prefer 11 ♗f4 g5 12 ♗xg5 ♕xe5+ 13 ♕e2) 11...♗d7 12 ♕e2 ♘xd5 13 e6 fxe6 14 ♕xe6+ ♘e7 15 ♘f3 ♕b4 (or 15...♕f6 16 ♕e2!) 16 ♘e5!.

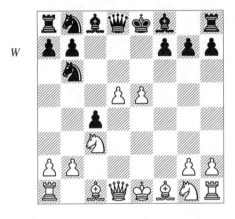

This has traditionally been considered the main position of this variation. The powerful centre pawn pair on the fifth rank looks menacing; one of them is passed to boot and both are mobile. However, they lack neighbours to support them and can only count on support from pieces. Black's last move opens a diagonal for the other bishop as well, preparing to attack a defender of the d5-pawn.

**10 d6**

Today this is considered the most critical continuation. Clearly, 10 ♗xc4?? ♕h4+ is no good and 10 a3 looks torpid. Let's consider the alternatives:

a) The immediate centralization of the queen by 10 ♕d4 is rarely seen. After 10...♘c6 11 ♕e4 ♘b4, 12 a3 ♘4xd5 13 ♘xd5 ♕xd5 14

♕xd5 ♘xd5 15 ♗xc4 leaves White no better; on the other hand, the line 12 d6 g6 13 ♗xc4 ♘xc4 14 ♕xc4 ♘c2+ 15 ♔f1 ♘xa1 16 ♘d5 ♗g7 17 ♘c7+ ♔f8 18 ♘xa8 leads to a fighting, unclear position.

b) Developing the dark-squared bishop first doesn't enjoy much popularity either. After 10 ♗f4 ♗b4 White cannot play 11 ♗xc4 ♘xc4 12 ♕a4+ ♘c6 13 dxc6 ♘xb2 and has to settle for 11 d6, but why let the enemy bishop out? Neither it is clear what the point of 10 ♗e3 might be.

c) The main continuation used to be 10 ♘f3, when Black replies by bringing out one of the bishops:

c1) 10...♗g4?! (D).

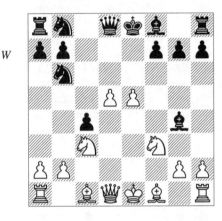

Black indirectly protects c4 but fails to pose a concrete threat to either centre pawn, which provides White with a certain respite. During the period when this system was fighting for recognition, Ljubojević played several games (as both colours!) that were important for its theory. Then the main debate was centred on the line 11 ♕d4 ♗xf3 12 gxf3 ♗b4 13 ♗xc4 0-0 14 ♖g1 g6 15 ♗g5 ♕c7 16 ♗b3 ♗c5 17 ♕f4 ♗xg1 18 d6 ♕c5 19 ♘e4 ♕d4 20 ♖d1 ♕xb2, and it seems that after 21 ♘f6+ ♔h8 22 ♖d2 ♕a1+! neither side has anything clearly better than a repetition of the moves, which is not a big achievement on White's part (if White wishes to play on, then 23 ♗d1 ♗e3! 24 ♕xe3 ♘c4 25 ♘g4 f6 26 ♕d4 leads to an unclear ending).

Such play, highly rich in content, has monopolized this sector of the theory, and the outwardly modest 11 ♗e2! has remained largely out of the spotlight. However, this move appears to cast grave doubt on Black's play in rather simple fashion. White has good chances to hold the centre until completing his development, although sharp lines like 11...♗c5 12 ♘g5 are also possible (and indeed considered very difficult for Black). Simple and interesting, though insufficiently tested in practice, is 11 ♗xc4 ♘xc4 12 ♕a4+ ♘d7 13 ♕xc4 ♗xf3 14 gxf3 ♘xe5 15 ♕e2 (weaker is 15 ♕e4 ♕h4+) 15...♕e7 (Barlov's piece sacrifice 15...♗d6 is interesting, but maybe not fully adequate) 16 0-0 0-0-0 (or 16...f6), when the white king feels clearly more secure than his opposing number.

c2) 10...♗b4 11 ♗xc4 for a long time wandered from one publication to another in the company of a line authored by Boleslavsky: 11...♘xc4(?) 12 ♕a4+ ♘c6 13 dxc6 ♗xc3+ 14 bxc3 b5 15 ♕b4 a5 16 ♕c5 ♕d3 17 ♗g5 with an advantage for White. Then in 1986 Shabalov offered a pawn sacrifice by 11...♗xc3+ 12 bxc3 ♘xc4 13 ♕a4+ ♘d7 14 ♕xc4 ♘b6 15 ♕b5+ ♕d7 16 ♕xd7+ ♗xd7, and Black's idea found a following (actually, it turns out that this had been played in a Finnish correspondence game as far back as 1976, but no one had noticed). In order to keep the pawn, White has to play 17 d6 (D).

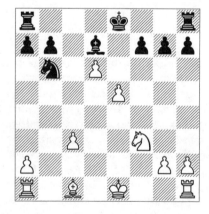

Black certainly has at least some compensation: the pawns are blockaded, the d7-bishop is the undisputed master of the light squares, whereas his dark-squared opponent is restricted and is potentially 'bad'. The subsequent play is likely to involve manoeuvring around the weaknesses on a2, c3 and e5; Black is not just playing for a draw, since if the e5-pawn falls, then its neighbour on d6 is doomed too. Nevertheless, there is no completely clear plan of

regaining the pawn, while White can also seek targets to attack, or at least to disrupt Black's activation of his forces. After 17...♖c8 18 ♗d2 (White can also seek safety by giving up the c3-pawn in return for activity; e.g., 18 ♗e3 ♖xc3 19 ♗xb6 axb6 20 ♔d2 ♖a3, leading to equality, and transposing to Shirov-Shabalov, Riga 1986), Black has a choice between the natural 18...♘a4, Bagirov's 18...♘c4 and Baburin's 18...♗b5 (or indeed 18...0-0 intending ...f6, as in Palmo-Nurmesniemi, Finnish corr. Ch 1976).

We now return to 10 d6 (D):

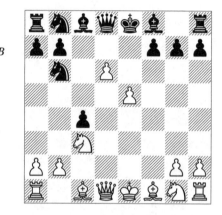

The text-move (10 d6) is the obvious choice, although it took a while for it to come into the spotlight. Its virtues are evident – the enemy bishop is locked in, which hinders castling, and the white queen's knight stares at the c7-square. Its defects are no mystery either: the pawn-centre's value is higher when the pawns stand side by side while remaining mobile; Black's task is to force one of them to step forward, which usually allows a blockade to be set up. Here White advances of his own accord and at the expense of his development to boot.

**10...♗e6**

The attempt to fianchetto the imprisoned bishop by 10...g6? creates chronically vulnerable holes on the dark squares.

The other main continuation is 10...♘c6?! (with ideas such as the controversial queen sacrifice line 11 ♗f4 g5 12 ♘e4 gxf4), but this leaves the c7-square without protection and White can set off for it immediately by 11 ♘b5!. Black's obvious recourse is an attempt to take advantage of the unguarded state of the e4-square, but this usually ends in the loss of the queen, and so far no one has managed to obtain sufficient compensation for it; for example, 11...♕h4+ 12 g3 ♕e4+ 13 ♕e2 ♕xh1 14 ♗g5! ♗e6 (14...f6 15 ♘c7+ ♔f7 16 e6+ ♔g6 17 0-0-0 is winning for White; as a desperate try, one might even consider 14...♗xd6 15 exd6+ ♗e6 16 ♘c7+ ♔d7) and now rather than 15 d7+?! ♔xd7 16 0-0-0+ (Fontaine-Rogulj, Kastav 2002), when 16...♘d5 does not seem clear, 15 0-0-0 is very good for White, as he threatens mate in two by 16 d7+, and so Black does not have time to gain a decent ransom for his queen; e.g., 15...♘d5 16 ♗g2 ♕xh2 17 ♗xd5! ♕xe2 18 ♗xc6+ bxc6 19 d7+ ♗xd7 20 ♘c7#.

If Black is desperate to make 10...♘c6 work, then perhaps he should look into Bronstein's old suggestion of meeting 11 ♘b5 with 11...♘xe5 12 ♘c7+ ♔d7. Some critical lines are then 13 ♘xa8 ♕h4+ 14 g3 ♕e4+ 15 ♕e2 ♘d3+ 16 ♔d2 ♕xe2+ 17 ♗xe2 ♘xa8 18 ♗xd3 cxd3 19 ♘f3 ♗xd6 20 ♔xd3 b6, and 13 ♘f3 ♗xd6 14 ♘xa8 ♖e8, when 15 ♘xb6+ ♕xb6 16 ♕a4+ ♔d8 17 ♗g5+ f6 18 0-0-0 fxg5 and 15 ♘xe5+ ♖xe5+ 16 ♗e2 ♔c6 17 0-0 ♗c5+ 18 ♔h1 ♕xd1 19 ♗xd1 ♘xa8 are both possible. In all three cases, the onus is still on Black to show that he can make his position work.

**11 ♘f3** *(D)*

The most natural, considering that the bishop is not likely to be tempted to spend two tempi to get to g4.

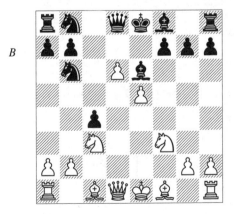

*B*

**11...♘c6**

Luther had previously essayed this variation twice. First in the game Korneev-Luther,

Gibraltar 2003 he chose the text-move and after 12 ♗e2 ♘d7 13 ♗f4 he continued to attack the e5-pawn by 13...♕a5 14 0-0, but did not risk actually taking it, and preferred 14...h6 instead (14...0-0-0!? is another idea). No direct refutation of 14...♘dxe5 is apparent, although the calm 15 ♘xe5 ♘xe5 16 ♔h1 poses Black awkward problems. In a later game Zelčić-Luther, Dresden 2003 he changed the move-order, forestalling the white knight's leap to b5: 11...♘6d7 12 ♗f4 ♘c6 13 ♗e2 (with this move-order, White has some extra options like 13 ♕a4), but avoided repeating the previous game and played 13...g6, but after 14 0-0 ♗g7 15 ♘d5 the version of the exchange sacrifice that followed left White with a strong passed pawn on d6, which eventually decided the game's outcome: 15...0-0 16 ♘c7 ♘dxe5 17 ♘xe5 ♘xe5 18 ♘xa8 ♕xa8.

**12 ♘b5**

12 ♗f4 ♘d7 transposes to the previous note, and may therefore be White's best option.

**12...♖c8**

Black doesn't mind giving up the exchange if he gets the d6-pawn into the bargain, of course.

**13 ♗g5 ♕d7 14 a4 h6**

Driving the knight off first by 14...a6 deserved consideration. Then after 15 ♘bd4 ♘xd4 16 ♘xd4 Black can initiate counterplay with 16...♖c5, while after 15 ♘c3 h6 the retreat 16 ♗e3 allows 16...♕d8, vacating the d7-square for the knight, when Black is not afraid of having a go at yet another version of the exchange sacrifice: 17 ♗xb6?! ♕xb6 18 ♗xc4? ♗xc4 19 d7+ ♔d8. If the bishop maintains control of the d8-square by 16 ♗h4, there can follow 16...♘b4 17 ♗e2 ♘6d5 18 ♘xd5 ♘xd5; e.g., 19 ♕c1?! g5 20 ♗g3 ♗g7 with an unclear game.

**15 ♗e3 ♘d5 16 ♗f2**

White could consider the grabbing a pawn by 16 ♗xa7!?.

**16...a6 17 ♘bd4 ♘xe5!?** *(D)*

In full accordance with the motto "it is better to die on one's feet than to live on one's knees". Black radically solves the problem of the enemy centre by giving up a piece for it. Objectively, White has the advantage in the resulting position, but he has to switch to defence and the price he may pay for a mistake increases drastically.

**18 ♘xe5 ♕xd6 19 ♘ef3?!**

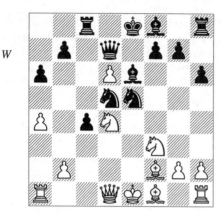

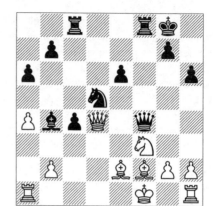

Maintaining the attack on e6 but letting the black queen onto an excellent square. The move with the other knight, 19 ♘df3, allows Black to keep the tension high too: 19...♕b4+ 20 ♕d2 ♘f6 21 ♕xb4 ♗xb4+ 22 ♔e2 0-0.

**19...♕f4! 20 ♗e2**

For now it's not the time for exchanges: 20 ♘xe6 ♗b4+ 21 ♘d2 ♕e5+ (21...fxe6 is also interesting) 22 ♗e2 ♕xe6 gives Black strong threats.

**20...♗b4+ 21 ♔f1 0-0 22 ♘xe6**

White has a lot of options. This exchange combined with the following manoeuvre is an obvious choice, but it seems that after the opening of the f-file Black's chances are no worse.

**22...fxe6 23 ♕d4** (D)

**23...♕xd4!?**

Even with the queens off, Black's activity is enough to maintain the balance. The subsequent play is of a forcing character.

**24 ♗xd4 e5 25 ♗xe5 ♘e3+ 26 ♔g1 ♘c2 27 ♖c1 ♗c5+ 28 ♔f1 ♘e3+ 29 ♔e1**

If White had seen the coming blow, he would perhaps have preferred to fight on in the endgame after 29 ♔f2 ♘g4++ 30 ♔e1 ♘xe5 31 ♘xe5 ♗b4+ 32 ♖c3.

**29...♘xg2+ 30 ♔d1 ♘e3+ 31 ♔d2?!**

Of course, White should have acquiesced to the repetition of moves.

**31...♖cd8+ 32 ♔c3??**

After 32 ♔e1 besides agreeing the draw Black, thanks to his activity, could have tried to seek the advantage with 32...b5, despite not having a full material equivalent for the missing piece.

**32...♖xf3!**

And now it is time to resign. However, that day fate saved the last gift for White – in a severe time-scramble Black repeated the position one time too many and the game ended peacefully.

**33 b4 ♘d5++ 34 ♔b2 ♖b3+ 35 ♔a1 ♖a3+ 36 ♔b2 ♖b3+ 37 ♔a1 ♖a3+ 38 ♔b2 ♖b3+??** ½-½

# Game 10
## Jean Christophe Olivier – Evgeny Yanev
*Grenoble 2007*

**1 e4 ♘f6 2 e5 ♘d5 3 d4 d6 4 c4 ♘b6 5 f4 dxe5 6 fxe5 ♗f5** (D)

If Black intends to develop the queen's knight to c6 during the next few moves, it is logical to start with that, since defending the pawn with the g1-knight then allows a more aggressive posting of the bishop to g4 (viz. 6...♘c6 7 ♘f3?! ♗g4). In this game we shall examine lines where the b8-knight is the last piece in the queue to develop.

**7 ♘f3 e6**

White has various possible orders by which to develop his pieces, and he should tailor these carefully in line with Black's move-order. Generally it is accepted that knights are the first to come out (unless there are specific reasons

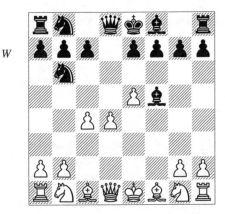

against it); in our case this rule is strengthened by the fact that c3 and f3 are definitely their best squares, whereas the situation with the bishops is not as clear.

However, it is more common to see the knight brought out to c3 first, increasing White's control over the d5-square; the text-move overprotects the e5-pawn and, in certain cases, rules out a check on h4. The order of the development of the knights is of no importance after 7...e6, but Black could have used White's move-order to play 7...♘c6. Then 8 ♘c3 ♗b4 is disruptive, while 8 d5 ♗b4 9 ♘d4 is no refutation because of 9...♗xb1 10 ♖xb1 e6, when the threat of the check on h4 allows Black to relieve the situation in the centre. Alternatively, White can agree to meet ...♗b4 with ♘a3 or spend a tempo on 8 a3.

**8 ♘c3**

As for White, any other move amounts to allowing ...c5. We should note that the destruction of the pawn-centre does not always lead to the loss of the opening advantage; a lot depends on the activity of the remaining pieces, and White's queenside majority is often an important factor. At this particular moment, both 8 ♗e2 c5 and 8 ♗e3 c5 lead to positions that are acceptable for Black. A few words about 8 ♗d3: the exchange of these bishops is often good for White: first, because it weakens Black's kingside defence, while White's space advantage and the half-open f-file suggest an attack in this sector; second, control is regained over an important diagonal and in particular the e4-square. Black has to be very careful; for example, after 8...♗xd3 9 ♕xd3 c5 10 0-0, he must avoid 10...cxd4? 11 ♘g5, when he can resign,

and instead play 10...♘c6 (with a view to 11 ♘g5? ♘xe5), keeping the chances even.

**8...♗b4?!**

Developing the bishop to this square is a tempting idea, especially when it can be linked with the aggressive ...c5 advance. However, there are some concrete problems with the move in this particular position, which is why it is rare in practice.

8...♗e7 *(D)* is more orthodox-looking, but if White responds accurately, Black will have nothing better than transposing to the main ...♘c6 lines.

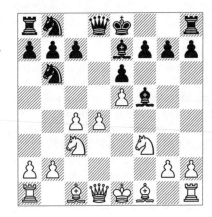

The point of this move-order is the preparation of the undermining ...f6 before developing the knight to c6, subsequently reaching a main-line position but without giving White the option of advancing by d5 with the gain of a tempo. Its main drawback is that the lack of pressure on d4 allows White ideas with a well-timed ♗d3. Then:

a) The immediate 9 ♗d3 widens Black's range of options; after 9...♗xd3 10 ♕xd3 the position of the queen hampers the d5 advance and gives Black time to prepare to castle queenside by 10...♘c6 11 0-0 ♕d7.

b) The more modest 9 ♗e2 allows Black by 9...0-0 10 ♗e3 ♘c6 11 0-0 f6 to achieve his goal and reach a well-known position which shall cover later via the move-order 6...♘c6 7 ♗e3 ♗f5 8 ♘c3 e6 9 ♘f3 ♗e7 10 ♗e2 0-0 11 0-0 f6, having side-stepped the sharp 10 d5 option.

c) White's most practical course is to play 9 ♗e3, inviting Black to transpose back to normal main lines by 9...♘c6. If Black persists with the plan of making the ...c5 advance and plays 9...0-0?!, then White can reply 10 ♗d3 to better effect, making good use of the fact that Black is not putting pressure on d4 (with ...♘c6 substituted for ...0-0, Black could meet 10 ♗d3?! with 10...♗g4! – see Game 12). After 10...♗xd3 11 ♕xd3 ♘c6, White can play 12 ♖d1 with a solid plus or even castle queenside himself: 12 0-0-0 a5 13 d5 ♘b4 14 ♕e4, Isaev-Zilberman, Moscow 2002. The attempt to undermine the centre at once with 9...f6 is rarely seen; without a knight on c6 the capture on e5 is not a threat, and 10 ♗d3 seems even more justified.

On b4, the bishop continues the struggle for the d5-square, and Black gets ready for the thematic ...c5.

**9 a3?!**

Outwardly the most natural reply, but it's not the best. While the d4-pawn is reinforced, its neighbour on c4 becomes vulnerable.

Black successfully implements his plan after 9 ♗e3?!, when the play can become very sharp, with chances for both sides; e.g., 9...c5 10 ♕b3 ♘c6 11 dxc5 ♘d7 12 0-0-0 0-0 13 ♗d3 ♗xd3 14 ♖xd3 ♗xc5, Fontaine – Santo-Roman, Cap d'Agde 2003.

The move that puts this line to a critical test is again that same 9 ♗d3! (D).

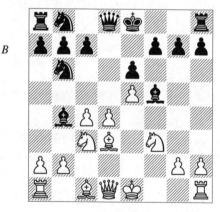

The position of the bishop on b4 is inferior to that on e7, as it doesn't control the g5-square and risks being cut off from d6. Black has no time to profit from the ...c5 advance, as can be seen from the line 9...♗xd3 10 ♕xd3 c5 11 0-0 cxd4 12 ♘e4 with numerous threats including a leap by one of the knights into g5, and the c5 advance. It would seem that Black can allow

the exchange on f5 and immediately strike in the centre; then he doesn't have to surrender the e4-square, while the c4-pawn is left without protection. However, White doesn't mind sacrificing it: 9...c5 10 ♗xf5 exf5 11 ♗g5 ♕d7 12 0-0 0-0 (after 12...cxd4 Black has to take into account 13 e6) 13 d5 ♘xc4 14 ♕e2 ♗xc3 15 ♕xc4 ♗xb2 16 ♖ab1 ♗d4+ 17 ♘xd4 cxd4 18 e6 and Black failed to repel the attack in Morozevich-Bagirov, Moscow PCA qualifier 1995. In reply to the counterattack on the d4-pawn by means of 9...♗g4 10 0-0 ♘c6 (here after 10...c5 the reply 11 ♘e4 is even stronger) White, with the diagonal reconquered, can afford to relinquish the d5 strongpoint temporarily: 11 c5 ♗xc3 12 bxc3 ♘d5 13 ♕e1, Velimirović-Martz, Vrnjačka Banja 1973.

**9...♗xc3+ 10 bxc3** (D)

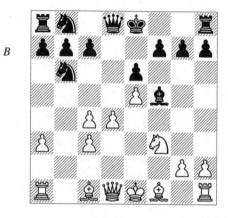

**10...c5**

Not so much to attack the centre as to fix the weakness on c4, which Black plans to attack with the other knight as well. Bagirov's idea of switching the moves around and beginning with 10...♘c6 deserves attention. Then the knight has time to reach a5, whereas the c5 advance by White has more cons than pros – it gives up the d5-square and gives Black a new target to undermine with ...b6.

**11 ♗e2**

Now White can prevent Black from reaching the planned set-up with the pawn raid 11 a4, followed by a further advance. On the other hand, 11 ♗d3 is not regarded highly despite the greater vulnerability of the enemy kingside, as the c4-pawn loses one of its defenders.

**11...♘c6 12 0-0 h6** (D)

Black engages in prophylaxis with the aim of setting up a solid defence in the most likely direction of the enemy offensive, but it costs time. 12...0-0 at once and 12...♕d7 have both been played rather successfully. The immediate attack by 12...♘a5 does not prevent 13 ♗e3, as for the moment the pawn is indirectly protected due to the possibility of a check on a4.

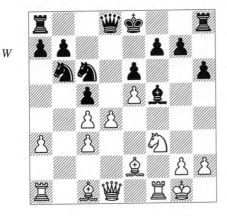

W

**13 ♗e3**

White may attempt to use the extra tempo for work in another direction by 13 a4. Then winning the exchange by 13...♘a5 14 ♗a3 ♘bxc4 15 ♗xc5 ♘e3 16 ♗b5+ ♘c6 looks very risky.

**13...♘a5 14 ♘d2**

The other option is 14 d5, when 14...exd5?! is quite dubious because of 15 ♗xc5, detaining the king in the centre; after 14...♖c8 15 ♘d2 0-0 the resulting pawn tension in the centre is hard for either side to relieve.

**14...0-0**

If undisturbed, Black plans to transfer the queen via d7 to a4. White must now decide upon a plan of concrete action.

**15 ♕e1**

The implementation of Black's counterplay involves the use of byways on the edge of the board, so it is logical that White should attack on the opposite flank.

**15...♘a4**

Not only attacking the c3-pawn but also eyeing the route to d3.

**16 d5 ♘xc3**

Pausing to defend the pawn by 16...♖c8 encourages White to wait for the knight to move again with 17 ♕g3 ♔h7 18 ♖ac1 ♘b2 and then sacrifice the exchange by 19 ♖xf5. Therefore

Black decides against postponing the relieving operation in the centre.

**17 ♗xc5 ♖e8?**

Of course, it was necessary to exchange by 17...♘xe2+, leaving the black light-squared bishop without an opponent.

**18 ♗b4?!**

White could have taken up an advanced post on h5 by 18 ♗h5.

**18...♘a4?!**

Black is too eager to keep a stable on the rim. Here too, it would be more prudent to exchange the bishop off; now White's initiative again acquires threatening proportions.

**19 ♕g3 ♖c8 20 ♗d3**

This is a rather conventional move. 20 ♖f4, bringing up the last reserves, is more interesting.

**20...♗xd3 21 ♕xd3 exd5**

After 21...♘b2 22 ♕f3 ♘axc4 23 ♕xf7+ ♔h8 24 ♘xc4 ♘xc4 25 d6 ♕b6+ 26 ♕f2 ♕xf2+ 27 ♖xf2 ♘xe5 28 ♖e1 ♘d7 29 ♖f7 ♖cd8 30 ♖e7 Black's defences are creaking.

**22 ♖xf7? (D)**

An untimely trip back to the 19th century; in the endgame after 22 ♕xd5 ♕xd5 23 cxd5 ♘c4 24 ♘xc4 ♖xc4 25 d6 White has a clear advantage.

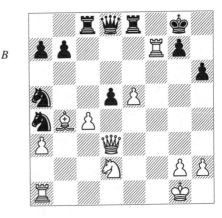

B

**22...♕b6+?**

Missing the opportunity: Black should play 22...dxc4! 23 ♕xd8 ♖exd8. After 24 e6 c3 the black passed pawn is in no way weaker than its white counterpart, while in the event of 24 ♗xa5 ♔xf7 25 ♗xd8 c3 26 ♗a5 cxd2 27 ♗xd2 ♔e6, there can be no doubt who has the better reasons to play for a win.

**23 ⃞f2 ⃞xe5?!**

23...⃞xc4? is bad due to 24 ♕xd5+ ♕e6 25 ⃞f8+, but 23...⃞c6 24 ♕xd5+ ⃞h8 is more resilient. Black remains a pawn down but brings his loose knight back into play and obtains some counterchances.

**24 cxd5?!**

24 ⃞f3 is more convincing. Then 24...dxc4? is no good because of 25 ♕d7 with a double attack on a4 and c8, while after 24...⃞h5? the simplest continuation is 25 ♗xa5 ♕xa5 26 ♕g6. The only way to avoid material losses is 24...⃞e6, but after 25 cxd5 the knights on a4 and a5 will not be much help against White's combined attack in the centre and on the kingside.

**24...⃞b2 25 ♕f3 ⃞bc4 26 ⃞xc4?**

26 ♕f7+ gives White a winning attack after 26...⃞h8 27 ♗c3 ⃞d6 28 ♕f4 or 26...⃞h7 27 ⃞e4. The exchange of the knights and the subsequent aimless shuffling of pieces presented Black with another gift.

**26...⃞xc4 27 ♕g4 ⃞c7 28 ♕f3 ♕e3 29 ♕xe3 ⃞xe3 30 ⃞f8+ ⃞h7** *(D)*

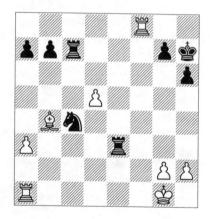

If Black can neutralize White's passed pawn, he can count on having the advantage – the knight is superior to the bishop and an outside passed pawn can be created.

**31 ⃞f3?**

In order to preclude the slightest chance of Black doubling his rooks on his seventh rank, White offers the exchange of rooks. However, this move allows Black to win a pawn and, with sufficient technique, the game. The easiest way to register the draw was 31 d6 ⃞d7 32 ⃞c8 ⃞xd6 33 ⃞d1 ⃞xc8 34 ⃞xd7 b5 35 ⃞c7.

**31...⃞xf3 32 gxf3 a5 33 ♗e1 ⃞d7 34 ⃞d1 b5?**

After 34...⃞xa3 35 ♗xa5 ⃞c4 no way to save the d5-pawn is apparent.

**35 ⃞d4 ⃞g6 36 f4?**

It is hard to understand this move: not only is the pawn weaker here, but the control over e4 is lost and a tempo that the king could use to get closer to the centre is wasted. Why not 36 ⃞f2?

**36...a4?**

Black immobilizes the weakness on a3 out of general considerations and lets another gift slip away; after 36...⃞xa3 37 ♗xa5 ⃞c2 White is in a bad way.

**37 ♗b4 ⃞f5 38 ⃞f2 g5**

It is illogical to exchange the enemy's weakness off and widen his rook's scope, but at the moment the black king has no entry points into the enemy camp, and forcing the pawn to advance by 38...⃞b6 39 d6 ⃞c4 gives White an easy draw after 40 ⃞d5+ ⃞xf4 41 ⃞xb5 ⃞xd6 42 ♗xd6+ ⃞xd6 43 ⃞b4+. After the text-move too, each side has a solid drawing reserve.

**39 fxg5 hxg5 40 d6 ⃞e6 41 ⃞e4+ ⃞d5 42 ⃞g4 ⃞xd6 43 ⃞xg5+ ⃞c4 44 ⃞e5 ⃞b3 45 ⃞e3+ ⃞c4 46 ⃞e5 ⃞f7+ 47 ⃞e2 ⃞f5 48 ⃞c5+ ⃞b3 49 ⃞d5 ⃞c4 50 ⃞c5+ ⃞b3 51 ⃞d5 ½-½**

## Game 11
# Hikaru Nakamura – Joel Benjamin
### *World Open, Philadelphia 2006*

**1 e4 ⃞f6 2 e5 ⃞d5 3 c4 ⃞b6 4 d4 d6 5 f4 dxe5 6 fxe5 ⃞c6**

The principal continuation in this position. It temporarily obstructs the c-pawn, but the attack on the d4-pawn is a little awkward for White. Defending the pawn with the natural ⃞f3 allows an unpleasant pin, so White is more or less forced to use his bishop, thus losing a little flexibility.

**7 ♗e3**

Nevertheless, 7 ⃞f3?! with the concrete idea of 7...♗g4! 8 e6 *(D)* is also played.

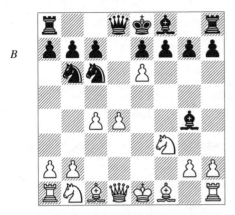

Black is forced to spoil his pawn-structure by 8...fxe6, since capturing with the bishop means giving up a piece for three pawns, which at this stage of the game is a very bad idea. However, to White's misfortune, Black's position after the capture with the f-pawn works well. White needs to parry the ...e5 advance by continuing 9 c5, but this cedes the d5-square to Black, which along with the extra pawn renders his chances rather better: 9...♘d5 10 ♗b5 ♕d7 (the most accurate; otherwise there will be only ruins left in the centre, and the e5-square is covered in time) 11 ♘bd2 g6 12 ♕a4 ♗g7. Instead, Black mustn't be too greedy: 9...♗xf3?! 10 ♕xf3 ♘xd4 11 ♕h5+ (also interesting is 11 ♕f2) 11...g6 12 ♕e5 leads to an unclear game.

**7...♗f5 8 ♘c3**

The move with the other knight, 8 ♘f3, allows 8...♘b4, which forces the reply 9 ♘a3. White will then be deprived of active options in the centre for some time, and Black can develop calmly, aiming for one of the typical counter-thrusts, ...c5 or ...f6.

**8...e6 9 ♘f3 (D)**

The alternative is to develop the bishop first by 9 ♗e2, which prevents some options for both sides. Specifically, the line 9 ♘f3 ♗g4, which occurs in our main game, is ruled out, which means that anyone who relies on that line as Black will need to have another reply ready in case White plays 9 ♗e2. However, if Black meets 9 ♗e2 with 9...♗e7, then White does not have the option of the aggressive d5 advance (as in the line 9 ♘f3 ♗e7 10 d5), and so the play will transpose to the quieter 9 ♘f3 ♗e7 10 ♗e2 0-0 11 0-0 f6 line (see Game 12). If Black prefers 9...♕d7 or 9...♗b4 (or indeed 9...♘b4),

then the order in which White develops his kingside minor pieces makes very little difference.

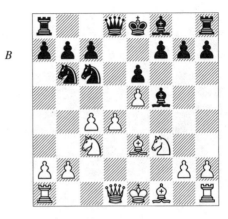

After the text-move, Black has five paths to choose from, some better investigated than others.

**9...♗g4**

The best explored, 9...♗e7, is the subject of the next game. Let's examine a few less well-travelled roads:

a) 9...♗b4 is safer than the ...♗b4 idea examined in Game 10, as White's extra move has placed the e3-bishop under possible attack from a knight on c4 in some lines. However, the fact that Black has blocked the c-pawn with his knight also robs Black's play of some of its sting, and his counterplay will now need to feature ...♘a5 before he can play ...c5, and while White must attend one way or another to the attack on c4, he will have additional time and options to start his kingside play. Now 10 ♗d3 is not considered to be very dangerous; after 10...♗g4 11 a3 ♗xf3 12 gxf3 White has the bishop-pair and a central pawn-majority, but his king's cover is less secure. The main continuation is 10 ♗e2, although 10 ♖c1 and 10 a3 are also seen. This whole line has not been seen much in recent years, and there is scope for further investigation here.

b) By choosing 9...♘b4, Black manages to carry out ...c5 and destroy the enemy centre, and this is the idea that was most actively developed during the early years of the opening's history. Gradually it became clear that the price Black has to pay is rather high. The operation is carried out at the expense of development, and the main factors in the subsequent struggle are White's active pieces and queenside pawn-majority. After 10 ♖c1 c5 (D), we have:

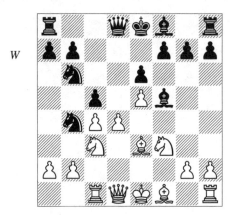

b1) The old analysis of the sharp 11 d5?! still stands – Black is OK.

b2) 11 a3 cxd4 12 ♘xd4 ♘c6 and now both captures – on c6 and on f5 – can be seen in practice.

b3) 11 ♗e2 is considered the most accurate continuation, for the moment not wasting time on the b4-knight (although eventually it will have to be driven off). Here is a recent example: 11...cxd4 12 ♘xd4 ♗g6 13 a3 (Levenfish's 13 c5 is unconvincing after 13...♘d7 14 ♕a4 ♗xc5 15 ♘xe6 ♘c2+) 13...♘c6 14 ♘xc6 ♕xd1+ 15 ♗xd1 bxc6 16 ♗f3 ♖c8 (16...0-0-0!?) 17 ♗xb6 axb6 18 ♘a4 ♗c5 and Black keeps his disadvantage fairly small, Predojević-Laketić, Serbian Team Ch, Vrnjačka Banja 2005.

c) 9...♕d7 (preparing to attack down the d-file with queen and rook) 10 ♗e2 (the advance 10 d5?! exd5 11 cxd5 ♘b4 12 ♘d4 used to be popular in correspondence chess, and today it may be of interest to aficionados of computer analysis; however, when compared to the main variation, the fact that the f5-bishop is protected should favour Black, who can play a temporary piece sacrifice such as 12...♘6xd5 13 ♘xd5 ♘xd5 14 ♘xf5 0-0-0) and now Black can put a rook on d8 in two different ways:

c1) 10...♖d8!? is by no means the obvious move, and it would require a true optimist to call the black king's position safer here than on c8, but there are lines where the king being on e8 turns out to be useful (you will notice that f7 comes under pressure in the lines after 10...0-0-0). 11 0-0

♗g4 12 ♘g5 (by analogy with line 'c2', 12 c5 is also possible) 12...♗xe2?! (12...♘xc4 leads to unclear play, with 13 ♗f2 ♗e7 14 ♘xf7 ♗xe2 15 ♕xe2 ♔xf7 16 ♗e3+ ♔e8 17 ♕xc4 ♘xd4 18 ♖ad1 c5 a critical line) 13 ♕xe2 ♘xd4 14 ♗xd4 ♕xd4+ 15 ♔h1 ♖d7 and here White has a choice of aggressive options, including 16 ♕h5 ♕xe5 17 ♖ae1 g6 18 ♕h4 ♕d4? 19 ♘xe6 1-0 Vocaturo-Vitri, Porto San Giorgio 2006.

c2) 10...0-0-0 (D).

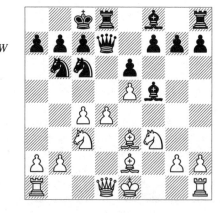

Black increases the pressure on the enemy centre, hinders its advance and plans to carry out the undermining ...f6. Nevertheless, the king is uncomfortable on c8, while the knights present targets for a queenside pawn offensive, and the f7-pawn can prove hard to defend. After the natural 11 0-0 Black has two plans:

c21) The immediate 11...f6?! is strongly met by 12 d5! ♘xe5 13 ♘xe5 fxe5 14 a4 a5 15 ♘b5 ♗b4 16 d6, which renders Black's position critical. This line has been known from correspondence games for a long time, and its first high-level over-the-board test, Kotronias-Short, Gibraltar 2003, did not succeed in changing its dubious status for Black.

c22) 11...♗g4 increases the pressure on the d4-pawn. Here too, the immediate attack on the f7-square with 12 ♘g5 leaves Black with the choice between 12...♘xc4 and 12...♗xe2 13 ♕xe2 f6. White more often prefers to cede d5 but to stabilize the situation in the centre and use the respite to organize a pawn offensive against the enemy king: 12 c5 ♘d5 13 ♘xd5 ♕xd5. Now 14 ♘g5 ♗xe2 15 ♕xe2 ♘xd4 16 ♗xd4 ♕xd4+ 17 ♔h1 ♕d2 18 ♕xd2 ♖xd2 19 ♖xf7 ♗xc5 20 ♘xe6 leads to a sharp endgame where Black should hold with careful defence. The alternative is the aggressive 14 b4, when Black has to take urgent steps with 14...♕e4. There are then two moves:

c221) 15 ♕b3 ♘xd4 16 ♘xd4 ♗xe2 17 ♖xf7!? (17 ♘xe2 ♖d3 18 ♕a4 ♕xe3+ 19 ♔h1 ♕xe2 20 ♕xa7 ♖d2 21 ♕a8+ ♔d7 22 ♕xb7 was successful in Minasian-Donchenko, Naberezhnye Chelny 1998, but 22...f5! is a good defence then; 17 ♖f4 is the old move, but Black's resources are fully adequate) 17...♗c4 18 ♕c3 may not be completely simple for Black.

c222) Recently White has enjoyed some success with 15 ♕d2!?, when Black should probably prefer 15...f6 (e.g., 16 h3 ♘xd4 17 ♘xd4 ♗xe2 18 ♖f4 ♕d3 led to a draw in Abel-Beikert, 2nd Bundesliga 2008/9) over 15...♘xd4?! 16 ♘xd4 ♗xe2 17 ♖xf7.

Let's return to the main game, where Black has just played 9...♗g4 (D).

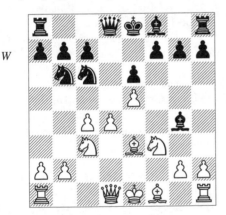

*W*

The second move by this already developed piece impedes the d5 advance and threatens to change White's pawn-structure (calling this change 'spoiling' would be too categorical). White is unable to prevent this.

**10 ♕d2**

Why this? Let's consider the most natural continuation, 10 ♗e2. The purpose of this move is not to recapture on f3 with the bishop, since after 10...♗xf3, the line 11 ♗xf3? ♘xc4 12 ♗xc6+ bxc6 13 ♕a4 ♘xe3 14 ♕xc6+ ♔e7 doesn't even give White a draw: after 15 ♕c5+ ♔d7 16 ♕b5+ c6 17 ♕b7+ ♕c7 18 ♕xa8 the white queen cannot get out without paying an extortionate ransom. Rather White is playing a developing move, acquiescing to 11 gxf3, when

the structure of the kingside as the white king's possible residence is weakened, but on the other hand White's presence in the centre is increased. After 11...♕h4+ 12 ♗f2 ♕f4 (D) White has to solve the problem of the d4-pawn's defence.

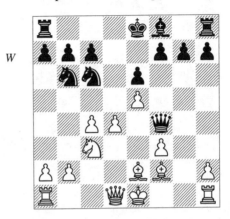

*W*

The immediate offer to exchange queens by 13 ♕c1 ♕xc1+ 14 ♖xc1 0-0-0 15 ♖d1 ♗b4 16 a3 (White cannot postpone the confrontation as the knight's leap to a4 is threatened) 16...♗xc3+ 17 bxc3 ♘a5 18 c5 ♘d5 leads to a complex ending where the knights successfully oppose the bishops.

Therefore 13 c5 has emerged as the main continuation. At this point 13...♘d7 used to be played, planning to put the d5-square to good use later, and maintaining the blockading character of the position. However, Black has struggled to find a reliable path to equality after 14 ♗b5!?; e.g., 14...♗e7 (14...0-0-0 15 ♗xc6 bxc6 16 ♕e2 with an attack; 14...f6 15 ♕e2 fxe5? 16 d5 – Black is not the only one who benefits from the d5-square being empty!) 15 0-0 ♗h4 (15...f6?! 16 d5!; 15...0-0!?) 16 ♗xc6 bxc6 17 ♕a4 is good for White. In the last decade, the endgame that arises after 13...♘d5 14 ♘xd5 exd5 15 ♕d2 ♕xd2+ 16 ♔xd2 g6 (D) has become topical.

This position had previously been considered to favour White, with his bishop-pair, space advantage and with segments of his pawn-chain still mobile. On the other hand, White's dark-squared bishop is restricted by the already immobilized part of the formation, and de Firmian perceived that with blockade possibilities added into the mix, it might be feasible to construct a reliable defence for Black.

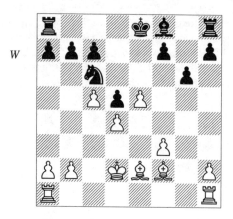

After 17 f4 ♗h6 18 ♗e3 ♘e7 19 ♗d3 (or 19 ♗g4) 19...♘f5 20 ♗xf5 gxf5 21 ♖ag1 (or 21 ♖hg1 ♔d7 22 ♖g3 ♖ag8 23 b4 ♖xg3! 24 hxg3 ♗f8, Atalik-de Firmian, San Francisco 2002) 21...♔d7 22 ♖g3 ♖ag8 23 b4 ♗f8! 24 ♔e2 ♖xg3 25 hxg3 h5 he achieves his aim, but it is interesting to play first 17 ♗e3 h5 and now not to hurry to lock in the bishop with f4 but to advance on the queenside for the time being; e.g., 18 ♗b5 ♔e7 19 ♗g5+ ♔e6 20 ♔c3 h4 21 h3 ♘e7 22 f4 ♘f5 23 ♗e2 b6 24 b4 a5 25 a3 ♗e7 26 ♗g4 ♗xg5 27 fxg5 ♔e7 28 ♗f3 ♖hd8 29 ♖hb1 and White went on to win in Pavasović-Nakamura, Austrian Team Ch 2008/9.

We now return to 10 ♕d2 (D):

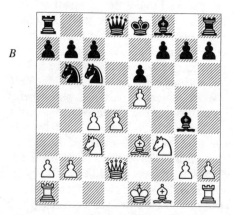

This is the other option, by which White places the f4-square under control.

**10...♗xf3**

Black is not obliged to take on f3 and can switch to one of the other standard plans, reckoning that the inclusion of the previous pair of moves favours him. After 10...♗e7 11 0-0-0

♕d7 12 h3 ♗f5 13 d5 the game usually takes on a sharp quality. A sly move (and indeed the most popular one in this position) is 10...♗b4, aiming to provoke 11 a3, weakening the light squares, when it is riskier for White to castle queenside, while in lines like 11...♗e7 12 ♘e4 ♕d7 13 b4 ♗xf3 14 gxf3 0-0-0 15 ♖d1 ♗h4+ 16 ♘g3 f6 Black has decent counterplay, Fedorov-Baburin, Istanbul Olympiad 2000. 10...♕d7, preparing queenside castling (or ...♖d8) while keeping open the option of transposing into the 9...♕d7 lines examined above, is also acceptable.

**11 gxf3 ♕h4+ 12 ♗f2 ♕h5**

The fact that Black cannot occupy f4 here is a possible argument against Black's 10th move.

**13 c5**

Not a particularly good novelty. White seeks an endgame similar to the one examined in the note about 10 ♗e2, but this version is more comfortable for Black. The previously played 13 ♗e2 and 13 ♕e3 promise more.

**13...♕xf3 14 ♖g1 ♘d5 15 ♗g2 ♕f4 16 ♘xd5 ♕xd2+ 17 ♔xd2 exd5 18 ♗xd5 ♖d8?** (D)

The long and relatively forced line is coming to an end, and now by continuing 18...♘xd4 19 ♗xd4 ♖d8 20 ♗xf7+ ♔xf7 Black could have steered the game toward the draw. Perhaps Black had higher aspirations?

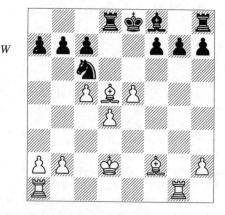

**19 ♗xc6+ bxc6 20 ♔c3 f5?**

If only Black could manage to complete his development and set up an airtight blockade on the light squares... The move is not so much laying the foundation of this blockade as the desire to get rid of the weakness on f7 that would not be easy to defend should White double his rooks on the f-file, especially as Black has to guard against the possibility of these rooks swinging across to the broken queenside pawns.

**21 b4?!**

White's advantage is obvious even after an exchange on f6. However, he could have secured an extra pawn by 21 ♗h4 ♖b8 (21...♖d7 22 ♖af1 g6 23 ♗f6 ♗g7 24 ♗xg7 ♖xg7 25 ♖xf5 fails to help) 22 ♖af1 g6 23 ♗f6 ♖g8 24 ♖xf5.

**21...♔d7 22 a4 ♖b8?**

Although Black's position is difficult, there was no need to loosen the control over the d5-square; now 23 b5 was winning.

**23 ♔c4?! a6 24 ♖ge1 ♔e6 25 ♖ab1?!**

This gives Black good drawing chances. The other rook should have been played to b1 (25 ♖eb1!), in order to be left with the more active rook on the a-file after the exchanges on b5.

**25...♗e7 26 b5 axb5+ 27 axb5 cxb5+ 28 ♖xb5 c6**

Forced. Black cannot simply exchange by 28...♖xb5? because of the zwischenzug 29 d5+.

**29 ♖b6 ♖xb6 30 cxb6 ♖b8 31 ♖b1 g5?**

The losing move. Black keeps good drawing chances after 31...♖b7 32 d5+ cxd5+ 33 ♔b5 ♖b8. White will get the bishop for his passed pawn, of course, but he has no pawns left that could aspire to an illustrious career.

**32 b7 ♔d7 33 d5 cxd5+ 34 ♔xd5 ♗c7 35 ♗b6+ ♔xb7 36 ♗c5+ ♔c7 1-0**

## Game 12
# Leinier Dominguez – Omar Almeida Quintana
### Cuban Ch, Santa Clara 2005

**1 e4 ♘f6 2 e5 ♘d5 3 d4 d6 4 c4 ♘b6 5 f4 dxe5 6 fxe5 ♗f5 7 ♘c3 e6 8 ♗e3 ♘c6 9 ♘f3 ♗e7 (D)**

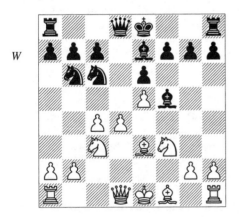

The most natural and common move. Black prepares to complete his development and carry out the undermining ...f6.

**10 d5**

This is the choice of the player who likes to live on the edge.

Here 10 ♗d3?! only makes the d4-pawn's life difficult; after 10...♗g4 11 0-0 ♘xd4 12 ♗xd4 ♗xf3 13 ♕xf3 ♕xd4+ 14 ♔h1 0-0 Black parries White's gambit with accurate play.

The main alternative is the calm 10 ♗e2, by which White does not interfere with the realization of Black's plan: 10...0-0 11 0-0 f6. This all but forces White to exchange on f6:

a) 12 ♘h4 is an attempt to make use of the newly available route for the knight, but after 12...fxe5 13 ♘xf5 exf5 14 d5 ♘d4 15 ♗xd4 exd4 16 ♕xd4 ♘d7 the black bishop is noticeably more comfortable than the white one.

b) 12 ♕e1 maintains a pawn on e5, even though it will be somewhat weak, counting on its role in supporting an attack. For this purpose, White must preserve his queen from exchange and direct it towards the kingside. Black then has several continuations, with 12...fxe5 13 dxe5 ♘d7 having an excellent reputation, while he can also try 12...♘b4. If 13 ♕g3 ♘c2 14 ♗h6 then 14...♗g6 and White has to sacrifice something. However, 13 ♖d1 is considered better; e.g., 13...♘c2 14 ♕f2 ♘xe3 15 ♕xe3 fxe5 16 dxe5 ♕e8 17 ♘b5 and Black must play carefully, Vega Gutierrez-Garza Marco, Spanish Ch, Palma de Mallorca 2009.

c) Naturally, the main continuation is 12 exf6 ♗xf6 (D).

By voluntarily creating a weakness in his own structure on e6, Black in return acquires certain pluses. He removes from e5 the enemy

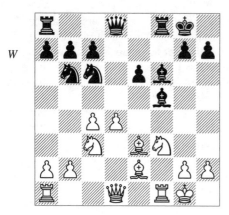

pawn that usually serves as a focal point of White's attack and hampers Black's ability to manoeuvre. Black also gains the freedom to operate along his second rank, useful both in protecting Black's own king and in building pressure along the d-file. The d4-pawn will now become subject to attack along the diagonal, and even though it is technically not an isolated pawn, it cannot count on the support of its fellows; hence it is a moot point which weakness is the more sensitive.

It is desirable to connect the rooks without forgetting the d4-pawn. Thus 13 ♕d2 is normal (at the same time angling for simplifications on g5). Now it is time for the black queen to declare her intentions as well. 13...♕e8 is sometimes played, with the view to a transfer to the kingside, but this loosens Black's control over the g5-square, and White benefits more from exchanges. 13...♕e7 is more common, indirectly parrying 14 ♗g5? with the counterblow 14...♘xd4!. Here 14 c5 ♘d5 15 ♘xd5 exd5 16 ♗b5 is played sometimes, not only helping Black to get rid of the weakness on e6 but also extinguishing the counterplay against the d4-pawn and initiating a struggle for the e5-square. The ideal goal is to place a knight there and leave Black with the light-squared bishop, but this is easier said than done. The main continuation is 14 ♖ad1 ♖ad8 15 ♕c1 with a manoeuvring struggle, where both sides have to be ready to meet, respectively, d5 for White or ...e5 for Black. Play can continue 15...h6 16 ♔h1 ♔h8 17 h3 ♗h7 18 ♗g1 ♖fe8 19 ♖fe1 ♕f7, and White will aim gradually to stifle Black's activity and play against his weaknesses.

**10...exd5**

Let's examine the immediate knight move 10...♘b4 (D).

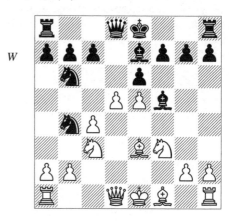

In comparison with exchanging first on d5 before putting the knight on b4, this move leaves the f5-bishop still protected, but means that Black is not yet threatening to take on d5 with a knight. This changes the play very considerably.

Getting down to basics, White has to cover the c2-square first of all. The situation might appear depressing for Black in the case of 11 ♘d4 ♗g6 12 a3 c5, but matters are not entirely clear. After 13 axb4 cxd4 14 ♕xd4 ♗xb4 Black is still holding on, while after 13 ♘xe6 fxe6 14 axb4 cxb4 (the attempt to play for a lead in development with 14...0-0 15 bxc5 ♘d7 was stymied by the riposte 16 dxe6 in Goloshchapov-Orlov, 2nd Bundesliga 2005/6) 15 ♘a4 0-0 (15...♘d7 16 ♕d4 ♕a5 17 d6 ♗d8 18 c5 b5 19 b3 is considered very good for White due to old theory that no one seems inclined to challenge) 16 ♘xb6 axb6 17 ♖xa8 ♕xa8, the line 18 d6 ♗d8 19 ♗e2 b3! (Gorges-M.Johnson, corr. 1990) is considered OK for Black, while 18 ♗e2 has been insufficiently tested, but here too 18...b3 must be the move to try.

But even if Black has solved his problems in that line, there is also 11 ♖c1 exd5 (11...f6 is powerfully met by Velimirović's pawn sacrifice 12 a3 ♘a6 13 g4!) 12 a3. Now 12...c5 13 axb4 d4 14 ♗xd4 cxd4 15 ♘xd4 ♕b8 has at times been thought acceptable, but 16 ♘xf5 ♕xe5+ 17 ♗e2 ♕xf5 18 c5 is to White's advantage. Recently Black has been trying to equalize with three pawns for the piece in the line 12...♘xc4 13 ♗xc4 dxc4, but it is an unenviable task.

We now return to 10...exd5 (D):

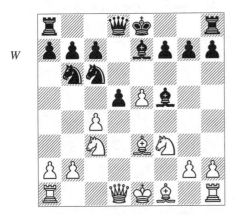

The preliminary exchange of pawns creates a concrete threat to the d5-pawn, but on the other hand it restores the e5-pawn's mobility.

**11 cxd5 ♞b4 12 ♞d4 ♝d7**

Reluctant as Black may be to obstruct one of the lines of attack on the d5-pawn, few are willing to allow 13 ♝b5+ and walk on foot to g8.

**13 ♕f3**

This move used to be a sideline, but has received renewed attention during the last few years. Before that, 13 e6 was heavily in the spotlight. The following line involving an exchange sacrifice is acknowledged as the best for both sides: 13...fxe6 14 dxe6 ♝c6 15 ♕g4 ♝h4+ 16 g3 ♝xh1 (D).

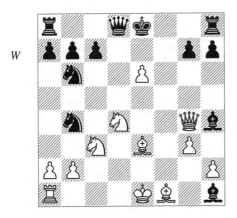

Here is a very brief summary of the main and most critical lines (the full analysis that has been devoted to this position could fill a small book!):

a) 17 ♝b5+ c6 18 0-0-0 0-0 19 gxh4 ♕f6 20 ♝g5 ♕f2 (or 20...♕e5 21 e7 and now 21...♖f2!?; or perhaps even 21...♖fe8?!, as successfully played in Grishchuk-Svidler, Odessa rapid 2009, although after 22 ♞f5! Black is yet to prove equality) 21 ♝e2 (21 e7 cxb5 22 exf8♕+ ♖xf8 is OK for Black) and now 21...h5 looks best.

b) The standard main lines are 17 0-0-0 and 17 gxh4, yet they come down to the same position: that after 17 0-0-0 0-0 18 gxh4 ♕f6. When it was established that 19 ♝g5? is well met with 19...♕xf1! (Kupreichik-Alburt, Odessa 1974), two other moves came to the forefront, both leading to immense complications with accurate calculation at a premium:

b1) 19 ♝e2 ♝d5 20 ♝g5 ♕e5 21 e7 ♖f2 22 ♕g3 ♕xg3 23 hxg3 and now 23...h6 looks fine for Black (and not 23...c5? 24 ♞db5!).

b2) 19 ♝b5 c5 (19...c6 transposes to the 17 ♝b5+ line; note that 19...♝f3? is bad due to 20 ♞xf3 ♕xf3 21 ♕xf3 ♖xf3 22 ♝xb6 axb6 23 e7) 20 ♝g5 ♕e5 21 e7 cxd4 22 exf8♕+ ♖xf8 23 ♖xh1 dxc3 (23...a6!? 24 ♕e2 ♕xe2 and 23...h6!? 24 ♝xh6 dxc3 are both viable alternatives) 24 ♕xb4 cxb2+ 25 ♔b1 ♞d5 is considered to lead to a forced repetition of moves in a number of lines.

While many of the details of these lines can (and no doubt will) be refined further, the general conclusion is well established: Black survives in this sharp line, and so White has been looking earlier for ways to deviate. Thus we return to the text-move, 13 ♕f3 (D).

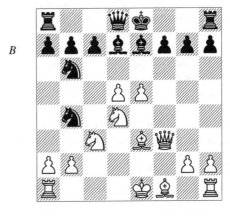

If White is to defend the d5-pawn with his queen, then f3 looks like a better square than b3, but Black's method of seeking counterplay remains the same.

**13...c5**

In the case of the immediate 13...0-0, there is a choice between two lines in which White's centre looks menacing, but Black hopes to find its vulnerable points: 14 0-0-0 ♗g5 15 ♘c2 ♘xc2 16 ♔xc2 ♕e7 (Morozevich-Ivanchuk, Amber Blindfold, Monaco 2002) and 14 a3 c5 15 axb4 cxd4 16 ♗xd4 ♗xb4, when 17 ♗d3 ♕h4+ 18 ♗f2 ♕e7 held firm in older high-level correspondence games, but White did not try the critical 19 ♕e4 g6 (19...f5 20 ♕d4) 20 d6.

**14 dxc6 bxc6** *(D)*

After 14...♘xc6 the reply 15 e6 is considered to be unpleasant, while the other recapture, 14...♗xc6, has not been sufficiently tested.

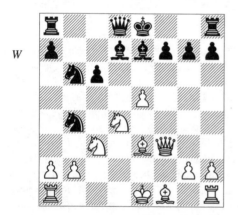

If after the text-move White continues with 15 e6?!, then 15...fxe6 leads to Black obtaining an outpost for his knight on d5, blocking the possible pressure along the d-file. A very nice idea analysed by Cafferty then runs 16 0-0-0 ♘6d5 17 a3 ♘xc3 18 ♘xe6 ♘ca2+! 19 ♔b1 ♗xe6 20 ♖xd8+ ♖xd8, with much more than enough compensation.

**15 ♗e2**

It is not easy to determine at once what White's claims for the advantage are based upon: his development is not better, the pawn-centre is only a memory and there are mutual weaknesses on the board. Still, there is one factor in his favour, and an important one at that: the black king has no other destination besides castling kingside, and here White has more space; his reserves can be quickly brought up, whereas Black's defenders are rather few. The

text-move is relatively new, but unlike 15 0-0-0 it prepares the evacuation of the king to a safe spot and does not allow simplifications, which are possible after 15 a3 c5!.

**15...0-0 16 0-0** *(D)*

This brings us to the critical position for the evaluation of White's idea.

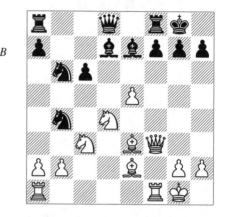

**16...♘4d5**

It is hard to make a categorical statement on the basis of so few practical examples, but it seems that the other knight had a better claim to this square: 16...♘6d5!? 17 ♗f2 ♕c7. One possibility is 18 a3 ♘xc3 19 bxc3 ♘d5 20 c4 ♘b6, as in Alavkin-Kravtsov, Novgorod 1997, but compared to our main game, White has spent a tempo on a3. In the line 18 ♗g3 ♗c5 19 ♖ad1 the b6-square will come in handy for the counterattack on the pinned knight on d4 by 19...♕b6; moreover, 19...♘c2 is also possible. 18 ♕g3 might be best, as played in Rebord-Rain, corr. 2004.

**17 ♗f2**

White doesn't object to having his queenside pawn-structure broken up; it is more important to deprive Black of the strongpoint on d5.

**17...♕c7 18 ♗g3 ♘xc3**

Black has no particular desire to exchange, yet he doesn't want to leave the knight on c3 either, as it possesses a considerable attacking potential and is preparing to jump to e4. 18...♗e6 does not lose material immediately, but the weakness that subsequently appears gives him little reason for joy.

**19 bxc3 ♕c8 20 ♗d3 g6?** *(D)*

This prophylactic defence against an attack on h7 was unnecessary and gives up a pawn without obtaining any compensation. Good or bad, 20...♘d5 had to be played, with a line like 21 c4 ♘b4 22 ♗e4 ♗g4 23 ♕c3 ♕d7, although the hopes to hold such a position are slim.

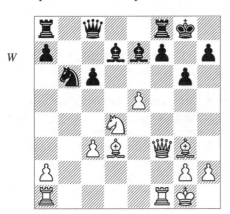

**21 ♗e4 ♗g4**

The attempt to hang on to the pawn by exchanging the bishop with 21...♗c5 22 ♔h1 ♗xd4 would lose in a few moves to an attack on the dark squares.

**22 ♕f2 ♘d5**

Here too, the retreat 22...♗d7 would give White an opportunity to settle matters with the enemy king: 23 ♗h4 ♗xh4 24 ♕xh4 ♕c7 25 ♘f3 ♘d5 26 ♕h6 (or 26 ♘g5 h5 27 ♕g3 with numerous threats).

**23 c4 ♘c3 24 ♘xc6 ♘xe4**

24...♗a3 is a better practical try, retaining more pieces in the game and, correspondingly, keeping it sharper. Of course, it doesn't change the overall evaluation of the position, viz. won for White.

**25 ♘xe7+ ♔g7 26 ♕f4**

For the time being, White avoids the exchange 26 ♘xc8 ♘xf2 27 ♘d6, remaining with opposite-coloured bishops, which is also sufficient for victory. Black's dark-square holes encourage White to keep the queens on the board.

**26...♕c5+ 27 ♖f2**

White must have been disturbed by something in the line 27 ♗f2 ♕xe7 28 ♕xe4 ♗f5 29 ♕f4 ♔g8 30 ♗h4 ♕c5+ 31 ♔h1 ♖fc8 32 ♗f6, although Black could have obtained roughly the same now as well by taking on e7. There is no immediate checkmate, but there can be no doubt about the outcome of the struggle.

**27...♗f5 28 ♗h4 f6?!**

Black could have tried fishing in troubled waters with 28...♖fb8.

**29 ♘xf5+?!**

Simpler is 29 exf6+ ♘xf6 30 ♘xf5+ gxf5 (30...♕xf5 31 ♕d6) 31 ♕g5+ ♔h8 32 ♕xf5 with two extra pawns.

**29...gxf5 30 ♕xf5 ♕xe5** (D)

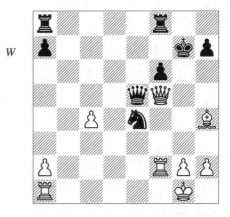

The factor of opposite-coloured bishops vanishes, and White goes into the technical phase that demands of him a certain accuracy, which he proceeds to demonstrate. Given that this is not an endgame book, further comments have little point.

**31 ♕xe5 fxe5 32 ♖e2 ♖f4 33 g3 ♘c3 34 ♖xe5 ♖xc4 35 ♖f1 ♘xa2 36 ♖e7+ ♔g8 37 ♖ff7 ♖g4 38 ♗f6 ♖g6 39 ♖g7+ ♖xg7 40 ♖xg7+ ♔f8 41 ♖xh7 ♖e8 42 ♖xa7 ♖e2 43 ♖b7 ♘c1 44 ♖b2 ♔f7 45 ♗h8 ♖e8 46 ♖f2+ ♔g6 47 ♗b2 ♘d3 48 ♖d2 ♖e3 49 ♗d4 ♖f3 50 ♗f2 ♘e5 51 ♔g2 ♖f7 52 h3 ♔h7 53 g4 1-0**

The system examined in this chapter is the most characteristic and original in our opening; the middlegame positions that result usually leave no doubt as to their ancestry. It is also considered the most pugnacious system, and with good reason, as it allows both sides to play for a win in a variety of ways. We can recommend the lines from Game 11 for players who like to maintain a certain level of solidity; on the other hand, those who appreciate more chaotic situations will prefer the play from Games 9 and 12.

# 4 The Old Main Line: 4 ♘f3 ♗g4

The subject of this chapter and the next is the position that arises after 1 e4 ♘f6 2 e5 ♘d5 3 d4 d6 4 ♘f3 (D).

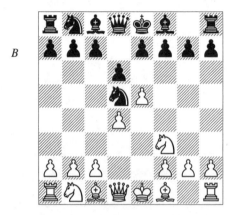

4 ♘f3 is the most frequently played move against the Alekhine Defence, and has been for many decades, and therefore can confidently be called the main line. Its popularity may to a certain extent be explained by the fact that it is a very natural and solid-looking move: White gives no ground and presents Black with only a small target for his counterplay. Moreover, unlike the Four Pawns Attack, it doesn't require a knowledge of many sharp lines, and an inaccurate move less often leads to fatal consequences. But while the struggle for the advantage proceeds at a moderate pace, this struggle is most definitely waged; 4 ♘f3 enjoys a reputation as the most testing reply to the Alekhine, and has the best score in practice of White's 4th-move options.

In reply, the pin of the knight by 4...♗g4 has traditionally been the main option (this is sometimes referred to as the Modern Variation, while in many sources this is the name given to 4 ♘f3 as a whole). However, in the last three decades, other continuations have been vying for the top spot (first 4...g6 and more recently 4...dxe5); we shall examine these in the next chapter.

The development of the bishop to g4 is totally natural and is based on two considerations: first, Black prepares to play ...e6 and doesn't wish to leave the bishop behind the pawn-chain, where it tends to get in the way; second, the fight against the enemy pawn on e5 is about to begin and, since the light-squared bishop is the only piece that cannot assault it directly, the attack is directed at one of the pawn's defenders, possibly followed by its exchange. White has a few trumps: his space advantage that is staked out by that same e5-pawn, and the potential advantage of the bishop-pair.

In Game 13 (J.Houska-Cornette) we shall examine lines, primarily those resulting from 5 ♗e2 c6, where Black seeks to exchange on f3 and put pressure on the e5-pawn.

The three remaining games of the chapter feature 5...e6. In Game 14 (Iordachescu-Chigladze) White waits for an opportunity to obtain an asymmetrical pawn-structure and himself exchanges on d6.

Games 15 (Acs-Tomashevsky) and 16 (Fedorowicz-Baburin) examine various methods of counterplay in the case where White strives to maintain his pawn on e5.

# Game 13
## Jovanka Houska – Matthieu Cornette
### *La Roche sur Yon 2007*

1 e4 ♘f6 2 e5 ♘d5 3 d4 d6 4 ♘f3 ♗g4 (D)
5 ♗e2

All the games in this chapter begin with this position. The modest placing of the bishop on

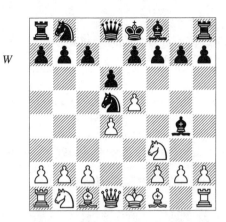

W

e2 is White's most effective option, but three other continuations had their place in the early days of the Alekhine's development. Although they are rarely seen in practice now, they deserve a few lines:

a) 5 ♗c4 promises little. Black must be careful not to fall for a tactical blow on f7 (5...♘b6?? 6 ♗xf7+), but both 5...e6 and 5...dxe5 are good.

b) With 5 h3 White clarifies the situation at once and reckons that the white queen's early deployment will exercise a useful influence over the position rather than just presenting Black with a target to attack. On the other hand, he is spending time to force an exchange that was on the cards anyway. Here is an example from recent practice: 5...♗xf3 (the retreat 5...♗h5 allows a standard, though not quite clear pawn sacrifice by 6 c4 ♘b6 7 g4 ♗g6 8 e6 fxe6 9 ♗d3, while it is also possible to return to the main road with 6 ♗e2) 6 ♕xf3 dxe5 7 dxe5 e6 8 ♗c4 ♘c6 9 ♕e4 ♘de7 10 ♗e3 ♘f5 11 ♘d2 (this move prepares castling queenside; the position after 11 0-0 is well known and is not considered dangerous, with 11...♕h4 accepted as the best reply) 11...♘xe3 (the opening of the f-file is fraught with dangers for Black; it is prudent to offer the exchange of queens by 11...♕h4 here as well) 12 fxe3 ♗c5?! 13 ♗a6 and Black failed to cope with the problems that subsequently arose in Sulskis-Chigladze, European Ch, Plovdiv 2008.

c) 5 c4 ♘b6 6 ♗e2 has its origin in two famous games by Alekhine (playing as White against 'his' opening). White doesn't aim to exchange the queens, of course, as after 6...dxe5 he either offers a pawn sacrifice by 7 ♘xe5 ♗xe2 8 ♕xe2 ♕xd4 that Black may very well

accept, or plays 7 c5, but the line 7...e4 8 cxb6 exf3 9 ♗xf3 ♗xf3 10 ♕xf3 ♘c6 also fails to scare Black. If he wishes, he can avoid these lines and insist on returning to the main continuations all the same by playing 6...c6, 6...e6, or even 6...♘c6!? (when he has reached the line 5 ♗e2 ♘c6 6 c4 ♘b6, having side-stepped 6 0-0).

We now return to 5 ♗e2 (D):

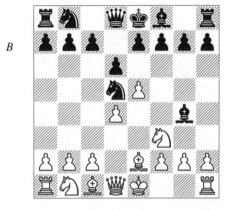

B

**5...c6**

Black's plan involves the exchange of bishop for knight on f3, followed by an exchange of pawns on e5. His subsequent development will then be focused around an attack on the e5-pawn. However, the move by the c-pawn is a necessary prophylactic measure, as shown by the line 5...♗xf3?! 6 ♗xf3, when 6...dxe5? fails to 7 c4 and ♗xb7, while 6...c6 can now be met by 7 exd6 ♕xd6 (after 7...exd6 8 ♗xd5 cxd5 the doubled d-pawns don't make Black's position any prettier) and his bishop-pair will have a more open position to operate in; perhaps 7 c4 ♘b6 (or 7...♘c7 8 ♕b3) 8 e6 is even stronger. Thus, Black does not want to make the exchange on f3 until he can be certain of saddling White with a vulnerable pawn on e5, and from this springs the idea of playing the move ...c6 first of all.

Let's have a look at another move that shields the b7-square from attack on the long diagonal and develops a piece at the same time: 5...♘c6 (D).

On the other hand, White now gets the opportunity to make the d5 advance with gain of a tempo, which may turn out to be rather unpleasant for Black. These are the main options:

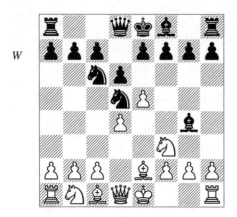

a) One attempt to exploit the position of the knight on c6 is to play the typical pawn sacrifice 6 e6 fxe6. The forcing sequence 7 ♘g5 ♗xe2 8 ♕xe2 ♘xd4 9 ♕d1 h6 10 ♘xe6 ♘xe6 11 ♕xd5 ♕c8 12 ♕h5+ ♔d8 leads to unclear play, but White can postpone concrete operations and for the time being occupy himself with development; e.g., 7 0-0 or 7 c3 with decent compensation.

b) White can also seek an Exchange Variation set-up by 6 c4 ♘b6 7 exd6, when Black has the standard choice of recaptures:

b1) 7...cxd6 fits less well with the knight on c6 than the recapture with the e-pawn, and is well met by 8 d5. At the moment the backward e7-pawn on the half-open file can hardly be called weak, but Black is unlikely to be able to get rid of it without creating new weaknesses.

b2) 7...exd6 is an acceptable form of the Exchange Variation, although Black has committed his knight to c6 less early than is ideal. White can resolve the position at once with 8 d5 ♗xf3 9 ♗xf3 ♘e5 10 ♗e2, or else wait and spend a move or two on development until Black is himself ready for the counter-advance ...d5. White's bishop-pair and advantage in space allow us to evaluate his chances as preferable.

c) The most critical reply is simply to get on with development by 6 0-0, challenging Black to find a useful follow-up. Now 6...e6 can be met by 7 c4 ♘b6 8 exd6 cxd6 9 d5 exd5 10 cxd5 ♗xf3 11 gxf3 (the bishop is needed on another diagonal) 11...♘e5 12 ♗b5+, when after 12...♘ed7 13 ♕d4 it is hard for Black to deploy the rest of his pieces, while 12...♘bd7 13 f4 ♘g6 14 ♖e1+ ♗e7 15 f5 ♘e5 16 ♘c3 is

also highly suspicious for Black, Oll-Kaunas, Clichy 1991. If Black inserts the preliminary exchange 6...dxe5, then in the line 7 ♘xe5 ♘xe5 8 dxe5 ♗f5 9 c4 ♘b6 10 ♕b3 White retains the initiative. That leaves 6...♘b6 (intending ...dxe5) to be considered, but then the traditional recipe is 7 h3 ♗xf3 8 ♗xf3 dxe5 9 ♗xc6+ bxc6 10 dxe5, and no one has ever mounted a serious challenge to the view that this favours White.

We now return to 5...c6 (D):

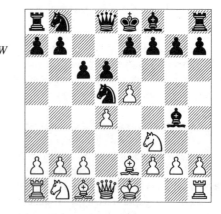

**6 0-0**

White simply allows Black to carry out his plan, and will seek to prove that the position Black is aiming for nevertheless favours White.

6 ♘g5 is a popular alternative, based on the belief that the knight is more useful in the upcoming struggle, and that an exchange of bishops is preferable from White's viewpoint. Then Black must decide whether to acquiesce:

a) Exchanging by 6...♗xe2 7 ♕xe2 leads to a quiet manoeuvring struggle where particular care has to be devoted to the control of d6. After 7...dxe5 8 dxe5 e6 9 0-0 ♘d7 10 c4 ♘e7, White should be somewhat better, but the temptation to rush Black at once can lead White to misfortune; e.g., 11 ♗f4?! ♘g6 12 ♕h5?! ♕e7 13 ♗g3 ♘gxe5 14 ♘e4 g6 15 ♕e2 f5 and Black managed to beat off White's 'attack', keeping the extra pawn, in Jonkman-Krasenkow, Wijk aan Zee 2007. 11 ♘c3 ♘f5 12 ♖d1 is a rather better way to proceed, when both 12...♗e7 and 12...♕c7 are met by 13 ♘ce4!, when Black has awkward problems to solve.

b) Therefore, Black more often chooses 6...♗f5 (D), which leads to livelier play.

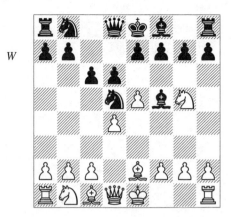

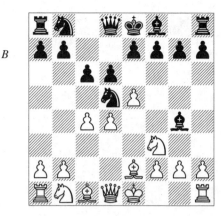

The motivation behind this move is not to avoid the exchange of bishops altogether, but only to make it in a way that leaves White's queen on a less ideal square than e2. In return though, White gains additional possibilities.

b1) Firstly, there is 7 e6. In the line that has been at the centre of the debate, 7...fxe6 8 g4 ♗g6 9 ♗d3 ♗xd3 10 ♕xd3 ♘f6 11 ♘xe6 ♕d7 12 ♕e2 ♚f7 13 ♘g5+ ♚g8 14 ♖g1 ♘a6 15 ♘c3, White's chances look preferable. After queenside castling, his king will be more secure and the development of the h8-rook may require some effort, although Black can try to free it immediately by 15...h5, as in Bondar-Beecham, corr. 1994.

b2) White can insist on the exchange by 7 ♗d3 ♗xd3 8 ♕xd3. Then the struggle is once again centred on the e5-pawn and the d6-square along roughly similar lines as in the case of the immediate exchange on e2, except that Black can hope to gain time and thus deploy his forces more harmoniously thanks to the white queen's position on d3. For instance, 8...e6! 9 0-0 (9 ♘e4 can be met by 9...♘b4 and ...d5, 9 c4 by 9...♘b4 10 ♕b3 dxe5 11 a3 ♗e7, and 9 ♕f3 by 9...♕c7 10 c4 ♘b4 11 exd6 ♗xd6 12 ♕e4 ♘d7 13 a3 ♘f6) 9...dxe5 10 dxe5 ♘d7.

Another line begins with pushing the knight out of the centre: 6 c4 (D).

First we shall have a look at the unconventional retreat 6...♘c7. Here the knight for a long time ceases to be a menace to the e5-pawn. On the other hand, it not only it neutralizes the threat of e6, but it plans to take advantage of that square for itself. White's advantage in space provides him with an abundant choice of set-ups: he can place the queen on b3 or unite the

knights first by 7 ♘bd2, or he can go into an attractive endgame with 7 0-0 ♗xf3 8 exd6 ♗xe2 9 dxc7 ♗xd1 10 cxd8♕+ ♚xd8 11 ♖xd1. Other popular plans involve the exchange 7 exd6 exd6 or the attempt to hobble at once or later the enemy knights with the d5 advance.

The more habitual 6...♘b6 creates a threat against the c4-pawn, but the knight's departure from the centre gives White additional freedom of action. The leap 7 ♘g5 at once or after the inclusion of 7 ♘bd2 ♘8d7 8 ♘g5 becomes more dangerous, as 8...♗xe2 can be met with 9 e6. After 7 ♘bd2 the exchange 7...dxe5 8 ♘xe5 gives rise to a pawn-formation common to many openings, but in this case the b6-knight's passive position complicates the struggle for equality. Painstaking defence is also required of Black in the line 7 exd6 exd6 8 0-0 ♗e7, though his pressure on the d4-pawn and the open file allow him to count on success; e.g., 9 b3 0-0 10 h3 ♗xf3 11 ♗xf3 d5 12 c5 ♘c8 13 ♘c3 ♗f6 14 ♗e3 ♘a6, carefully edging his way toward equality, Kritz-Zhigalko, Hengelo 2001.

**6...♗xf3 7 ♗xf3 dxe5 8 dxe5 e6 (D)**

It is this position that Black was aiming for when choosing 5...c6. He can quickly enough raise three attackers against the e5-pawn; it is less obvious but not out of the question that he can also involve his bishop and even the rooks after developing them to the flanks. Unless he is careless, White can easily drum up three defenders, but finding more is harder. Supporting the pawn with its neighbour, the f-pawn, would solve this problem, but White would like to avoid playing this move, as it closes the position and weakens a whole complex of squares.

W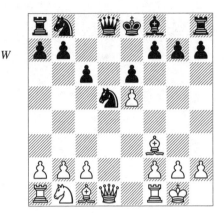

B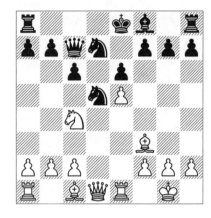

Moreover, it doesn't suit White to concentrate on defence; he must seek to use his trumps: his space advantage, the bishop-pair and the weakness on d6.

**9 b3**

White puts the bishop in charge of initiating the process of supporting the e5-pawn; this is a quite playable continuation but not the only one. The least logical course is to exchange the queens by 9 c4 ♘e7 (note that this is the knight's standard route in this variation) 10 ♕xd8+ ♔xd8. White drives the knight to a better position, while robbing the black king of his castling rights is not a real achievement (he is quite comfortable on c7), whereas there's nothing to attack the f7-pawn with. After 11 ♗e4 ♘d7 White has to decide: if 12 f4, the knight goes to f5, whereas after 12 ♗f4 the g6-square looks more attractive, forcing the exchange of the light-squared bishop.

For some pieces, natural posts beckon to them: for the knight it is the c4-square, and for the rook e1, and they can be occupied in various orders, such as 9 ♘d2 ♘d7 10 ♖e1 ♕c7 11 ♘c4 (D) (11 ♕e2!? should keep an edge in a protracted manoeuvring struggle).

Now 11...b5? meets the elegant riposte 12 ♗xd5 cxd5 13 ♘d6+ ♗xd6 14 ♕xd5 with a large advantage for White, while after the superior 11...♘7b6 White can choose between sacrificing a pawn by 12 ♘d6+ ♗xd6 13 exd6 ♕xd6 14 c4 ♘xc4 15 ♕d4 ♘cb6 16 ♕xg7, unleashing the bishops, and 12 ♕e2 ♘xc4 13 ♕xc4 0-0-0, when opposite-side castling promises an interesting struggle.

Another popular set-up utilizes the c4-square for different purposes: 9 ♕e2 ♘d7 10 c4 ♘e7.

Here the dark-squared bishop supports the e5-pawn along one diagonal from b2 or c3, although it can also settle on another diagonal via the f4-g3 route. The light-squared bishop seeks work on g4 or h5, at the same time clearing the road for the f-pawn. However, this set-up tends not to be too effective; for example, 11 ♗g4 h5 12 ♗h3 ♕c7 13 f4 ♘f5 14 ♘c3 0-0-0 15 ♗xf5 exf5 16 ♗e3 ♗c5 17 ♘a4 ♗xe3+ 18 ♕xe3 ♘b6 19 ♘xb6+ ♕xb6 20 ♕xb6 with an approximately even rook endgame, Arakhamia-Baburin, Liechtenstein 2007.

**9...♘d7 10 ♗b2 ♕c7 11 ♕e2 (D)**

This defence gives Black an opportunity to transfer the knight for the attack of the e5-pawn with the gain of a tempo. However, the transfer of the queen to e4 has its advantages too: the pressure on c6 deprives the enemy b-pawn of its mobility and the development of the bishop to b4 is hindered. 11 ♖e1 is another possibility, but then there is the issue of ...♗b4, gaining a tempo attacking the rook and so causing disruption in White's position.

B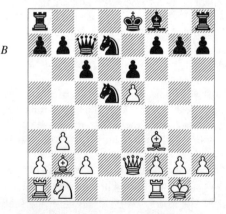

**11...♘f4 12 ♕e4 ♘g6 13 ♖e1**

It is worth noting that the tempting 13 ♗h5?! ♘gxe5 14 f4 ♘g6 15 f5 is ineffective due to 15...0-0-0!, when 16 fxg6? hxg6 opens up an attack against h2. This idea crops up in several similar lines.

**13...♖d8**

What is preferable – this or 13...0-0-0? That's largely a matter of taste; the pros and cons of the king's position on c8 are obvious enough. Note that after the development of the bishop to e7 (or c5) there appears the tactical threat of mass exchanges on e5 followed by winning back material on the long diagonal with ...♗f6 (or ...♗d4). If Black succeeds in grabbing a whole rook there are no further questions, but if White manages to bail out for the price of the exchange then the bottom line is Black's rook and a pawn versus White's two minor pieces. The evaluation of such a material balance is not entirely simple, although generally it hovers around equality. In an open position, an outside passed pawn supported by a rook usually secures its owner the advantage; and vice versa, if the rook is restricted, the side with the minor pieces has the better chances.

**14 a4 a5 15 ♘a3 ♗b4 16 ♘c4 (D)**

Although it looks showy, this move is practically forced if White intends to continue the struggle. 16 ♖e3 invites Black to repeat moves with 16...♗c5, while 16 ♖e2? disrupts the control over the d1-square and loses a pawn to 16...♗xa3.

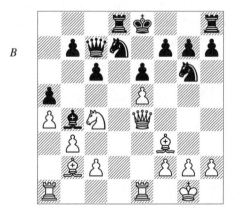

**16...♗xe1 17 ♖xe1 0-0 18 ♗a3 f5?!**

It appears that Black's play was stronger in the stem game: 18...b5 19 ♗d6 ♕a7 20 ♘a3 (in

1981, long before this idea had occurred in practice, Curt Hansen analysed 20 ♘e3 ♖fe8 as slightly favouring Black) 20...♕b6, Zambrana-Lima, São Paulo Zonal 2003, and now White could have played for a small advantage by continuing 21 axb5 cxb5 22 ♕e2. The text-move retains the exchange but activates the white bishops, exposes Black's king and creates a weakness on e6.

**19 exf6 ♖xf6 20 ♗d6 ♕c8 21 ♗g4 ♔h8 22 ♗g3**

The position is not of a forcing character. It is clear that White's active pieces are sufficient compensation for the sacrificed exchange, but it is desirable to transform this activity into either the creation of new weaknesses in the enemy camp or into material gains. Here and on the next move the capture on a5 deserved consideration. Perhaps White didn't want to open the road to d5 for the enemy knight, but even then Black wouldn't create any serious threats, whereas winning back even part of the sacrificed material would boost White's confidence.

**22...♖df8 23 h4?!**

Although the idea behind the raid by the h-pawn is not bad in itself, it could have waited a bit. Now Black's pieces manage to come to life.

**23...♕a8**

Strange as it may seem, the queen is placed well on this square and operates in all directions.

**24 ♕d4 b5 25 ♘d2 (D)**

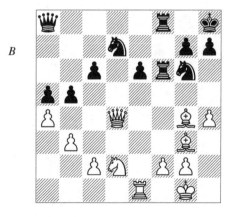

**25...e5?**

With this move, the advantage swings back to White, and decisively so. Although the simplifications theoretically should suit Black, their price turns out to be exorbitant – the white queen becomes too active. Black could have maintained even chances with 25...♖d8.

**26 ♕xd7 ♖d8 27 ♕c7 ♖xd2 28 h5 ♘f4 29 ♖xe5?!**

We can only guess that White was in time-trouble. It's not apparent what Black can do after 29 ♕xe5, but even the text-move is good enough.

**29...♕f8 30 h6 gxh6 31 ♖e4?**

With this move, White lets a significant part of her advantage slip away. The immediate 31 axb5 is much more convincing.

**31...♘g6 32 axb5 cxb5**

Black could have opted for the line 32...♖fxf2 33 ♗f3 ♖xf3 34 gxf3, when both kings are in danger, although the black one is more so.

**33 ♗d7??**

Here 33 ♕c3 would drive the active enemy rook away and neutralize Black's counter-threats. After that, White could turn her attention to the enemy pawns on the queenside.

**33...♕f7??**

Once again a single move turns the evaluation of the position upside down. 33...♖fxf2! is correct, when White loses in case of 34 ♖e8? ♖xg2+ 35 ♔h1 ♕xe8 36 ♗xe8 ♖ge2, whereas after 34 ♕c3+ ♕f6 35 ♕xf6+ ♖xf6 36 ♗xb5 ♖xc2 it is Black who has the winning chances.

**34 ♕c8+?!**

The correct way was 34 ♕b8+!, in order to maintain control over the a7-square.

**34...♔g7 35 ♗e8?!**

35 ♗xb5 is better.

**35...♕d5?**

35...♕a7! leads to a double-edged position, whereas now the black king has to set off on a final journey.

**36 ♗xg6 ♔xg6 37 ♕e8+ ♕f7 38 ♖g4+ ♔h5 39 ♖h4+ ♔g6 40 ♖g4+ ♔h5 41 ♕e4 ♖f5 42 f3**

White takes advantage of the extra minute obtained via the repetition of moves to work through one of several winning continuations.

**42...♕d5 43 ♕e8+ ♕f7 44 ♕e3 ♖d1+ 45 ♔h2 ♖g5 46 ♕e4 ♕f5 47 ♕e8+ ♖g6 48 ♖h4+ ♔g5 49 ♖e4 1-0**

# Game 14
# Viorel Iordachescu – Iveri Chigladze
*European Ch, Plovdiv 2008*

**1 e4 ♘f6 2 e5 ♘d5 3 d4 d6 4 ♘f3 ♗g4 5 ♗e2 e6** (D)

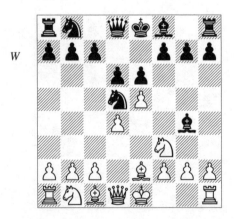

This is the main thoroughfare of the system examined in this chapter. The idea behind Black's last move does not require any comments – it is obvious. Note that it cuts out the option of recapturing on d6 with the e-pawn, which makes this version of the Exchange Variation more attractive for White – there is more fight in asymmetrical structures, and Black's most harmonious set-up in the ...cxd6 lines, the fianchetto, is ruled out too.

White is faced with a strategic choice: either to aim for the exchange on d6, in which case he must also decide when to execute it, or to keep a pawn on e5, securing the advantage in space. In this case he must be constantly on the lookout in order to meet advantageously the exchange on this square.

Another important question is whether to force the g4-bishop to declare its intentions by playing h3, which is almost always met by ...♗h5. In most cases it is useful for White to drive the bishop off to h5 and take away one of its diagonals, but whether the pawn is better placed on h3 or h2 depends on the particular variation; sometimes it is better on h3, while in other lines it only helps Black, and in some it makes little real difference. The upshot is that throughout the theory of this variation, there are two slightly different versions of most of the main lines, and one must never assume that the difference is irrelevant. It is possible for Black even to construct his repertoire around this point, playing one line when White includes h3 ♗h5, and a completely different one when he does not.

In this game we shall be examining variations where White exchanges on d6. It's not feasible to examine every possible case; that's why we shall limit ourselves to the most popular move-orders and aim to single out the general points applicable to all cases.

**6 h3**

If White is intending to exchange on d6, then it is useful to include this move, so White decides to play it at once. In reply, Black has nothing better than dropping back to h5, since 6...♗xf3 7 ♗xf3 poses the problem of the b7-pawn's defence, so Black is unable to follow up by exchanging on e5, which would be the only way to justify giving up bishop for knight. After both 7...c6 8 exd6 and 7...♘c6 8 c4 ♘b6 9 exd6 cxd6 10 d5 exd5 11 ♗xd5 White retains an advantage.

However, we should also examine the case of White exchanging on d6 without playing the move h3, especially as these lines are important from a transpositional viewpoint: 6 0-0 ♗e7 7 c4 ♘b6 8 exd6 cxd6 *(D)*.

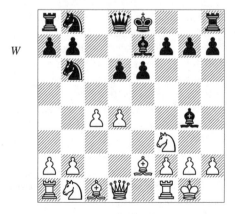

It makes sense to chase the knight away from d5 before exchanging in order to cut out the option of retreating to f6, and because on

d5 it interfered with White's piece development.

Black's main strategic goal is the advance in the centre by ...d5. White can either allow this, or pre-empt it by playing d5 himself. Black also has the option of playing ...♘c6 in preparation for ...d5, but in this case White will almost certainly reply with d5, as it then comes with gain of tempo and the prospect of leaving Black with exposed structural weaknesses. If after multiple exchanges on d5 a white piece ends up on that square, the weakness of d6 may become sensitive; on the other hand, it is more acceptable for Black for a white pawn to end up on d5, as this blocks the frontal attack on d6. We should note that the ...♘c6 line's principal importance stems from lines like 6 0-0 ♗e7 7 c4 ♘b6 8 ♘c3 0-0 9 ♗e3 ♘c6, with White making the exchange on d6 only then, as a specific response to ...♘c6. We can thus see why White might have omitted the move h3: he was in fact steering for the 9...d5 10 c5 ♗xf3 11 gxf3 main line, where the pawn is better on h2 than on h3, and Black is seeking to avoid this line.

Let's proceed further from the diagram position: 9 ♘c3 0-0 *(D)*.

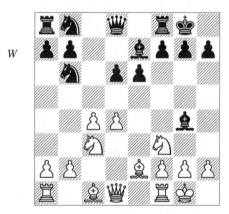

Now there are three candidates for the next move.

The most natural is 10 ♗e3, when after 10...♘c6 11 d5 exd5 White has a choice between 12 ♗xb6 ♛xb6 13 ♘xd5 and 12 ♘xd5 ♘xd5 13 ♛xd5 ♗e6 (preventing this is one reason why White would like to have driven the bishop to h5 – indeed, the whole ...♘c6 approach is a lot less palatable in that case, but the saving grace is that the main line seen in Game

16 works a little less well for White if he *has* played h3) 14 ♕d2 (14 ♕b5 is also good) 14...d5 15 c5. A useful waiting move is 10...a6; among other things it threatens the c4-pawn after the exchange on f3 as the rook acquires a flight-square on a7, but it weakens the b6-knight's position and White can attempt to profit from this with 11 ♕b3.

White may observe that a drawback of the development to e3 is that the knight will leap in some lines to c4, threatening to exchange the bishop off, so 10 ♗f4 suggests itself, but this in turn makes 10...a6 a safer reply.

Finally we have 10 b3, but this basically loses a tempo, since White's plans include an offensive with the queenside pawns. More concretely, it also allows 10...♘c6 in improved circumstances, as the line 11 d5 exd5 12 ♘xd5 ♘xd5 13 ♕xd5 ♗f6 is more likely to favour Black as the long dark diagonal is weakened.

On the basis of these considerations we can single out the two most popular continuations. The first is 10 ♗e3 d5 11 c5 ♗xf3 12 ♗xf3 (the recapture 12 gxf3?! doesn't allow the knight leap; after 12...♘c4?! 13 ♗xc4 dxc4 14 ♕a4 White is a clear pawn to the good, at the expense of the spoiled kingside pawn-structure; on the other hand, White's position would work better in this case if he had not already exchanged on d6, as we shall see later) 12...♘c4 *(D)*.

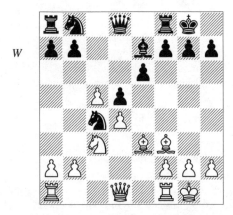

Now White usually plays 13 ♗c1 or 13 ♗f4 followed by a queenside pawn advance, while Black's counterplay is based on the undermining ...b6 and the counterattack against the d4-pawn.

The other continuation is 10 b3 ♘c6 11 ♗e3 d5 12 c5 ♘c8 (a route typical for this opening; the knight is bound via e7 for f5 to attack the pawn on d4) 13 b4 a6 14 ♖b1 ♗f6 15 a4 ♘8e7 *(D)* (note that if h3 and ...♗h5 have been played, White has the possibility of g4-g5, so before playing the knight to e7 Black must insert the exchange on f3).

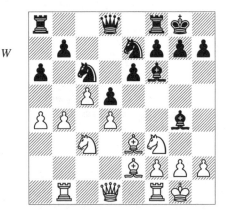

In these variations Black's counterplay is quite substantial, so another set-up for White has gained popularity, one that is less active but aims to restrict Black's options in the centre and to postpone active play until White's mobilization is complete. Let's return to the position after 6 0-0 ♗e7 7 c4 ♘b6 8 exd6 cxd6 and pick another continuation: 9 ♘bd2 ♘c6 10 b3 0-0 11 ♗b2. The main focus is the control of the squares d4 and e5. However, there are no immediate threats and Black can also avoid forcing matters and make useful waiting moves: 11...a5 12 a3 d5 (if Black wishes, he can improve the bishops' positions by first transferring them to f5 and f6) 13 c5 ♘d7 14 ♗c3 b6 15 b4 bxc5 16 dxc5 (the formation after 16 bxc5 is wholly satisfactory for Black) 16...e5 17 b5 d4 18 bxc6 ♘xc5 with complications, Bryzgalin-Sorokin, Russian Ch, Kazan 2005.

The above lines do not exhaust White's options; for instance, there is the immediate queenside raid 9 a4, and the recently employed 9 b4 is interesting as well.

**6...♗h5 7 c4 ♘b6 8 exd6 cxd6 9 ♘c3** *(D)*

White can generally speaking play his last few moves in several orders, and if he wishes, he can castle at some point in the sequence.

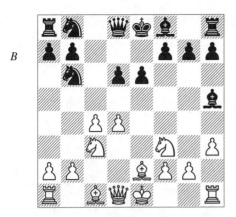

However, the plan we shall consider below involves foregoing castling altogether.

**9...♗e7**

Naturally, White now has the same set of options as in the position we examined earlier without h3, but with some differences that are in his favour, as mentioned above.

**10 d5 (D)**

This is the most radical way to prevent the ...d5 advance. Unlike the same advance we saw earlier, here it occurs without attacking a knight on c6 and allows the reply...

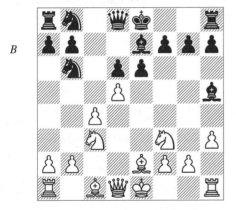

**10...e5**

The resulting formation occurs in other openings as well, including many Sicilian lines. In itself, this pawn-structure is pleasant for Black if he can form a pawn phalanx e5 + f5, but the defining factor is the piece placement.

**11 c5?!**

This reckless thrust has hardly been played. It looks tempting but doesn't seem to achieve anything tangible.

With the bishop already driven off to h5, White can take advantage of its position to initiate active operations on the kingside by 11 g4!? ♗g6 12 h4 (D).

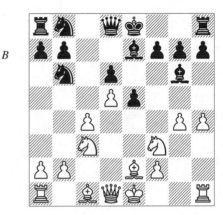

Of course, this is not played in the simple hope of winning a piece; the main goal is to devalue Black's kingside majority and win the battle for e4 while preserving White's own pawn-majority on the queenside. On the other hand, if Black succeeds in setting up a blockade on the queenside, the white pawn-chain there may as a result turn into a chronic weakness.

This plan has only become popular in the Alekhine in the past few years, and has so far scored well. It leads to non-standard yet interesting positions; for example, 12...h6 13 ♗d3! ♕c8 (counterplay is more important than a spoiled pawn-structure) 14 ♗xg6 fxg6 15 ♘d2 (the only move to defend both pawns, eyeing e4 at the same time, though at the expense of development) as in Bologan-Agdestein, Erevan Olympiad 1996. White is better, but Black retains counter-chances.

**11...dxc5!**

After 11...♘6d7?! (or 11...♘c8?!) the passed d5-pawn secures White a small advantage.

**12 g4 ♗g6 13 ♗b5+ ♘8d7**

13...♔f8, not allowing the following play, is also possible, as losing the right to castle is quite acceptable.

**14 d6 ♗h4 (D)**

**15 ♗xd7+**

There were various ways to take the e5-pawn that lead to acceptable positions, such as 15 ♘xe5 a6 16 ♘xg6 hxg6 17 ♗e2, but none that promise White the advantage. Interesting

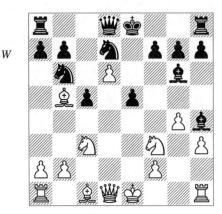

**22...♘f6 23 0-0-0 ♕f3 24 ♘d5** *(D)*

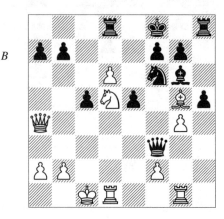

complications arise after 15 g5 ♗h5 16 ♖g1 threatening ♖g4, although Black's chances still look preferable. With his actual choice, White tries to prove that the black queen is overloaded, but now the pawn sacrifice becomes permanent.

**15...♘xd7 16 ♕a4?!**

Hindering Black's castling and creating the threat of ♘d5, but Black manages to consolidate. 16 ♕d5, again threatening g5, looks stronger and if 16...h6 then 17 ♘xh4 ♕xh4 18 ♕xb7 leads to roughly the same type of play but with an equal pawn-count.

**16...♕f6 17 ♘xh4 ♕xh4 18 ♘d5 ♖d8 19 ♘c7+ ♔f8**

White's initiative evaporates, while in addition to the extra pawn Black acquires counter-threats.

**20 ♗e3 h5 21 ♖g1 ♕xh3 22 ♗g5?!**

This only helps Black to untangle himself. 22 0-0-0 at once is better, when despite the two-pawn deficit, White's chances to complicate matters haven't been exhausted yet.

**24...♖xd6**

24...♘xd5!? would give Black an extremely strong attack after 25 ♗xd8 ♘c3 and now 26 ♗e7+ ♔g8 27 d7 ♘xa4 28 d8♕+ ♔h7, 26 ♕b3 ♕f4+ 27 ♔d2 ♘e2+ 28 ♔d1 ♘xg1 or 26 ♕c4 ♘e2+ 27 ♔d2 ♘d4.

**25 ♘f4?!**

White eliminates the terrible bishop, but exposing the enemy king with 25 ♘xf6 gxf6 26 ♖xd6 fxg5 27 ♖xg6 was a better chance.

**25...♖d4 26 ♘xg6+ fxg6 27 ♕a5 ♕c6 28 ♗e3 ♖xd1+ 29 ♖xd1 ♔f7 30 ♕c3 hxg4 31 ♕xe5 ♖h1 32 ♗xc5?!**

Naturally, after 32 ♕xc5 ♕xc5+ 33 ♗xc5 ♖xd1+ 34 ♔xd1 a6 35 ♔e2 ♔e6 36 ♔e3 ♔f5 37 ♗f8 ♘e4, followed by giving up one of the g-pawns and exchanging off another, Black would realize the third one without much effort. However, this way White saved himself and his opponent each about two hours of free time.

**32...b6 0-1**

# Game 15

# Peter Acs – Evgeny Tomashevsky

*Pardubice 2001*

**1 e4 ♘f6 2 e5 ♘d5 3 d4 d6 4 ♘f3 ♗g4 5 ♗e2 e6 6 c4 ♘b6 7 0-0 ♗e7 8 ♘c3** *(D)*

In this game and the next we examine another strategic approach, and one that has over the years done the most to dent the solid reputation of the old main line of the Alekhine. Taking advantage of the fact that the exchange

on e5 activates White's forces and suits him just fine, he refrains from taking on d6, which would free Black's game somewhat, but keeps the option of transposing into those variations should the knight be developed to c6, for instance.

**8...0-0 9 ♗e3**

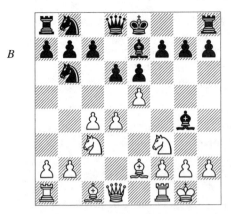

*B*

If White does not exchange first on d6, it is disadvantageous to deploy the bishop further up the board by 9 ♗f4, since Black can calmly reply with 9...♘c6, as the line 10 exd6 ♗xd6 11 ♗xd6 cxd6 12 d5 exd5 13 ♘xd5 ♗xf3, exchanging the dark-squared bishops, is perfectly fine for him.

**9...a5**

We shall examine 9...d5 in the next game, in the context of the analogous line with h3 and ...♗h5 included.

We have already mentioned in the previous game how events develop in the case of 9...♘c6. Note, however, that with 9 h3 ♗h5 included (which, naturally, can be inserted earlier as well) 10 ♗e3 ♘c6 is a lot less attractive. In most games in this version Black settles for 11 exd6 cxd6 12 d5 ♗xf3 13 ♗xf3 ♘e5 14 dxe6 fxe6 15 ♗g4, which clearly favours White.

Our main focus in this game is on Black's ways to avoid forcing matters and making a useful but non-committal move instead. Besides the text-move, there are two other continuations:

a) 9...a6 is an idea that we have already seen. This move is useful in the construction of defensive fortifications against the enemy queenside offensive, and it makes the capture on c4 a real threat. After 10 b3 Black can congratulate himself on winning a tempo (as White's plans involve a further advance of the b-pawn), and a new plan of counterplay appears: 10...d5 11 c5 ♘6d7 followed by the undermining ...f6 (when White should urgently worry about preparing the supporting f4). The other possible reaction has already been mentioned: 10 exd6 cxd6 11 ♕b3 or at once 10 ♕b3, striving to take advantage of the b6-knight's weakened position.

b) By playing 9...♘8d7, Black ensures that White's possible d5 advance does not gain a tempo, but the knight is not positioned very well here: it is on a poor circuit for the likely structures after an eventual ...d5 advance, and it fails to take part in the attack on the d4-pawn. On the other hand, it does pose a threat to take on c4 (after exchanging on f3, of course). In the case of 10 b3 Black has good prospects of equality after 10...dxe5 11 ♘xe5 ♘xe5 12 ♗xg4 (an exchange of queens by 12 dxe5 ♕xd1 leaves Black even more OK) 12...♘xg4 13 ♕xg4. Note that here too, it is useful for White to have shooed the bishop away to h5 at an earlier point; then in the line 11 b3 (we increased the move numbering by one because of h3 and ....♗h5) 11...dxe5 12 ♘xe5 ♘xe5 13 ♗xh5 White has a better claim for the advantage as the white bishop remains on the board. Without those moves included, White usually plays 10 exd6 cxd6 and only then 11 b3, retaining more space, more pieces and, accordingly, more fighting resources.

We now return to 9...a5 *(D)*:

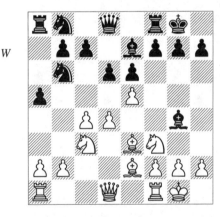

*W*

The move in the game is multi-faceted. It fulfils defensive functions against the coming pawn offensive, while creating an attack on c4 and also adds (unlike 9...a6) the option of developing the knight to a6.

White must now choose once more what formation to meet ...d5 with. If he includes the exchange on d6, then the standard play will see the knight retreat to c8, bound for the favourite e7-f5 route.

**10 b3**

White opts to keep the spearhead of his formation on e5.

Taking into account the fact that ...a5 weakens the queenside squares, the plan of creating a queenside majority by 10 exd6 cxd6 11 c5 has some appeal.

**10...♘a6**

After 10...d5 11 c5 the f6-square is not available to the black bishop, so it is more logical to retreat with 11...♘6d7 to support the undermining ...b6 and ...f6.

Black instead prefers to continue developing for the time being, although the position of the knight on a6 doesn't really fit with a later ...d5. However, other operations in the centre are possible, such as preparation for the exchange on e5.

**11 exd6**

White decides to take positive action, rather than wait any longer for Black to declare his intentions. 11 ♖c1 is considered a good alternative that makes it hard for Black to equalize, but experience with the whole line is limited. Note that 11 h3 ♗h5 12 g4 ♗g6 13 h4 h6 14 g5 hxg5 15 hxg5 ♘d7 is considered playable for Black.

**11...cxd6 12 d5** *(D)*

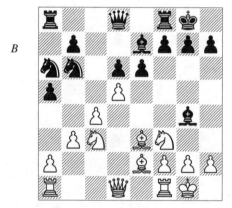

This hadn't been played before. Black's last few moves are useful for a blockade of White's queenside pawns, but White nevertheless decides to go for the formation familiar to us from the previous game.

**12...♗f6?!**

The desire not to leave the bishop locked in behind the pawn-chain is understandable, but the exchanging manoeuvre permits White to open up the centre. While 12...e5 forms a pawn-chain along dark squares, it is not permanently

fixed, and doesn't therefore deprive the e7-bishop of hopes for a decent future. If Black wishes to adopt the approach chosen in the game, it would be more precise to exchange off the other bishop first by 12...♗xf3 13 ♗xf3 and only now 13...♗f6.

**13 ♖c1**

Black's inaccurate move-order allows White the attractive continuation 13 ♘d4 ♗xe2 14 ♘dxe2.

**13...♗xc3 14 ♖xc3 ♗xf3**

If 14...e5 at once, then after 15 ♘g5 White has an attack that Black helped to intensify by inviting a rook to the third rank.

**15 ♗xf3 e5** *(D)*

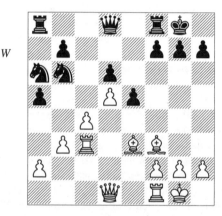

We have a showdown between the bishop-pair and the knight duo. Black hopes to set up a secure checkpoint on c5, when his prospects will look rather good. His likely next move is with the knight to d7.

**16 c5!**

Tomorrow may be too late. White sets his bishops loose and to that end plans to sacrifice the exchange for a pawn.

**16...dxc5**

It would seem that it makes more sense to get rid of the knight on the rim and, at the same time, of White's bishop-pair, yet after 16...♘xc5 17 ♗xc5 dxc5 18 d6 (if White allows the blockade to be set up a square further up the board by 18 ♖xc5 ♕d6, then the advantage is more likely to be with Black) White will regain his pawn and the remaining bishop will be definitely stronger than the black knight, while the passed pawn may also become dangerous.

**17 d6 ♕d7 18 ♗xc5** *(D)*

It is quite likely that the simple 18 ♕d2 is at least as strong. White then has numerous ways of strengthening his position, in particular by returning the bishop to e2 in order to break the blockade of the passed pawn. However, it is also tempting to open the game fully for the bishops, and then sit back and admire their work.

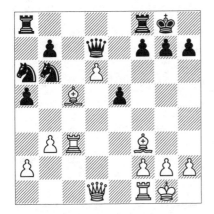

**18...♖ac8?!**

18...♖fc8 is possible. After 19 ♗g4 f5 20 ♗xb6 ♖xc3 21 ♕d5+ ♔h8 22 ♕xe5 ♖d3 23 ♗xf5 ♕xd6 Black holds the position.

**19 ♗xb6 ♖xc3 20 ♗xa5 ♖cc8 21 ♖e1 ♘b8 22 h3**

Not only opening an emergency escape hatch but also allowing the bishop to spring to g4 at a favourable opportunity.

**22...♘c6 23 ♗b6**

Winning back the exchange by 23 ♗c7 ♖xc7 24 dxc7 ♕xc7 would be too small an achievement, although even then the advantage is with White. He has a clear plan of further strengthening the position that involves the advance of the queenside pawns, and it is hard to see a way to neutralize it. Black lacks counterplay, and any attempt to generate it entails the appearance of new weakness.

**23...f5**

Black cannot get by without this move, but a further advance of this pawn allows the already mentioned ♗g4.

**24 ♕d5+ ♔h8 25 ♖d1 ♖f6** (D)

Not so much to attack White's passed pawn as to try to use the rook along its third rank in support of the counterplay against the white king.

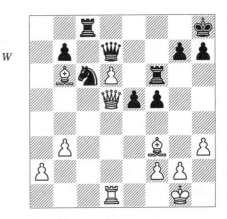

**26 a4 e4 27 ♗e2 ♖e8 28 a5 ♖e5 29 ♕d2 ♖f8 30 ♕f4 ♖fe8 31 ♕d2**

Repeating the position a couple of times usually favours the side with the initiative, not just to gain time on the clock (the opponent gains as much) but also out of psychological considerations: even though reason does not believe in further repetition and the possibility of the end of suffering, when the opponent resumes the fight there is nevertheless a certain sense of disappointment.

**31...♖f8 32 b4 f4** (D)

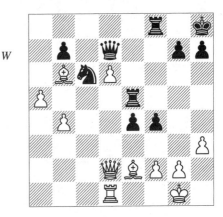

Not wishing to submit passively to his fate, Black charges headlong into a desperate counterattack.

**33 b5?!**

The idea of advancing the pawn-majority is hard to criticize, but in this case it was more important to let another soldier make his next to last step: after 33 ♗g4 ♕f7 34 d7 h5 35 ♗e2 f3 36 ♗f1, Black's threats are not serious, whereas the passed pawn is only one step away from rising in rank. Instead, White drives the enemy knight where it wants to go.

**33...♘d8 34 ♕d4?!**

Now 34 ♗g4 gives up the pawn on b5, but was nevertheless better than the idea carried out by White in the game.

**34...♘f7 35 f3?!**

White destroys Black's phalanx but the price is too high: his king's residence is weakened and all the enemy forces are ready to take part in his persecution.

**35...♖g5?**

Black misses his first chance: after 35...♖e6 36 ♗c7 ♘g5 (D) the game becomes completely unclear.

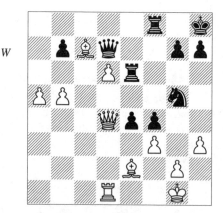

The recently passive black pieces have become coordinated and taken up menacing posts, creating a dangerous attack.

**36 ♕xe4 ♖e8**

Black loses after 36...♘xd6? 37 ♕b4 ♖f6 38 ♗f1 ♖gg6 39 a6, and while he disentangles himself, the a-pawn will decide the game.

**37 ♕c4 ♕xh3?**

Here it was mandatory, even with the loss of time, to try to eliminate the most dangerous enemy – the passed d-pawn – by playing 37...♖g6. Black retains the option of taking on h3 to gain a tempo for unpinning. This leaves Black with some defensive resources, but the advantage remains with White.

**38 ♗f1 ♘e5 39 ♕xf4 ♕h6**

Any capture on f3 ends in the knight remaining *en prise* and the passed pawn free to advance. Therefore Black tries to lay some tactical traps.

**40 ♕e4?!**

Much simpler is 40 ♗e3 ♖f5 41 ♕xh6 gxh6 42 d7 ♖d8 43 f4 ♖xd7 44 ♖d4 or 40 d7 ♘xd7 41 ♗e3.

**40...♕h5 41 ♖e1 ♖f8 42 d7 ♘xd7 43 ♗d4 ♖g6 44 ♕xb7 ♘f6 45 ♕e7 ♖g8 46 ♕e3 ♖h6 47 ♕f4 ♕h1+ 48 ♔f2 ♖g6 (D)**

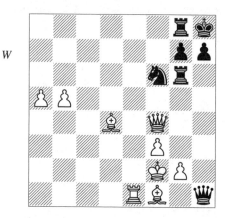

**49 ♗xf6?!**

A few of the preceding moves were not compulsory, and it is probable that each side could have played at certain moments a bit stronger or more ingeniously, but the actual course of events hasn't changed the overall evaluation of the position as won for White. The exchange on f6 also doesn't throw the win away, yet it unnecessarily complicates things and exposes the white king. The simplest way to parry Black's counterplay with ...♘h5 was to play 49 ♗e5 with the threat of ♕h2. If 49...♖f8 White shouldn't worry about the possibility of having to sacrifice the queen, as after 50 b6 ♘g4+ 51 fxg4 there is nothing to stop the passed b6-pawn.

**49...gxf6 50 g4 ♕h4+ 51 ♕g3 ♕g5 (D)**

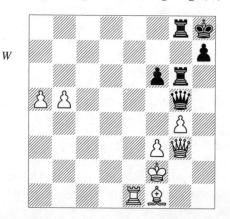

All the same, Black's chances to fish in troubled waters appear to be illusory. Both rooks are facing the wall of white pawns and activating them takes time, as Black must break up the white pawns by ...h5. Meanwhile, the pair of passed pawns gains in value with every step forward. Only the black queen is doing a good job; at the moment it threatens to take on a5 after a check on d2.

**52 ♖d1??**

A fine example of how to lose in one move from an excellent position. When short of time and with the king exposed, it is a very good general guideline to keep all the pieces protecting one another. Out of several moves that retain the winning chances, the step forward by 52 a6 is the most convincing.

**52...♕c5+ 53 ♔e1**

Naturally, 53 ♔g2 is met with 53...♕c2+.

**53...♖e8+ 54 ♗e2 ♕xb5 55 ♕f2 ♖h6 0-1**

## Game 16
# John Fedorowicz – Alexander Baburin
### San Francisco 2002

**1 e4 ♘f6 2 e5 ♘d5 3 d4 d6 4 ♘f3 ♗g4 5 ♗e2 e6 6 0-0 ♗e7 7 c4 ♘b6 8 ♘c3 0-0 9 h3**

This move can also be included on the sixth, seventh or eighth move, or not at all, but this is White's last opportunity to enter the subsequent events with the pawn on h3.

The line that occurred in this game is at least as attractive for White with the pawn on h2 (the h3-square can be put to good use and the white king is more secure), but then Black has more scope to get off the beaten path at an earlier stage, for instance by developing the knight to c6 before advancing ...d5.

**9...♗h5 10 ♗e3 d5** *(D)*

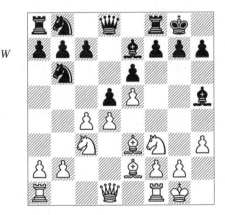

*W*

White has refrained from exchanging on d6 and retained the cramping e5-pawn, but in this version the move ...d5 is still the main method of clarifying the situation in the centre. By luring another enemy pawn into his camp, Black

relies on creating counterplay by undermining the white pawn-chain from both sides.

**11 c5**

What other replies does White have? First, there is 11 b3, preparing c5 while forestalling the knight's leap forward, which makes the idea of exchanging on f3 less attractive. Black can try to profit from the unhurried manner of the b-pawn's advance by 11...♘c6 and after 12 c5 ♘c8 carrying out the undermining ...b6, or he can increase the position's dynamism by including the preliminary exchange 11...dxc4 12 bxc4 before playing 12...♘c6. Black's pressure on White's pawns has noticeably increased, but the white centre has acquired mobility.

Another lively continuation, popular some thirty years ago, is 11 cxd5 *(D)*

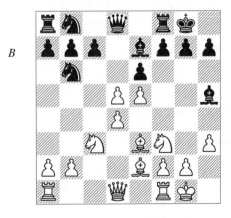

*B*

The initial impression is that White is freeing Black's game, ceding the d5 strongpoint into the bargain. However, it turns out that Black has no time to seize it, as 11...♘xd5 is met by 12 ♕b3. After the retreat 12...♘b6 White has a pleasant choice – he can weaken Black's queenside with 13 a4 a5 first, or play in the centre with 13 ♖fd1 or even the immediate 13 d5. The activity of the white pieces also acquires threatening proportions in the case of 12...♘xe3 13 fxe3 b6 14 d5. The other capture, 11...exd5, therefore became more popular. White has acquired a kingside pawn-majority, and advancing the f-pawn looks logical. White can clear its path at once by 12 ♘e1, but then the light-squared bishops are exchanged, which favours Black who has less space. They can be kept on the board by playing 12 g4 ♗g6 first, followed by 13 ♘e1. While White is on the offensive, which requires a numerical advantage in this sector of the board, he is not worried about the weakening of his king's position, but if the attack fails, the white king may feel less comfortable. Black will meet the f4 advance with ...f5 and strive to set up a blockade on light squares.

Now we return to the position after 11 c5 (D).

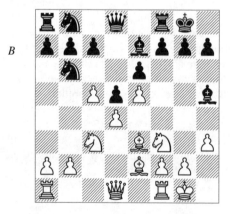

**11...♗xf3**

What are Black's reasons for this exchange? One is concrete: if White recaptures with the bishop then the knight can remain in the thick of things by moving to c4 instead of having to retreat to c8; or else White has to take with the pawn, weakening his spoiled pawn-structure. There is also a strategic theme: a piece that is not very useful in the attack on the dark-squared pawn-chain is exchanged for a knight that interacts very well with this chain.

**12 gxf3**

During the early stage of this system's development, the dominant recapture was 12 ♗xf3, with Black, naturally, replying 12...♘c4 (D).

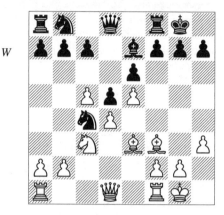

The interest in the development of a new opening variation depends to a significant degree on who the players who introduced it into practice were. The diagram position could not have started its life in a higher-profile event: it occurred in Spassky-Fischer, World Ch (19), Reykjavik 1972. White chose not to keep the bishop and played 13 b3 ♘xe3 14 fxe3, which gives White the additional option of playing in the centre with an e4 advance. Fischer replied 14...b6 and after 15 e4 held the game only with difficulty; later it was concluded that 14...♘c6 first is more reliable. Subsequently, respect for the bishop-pair brought 13 ♗f4 to the forefront. Black can meet this in two ways:

a) 13...b6 immediately starts the undermining of White's pawns. After 14 b3 ♘a5 the piece sacrifice 15 ♖c1 bxc5 16 dxc5 ♘ac6 17 ♖e1 underwent several practical tests. The idea is to meet 17...♘d7? with 18 ♘xd5!, but if Black inserts 17...♗g5, then his chances are not worse. The continuations 15 ♘a4 and 15 b4 have also been employed, but the following game is the only recent contribution of interest: 15 b4 ♘c4 16 ♗e2 a5 17 b5 bxc5 18 ♗xc4 dxc4 19 d5 with some initiative for White, Kurenkov-Orlinkov, Moscow 2006.

b) With 13...♘c6 Black avoids an immediate weakening of the long light-square diagonal, which makes the sacrifice on d5 look less tempting. The usual continuation is 14 b3 ♘4a5 15 ♖c1, when in addition to the main counterplay with 15...b6 Black has the bishop exchange 15...♗g5, with a subsequent transfer of the knights via the newly vacant e7-square, and the prophylactic 15...♕d7, covering e6 in advance and aiming to undermine the centre with ...f6.

Since Black's game is acceptable in these variations, the recapture with the pawn became more popular.

**12...♘c8** (D)

Now the leap forward 12...♘c4? leads to the loss of a pawn after 13 ♗xc4 dxc4 14 ♕a4, when Black's compensation is considered insufficient.

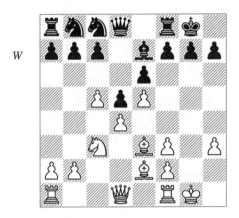

W

In the resulting position, White can list to his credit his advantage in space, bishop-pair, better development and the half-open g-file that can serve as an avenue of attack. However, the game is of a closed nature, and White's somewhat spoiled pawn-structure renders his prospects of opening the game more difficult. On the queenside his achievements will be limited to a single open file, while on the kingside much depends on whether the f4-f5 advance can be carried out under favourable conditions. Besides the variations where this advance leads only to the exchange of the doubled pawn and freeing the bishops, also possible are lines where the f-pawn gives itself up to deprive the d5-pawn of its support, when White restores the material parity and gains the upper hand in the centre.

Note that in this variation the omission of h3 and ...♗h5 favours White (i.e. 6 0-0 ♗e7 7 c4 ♘b6 8 ♘c3 0-0 9 ♗e3 d5 10 c5 ♗xf3 11 gxf3 ♘c8, the only difference now being the pawn's location on h2 rather than h3), who retains the

option of using the h3-square for his queen or a rook, which allows him to create additional threats along the h-file as well as the g-file, or to evict the black bishop from h4. There are also some lines where Black's chances of counterplay are reduced because the white king is safer with the pawn on h2.

For the time being Black is cramped; one look at his knights is enough to confirm this. One of them would like to get to f5 where it will blockade the white pawns and feel a worthy piece, but the transfer via e7 is beset with difficulties.

**13 f4** (D)

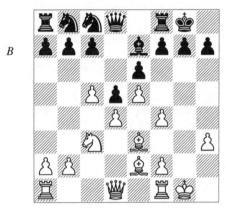

B

This is the first move to consider. White locks in one of the bishops, hoping it to be only a temporary concession, and clears the path to the kingside for the other and, given a chance, for the queen as well. Moreover, the pawn is ready to step forward to f5. In the version with the pawn on h2, the move 12 ♔h1, intending ♖g1, is also highly potent.

**13...♘c6**

In practice Black employs two defensive plans, which differ mainly in their use of the f5-square. Either a knight will attempt to settle here, as in our main game, or a pawn will be assigned the blockading duty, which can be done right now with 13...f5. This move closes the position to an even greater extent, though the black pieces become even more cramped. White's kingside chances approach zero and the conflict shifts to the queenside, where his chances to break through Black's defences are also doubtful. Still, at the moment Black is strictly on the defensive, and the grounds for active operations will appear only if the white pieces get bogged down far from the possible counterplay, which can be initiated with the ...g5 advance. Once again, in the version with the pawn on h2, the line 12 f4 f5 13 ♔h1 is a good deal less secure for Black.

In order for the knight to assume blockading duties, the transit square e7 needs to be freed for him, which can be done at once by 13...♗h4 *(D)*, but the bishop is not secure here.

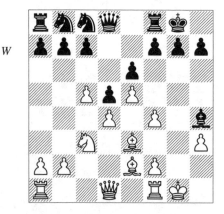

W

Black is ready for the immediate 14 f5, as after 14...♘e7 he has everything in order. The preliminary 14 ♗d3 is more dangerous, as it hinders the immediate knight transfer: 14...♘e7 15 ♕g4 (or 15 ♕h5) 15...♘g6 (the pawn sacrifice 15...♘f5 16 ♗xf5 exf5 17 ♕xf5 ♘c6 18 ♕g4 f5 19 ♕f3 ♘e7 20 ♔h2 c6 21 ♖g1 ♘g6 proved inadequate in Blanco Gramajo-Machycek, corr. World Ch 2007-9) 16 f5 with the advantage for White. Black usually replies with the prophylactic 14...g6 and again doesn't fear 15 f5 exf5 16 ♕f3; now 16...c6 is passive and fails to hold the pawn after 17 ♗h6 followed by the capture on f5, but 16...♘c6 gives Black good counterplay. Therefore White chooses 15 ♕g4, again not allowing the knight to move, when the usual reply is 15...♔h8. Subsequently it is risky to drive the queen away with ...h5 as it weakens the king's cover too much; there remains ...f5, but then Black has to give up the idea of the knight transfer.

The developing text-move postpones determining Black's set-up for the time being.

**14 b4**

Let's note that this move rules out any ideas with ...♗xc5, based on a pawn fork by ...d4, not

that this would necessarily be a good idea for Black any time soon.

Again 14 f5, with the idea of exchanging off the doubled pawn for Black's d-pawn, is an alternative. The main variation runs 14...exf5 15 ♗f3 ♗g5 16 ♘xd5 f4 17 ♗xf4 (after 17 ♘xf4 ♗xf4 18 ♗xf4 ♕xd4 19 ♕xd4 ♘xd4 20 ♗g4 ♘e7 the white pawns are weaker than their black counterparts, which nullifies the advantage of the bishop-pair) 17...♗xf4 18 ♘xf4 ♘8e7!, preparing to regain the pawn in the optimal way; this was first played in Aseev-Bagirov, Berlin 1990, and it retains a solid reputation.

Another continuation, 14 ♗d3, also looks familiar. However, with this move-order Black can try 14...g6, seeking to rule out 15 f5 due to the rejoinder 15...exf5 16 ♕f3 ♗xc5 17 dxc5 d4 18 ♗h6 dxc3, when 19 ♗xf8?! ♕xf8 gave Black more than enough compensation for the exchange in Chiburdanidze-Bagirov, Minsk 1983. The critical line is 19 e6, which has scored well in practice. However, 19...fxe6 20 ♗c4 ♖e8 and 19...cxb2 20 ♖ad1 fxe6 (or 20...♕h4) may not be completely clear.

**14...♗h4 *(D)***

14...a6 creates another defensive set-up on the queenside. Now the advance with a4 and b5 requires preparation and leads to the opening of the a-file. While this file will fall into White's hands, the number of the combat units will decrease. Recapturing on b5 with a piece opens the line of attack on the b7-pawn, but on the other hand weaknesses appear in White's own camp as well.

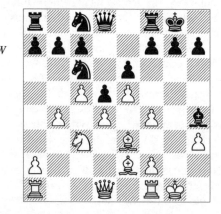

W

**15 ♖b1**

White is not in a hurry to clarify the situation on the queenside with 15 b5 while Black can reply 15...♘a5, when it is harder to open new lines, whereas on the other half of the board in reply to the standard play with 16 ♗d3 g6 17 ♕g4 Black has tested 17...h5, 17...f5 and 17...♔h8. Overall, his position is solid, but he has no active prospects. Another reply, 15...♘6e7 followed by the knight's transfer to f5 and, quite likely, its exchange on that square, reduces the already modest potential of the c8-knight, which would hardly be able to find a way to get to the resulting blockading square e6.

**15...♘8e7 16 ♗d3 g6 17 ♔h2** *(D)*

In the case of 17 ♕f3, at once taking control of d5 and threatening f5, Black can afford to play 17...♘f5 18 ♗xf5 gxf5, agreeing to give up a pawn in case of the exchange of queens: 19 ♕h5 ♔h8 20 ♔h2 ♖g8 21 ♕xf7 ♕e8, and White's extra doubled pawn is of no significance. More interesting is the plan 17 ♕g4 ♘f5 18 ♗xf5 exf5 19 ♕f3 ♘e7 and now White should set the opening of the a3-f8 diagonal as the goal of his queenside offensive, in order to attack a defender of the d5-pawn with the bishop.

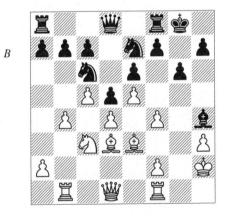

**17...♘f5 18 ♗xf5 exf5 19 ♖g1?!**

This allows Black to prepare another way of defending the d5-pawn. White now had even more reasons to try to carry out the plan from the previous note by playing 19 ♕f3 or 19 b5 ♘e7 at once (19...♘a5?! 20 c6 bxc6 21 ♕a4 leads to the creation of new targets to attack in Black's camp).

**19...♕d7 20 ♕f3 ♖fd8 21 ♕h5 ♗e7 22 ♕d1 a6 23 ♘e2**

The queen's rushing to and fro has failed to achieve anything. White thought it inexpedient to drive the enemy knight to a5 and decided to transfer his own to f3, but the black knight can now occupy an even better square.

**23...♔h8 24 ♕c2 ♖g8 25 a3 ♘d8** *(D)*

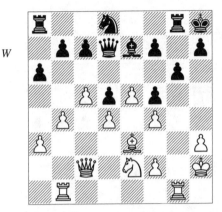

With the knight coming to e6, Black no longer considers himself to be on the defensive, yet the closed character of the position curbs both sides' ambitions.

**26 ♖g3 ♘e6 27 a4 c6 28 ♖b3 ♗f8 29 ♕b1 ♗h6 30 h4**

Such an advance only weakens White's position. On the other hand, Black's only chance to generate counterplay involves the undermining ...f6, but such play didn't seem promising enough to Black.

**30...♘g7 31 ♖h3 ♘h5 32 ♕c1 ♕e6 ½-½**

There are few reasons to consider the system that occurred in this game to be experiencing a crisis, yet its popularity remains low. The prospect of tedious, painstaking defence doesn't improve the variation's reputation, and few players are willing to settle for such play in contemporary chess. After 5...e6 the course of subsequent events is largely for White to decide. Meanwhile, 5...c6 (Game 13) may offer more enticing practical prospects to Black, but in this line there are also some significant theoretical problems yet to be solved. Consequently, Black's alternative fourth moves are gaining in popularity, and we shall examine them in the next chapter.

# 5 The New Main Line and 4th Move Alternatives

The overwhelming majority of Alekhine Defence games start with the moves 1 e4 ♘f6 2 e5 ♘d5 3 d4 d6 *(D)*.

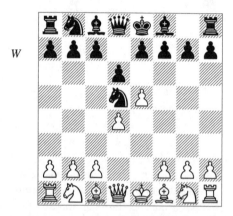

The two most popular moves here are 4 ♘f3 and 4 c4, both of which we have partially covered so far in the book. We shall revisit 4 c4 in the next chapter, in the guise of the Exchange Variation, while in the current chapter we shall complete the coverage of 4 ♘f3 by examining all of Black's alternatives to 4...♗g4, of which the most important is 4...dxe5, in particular with the follow-up 5 ♘xe5 c6. However, these continuations do not exhaust White's 4th-move options and Game 17 (Conquest-Baburin) shall shed light on 4 ♗c4 and other moves by which White seeks to maintain a modest presence in the centre while generating piece play.

But our main focus is the position after 4 ♘f3. As we noted in the previous chapter, the traditional main line 4...♗g4 has in recent years lost a great deal of its popularity, partly as a result of fashion, but mainly because the resulting positions do not seem terribly attractive to modern players, with Black struggling to equalize or create realistic chances of playing for a win.

In Game 18 (Kariakin-Vaganian) we examine 4...g6 (together with less common moves), a line that was highly topical in the 1980s due to its use by Lev Alburt. It still has a following and remains playable, but is not such a hot topic any more.

The remaining three games focus on 4...dxe5, a line originally popularized by Bent Larsen in the 1960s. Black allows White to activate the knight by 5 ♘xe5 *(D)*, planning to offer its exchange by ...♘d7; if White declines in order to keep Black cramped, it will cost him two tempi.

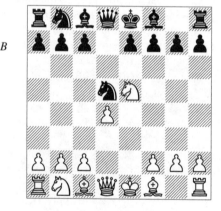

In Game 19 (Oleksienko-Prokopchuk) we begin our coverage of the highly topical line 5...c6, which was hardly known at all before the late 1990s, yet is now played in quite a large proportion of all Alekhine games. We also cover, in the notes to this game, the original Larsen treatment with the provocative 5...♘d7?!, and the move 5...g6, which enjoyed considerable popularity in the 1990s before it was edged out by the more flexible move with the c-pawn. The main game features (after 5...c6) 6 ♗e2, a modest-looking move that has been very popular in the most recent events and that can be followed up in highly aggressive fashion. The remaining two games deal with other ways for White to develop his king's bishop: Game 20 (Peru-nović-Ki.Georgiev) features 6 ♗c4, while 6

♗d3 is covered in Game 21 (Topalov-Carlsen), a striking victory for the young Norwegian superstar that will no doubt do much to popularize this variation, and our opening as a whole.

## Game 17
# Stuart Conquest – Alexander Baburin
### *Irish Ch, Dublin 2008*

**1 e4 ♞f6 2 e5 ♞d5 3 d4 d6 4 ♗c4**

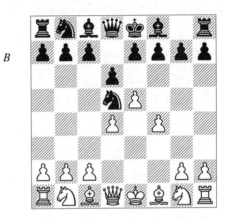

It is hard to find fault with 4 ♞f3; it is the most natural continuation, though of course not the only one. We have already seen 4 c4 as the introduction to the Four Pawns Attack, and another important follow-up to this move will be examined in the next chapter.

4 ♗e2 for the moment prevents the development of its opposing number to g4, but after 4...dxe5 (4...g6 is also perfectly reasonable) White only has 5 dxe5 (when 5...♗f5 is a solid option); generally the claim for the advantage is based on the possibility of recapturing with the knight. One point worth noting is that Black should avoid the line 5...♞c6 6 ♞f3 ♗g4 7 c3 e6?! 8 ♕a4 ♗xf3 9 ♗xf3 ♕d7 10 ♕e4 ♞de7 11 ♗f4 ♞g6 12 ♞d2 0-0-0 13 0-0-0 ♕d3 14 ♕a4, when old analysis by Kupreichik gave the spectacular 14...♗a3 as saving Black. However, it loses to the laconic 15 ♞b1!.

The immediate exchange 4 exd6 has no advantages over the normal Exchange Variation (4 c4 ♞b6 5 exd6), whereas Black gains additional squares for the retreat of the knight: f6, and in the case of 4...cxd6 also c7; moreover, 4...♕xd6 is a completely viable reply.

Therefore, besides the move in the game we shall dwell briefly only on 4 f4 *(D)*.

Now 4...g6 leads, as a rule, to a difficult branch of the Four Pawns Attack, so Black generally chooses one of the two other replies:

a) After 4...♗f5, if White plays 5 c4 then the 5...♞b4 thrust looks rather favourable for Black, so White prefers 5 ♞f3 e6 6 ♗d3 ♗xd3 7 ♕xd3. Despite the exchange of the light-squared bishops (which on general grounds favours Black), White retains a certain initiative, thanks to his advantage in space and freer development.

b) Black's most consistent continuation is 4...dxe5 5 fxe5. White acquires a half-open file

and a pawn-majority in the centre, but his pawn-chain encourages the undermining thrust, ...c5.

b1) Out of the continuations employed here, 5...♞c6 looks the least enterprising – a developing move that postpones active counterplay in the centre to a later stage. White can transpose into the Four Pawns Attack, but this would tend to justify Black's last move – and in any case, having avoided the Four Pawns earlier, he is not likely to be tempted now, unless Black allows a favourable version of it. White usually plays 6 ♞f3 or 6 c3, reinforcing the centre and aiming for a small but enduring advantage.

Black's main continuations seek to make a return to Four Pawns territory dubious for White:

b2) 5...♗f5 has the point that in reply to 6 c4 the knight will display more aggression by 6...♞b4, and with good reasons. Heberla-Grabarczyk, Polish Ch, Opole 2007 is typical: 6 ♞f3 e6 7 ♗d3 ♗xd3 8 ♕xd3 c5 9 0-0 ♗e7 (9...h6!?) 10 dxc5 ♞c6 11 ♔h1 ♗xc5 12 ♕e4. If an endgame is reached, the e5-pawn may become a sensitive weakness, but at the moment it creates favourable conditions for a kingside attack by taking away the important f6-square from Black's defenders. White can also lead an offensive on the other side of the board, where he has a pawn-majority. Black will only acquire counterchances after completing his defence successfully.

b3) The immediate blow in the centre, 5...c5, is without doubt the most pugnacious continuation. In the line 6 ♘f3 (6 c4? ♘b4!) 6...cxd4 (6...♗g4!?) 7 ♕xd4 ♘c6 8 ♕e4 g6 9 ♗c4 ♘b6 10 ♗b3 ♗f5 the conflict centred on the e5-pawn immediately becomes concrete in nature, and energetic play is demanded of both sides.

The text-move (4 ♗c4) attacks the knight, offering Black two logical replies.

**4...♘b6**

We shall pass over 4...e6, voluntarily locking in the bishop, as White is spoiled for choice: 5 ♘f3, 5 ♕e2 or 5 ♕g4. The line 4...dxe5 5 dxe5 c6 6 ♘c3 e6 suffers from the same defect, while if 6...♗e6 then the bishop will come under attack after 7 ♘e4 or 7 ♘f3.

Thus the only serious alternative to the text-move is 4...c6 *(D)*.

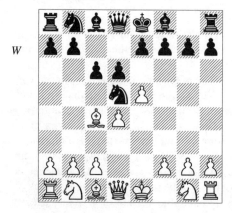

Black strives to maintain the knight on its centralized post, which for the moment cannot be threatened by the white c-pawn. Let's examine the most significant replies for White:

a) 5 f4 is based on a view that ♗c4 is a more useful move than ...c6. Transplanting Black's plans from the 4 f4 lines considered above entails a loss of time, and the white knight acquires another route with the idea of taking advantage of the weakened d6-square: 5...dxe5 6 fxe5 ♗f5 7 ♘e2 e6 8 0-0 ♗e7 9 ♘g3 ♗g6 10 ♗d3 0-0 11 ♗xg6 fxg6 12 ♖xf8+ ♗xf8 13 c4 ♘b6 14 ♕g4 ♕d7 15 c5 and it is hard to prevent

the knight from getting to d6, Glek-Konopka, Austrian Team Ch 2002/3. Lines where Black aims to close the game become more attractive; for instance, 5...♘b6 6 ♗b3 ♗f5 7 ♘e2 d5.

b) 5 ♕f3 restricts the c8-bishop's freedom of development and takes aim at f7. However, the e5-pawn is deprived of its main defender – a knight on f3 – and after 5...dxe5 6 dxe5 ♗e6 followed by ...♘d7 White has to spend time to find another way of supporting it, whereas Black will overcome the slight delay in his development.

c) 5 ♕e2, reinforcing the e5-pawn in advance, invites the enemy bishop to settle for the post on f5. After 5...dxe5 6 dxe5 ♗f5 7 h3 e6 8 ♘f3 ♘d7 9 0-0, Black has a solid, although slightly passive, position.

d) The most natural move, 5 ♘f3, leads after 5...♗g4 6 h3 ♗xf3 7 ♕xf3 dxe5 8 dxe5 e6 to a standard Alekhine position that is considered to be solid enough for Black. We have seen a similar position in Game 13, with the knight instead of the pawn on c6, which is admittedly slightly more pleasant for Black, but he has no reason to avoid the line examined above either.

**5 ♗b3** *(D)*

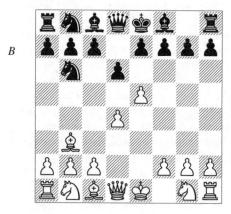

**5...♗f5**

Black can close the game by 5...d5, which looks quite acceptable by analogy with French Defence lines, but psychologically it is not easy to go for a position that Black can achieve in another variation with an extra tempo (1 e4 ♘f6 2 e5 ♘d5 3 ♗c4 ♘b6 4 ♗b3 d5 5 d4). The continuation 5...♘c6 provokes the old familiar pawn sacrifice 6 e6 fxe6; in this version it leads to a double-edged struggle.

The principal move here is 5...dxe5. Now, it is obvious that White didn't embark on this variation in order to exchange queens, so he has to attack f7, forcing ...e6 and leaving the c8-bishop imprisoned for some time. There are two ways to do it:

a) The less common method is 6 ♕f3 e6 7 dxe5, when Black chooses between 7...♘c6, to be followed by the leap of the queen or the knight to d4, and 7...a5 8 c3 a4, creating yet another possibility of attack on the e5-pawn with the rook-lift to a5. The transfer of the bishop to b5 in order to use the weakened d3-square is also interesting.

b) After 6 ♕h5 e6 7 dxe5 (D) the e5-pawn is protected and the f3-square is available to the knight, which secures White greater freedom in choosing a development plan.

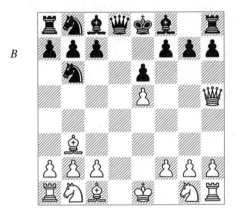

B

Black again has to decide whether to play 7...♘c6 or to harass the enemy bishop first and seize space with a queenside advance, viz. 7...a5 or 7...c5.

b1) After 7...♘c6 the opening's outcome depends on the success of the counterplay against the e5-pawn, which should not be delayed: 8 ♘f3 ♘d4 9 ♘xd4 (9 ♘bd2, not clinging to the bishop and striving to develop as rapidly as possible, is interesting) 9...♕xd4 10 0-0. If White manages to maintain his stronghold in the centre and avoid excessive simplification, he can retain the advantage. If Black instead opts for routine development, leaving his queen on d8, he will be too cramped once a white rook appears on d1.

b2) 7...a5, besides seizing space, creates a concrete threat. It turns out that after 8 c3?!

♕d3 with the threat of ...a4-a3 White has to offer an exchange of queens, while in the line 8 a3?! a4 9 ♗a2 ♘c6 10 ♘f3 ♘d4 11 ♘xd4 ♕xd4 it is difficult to defend the e5-pawn, which Black plans to attack yet again with the rook from a5. Thus 8 a4 has emerged as the most principled continuation, although it allows the bishop to be exchanged by ...♘a6-c5 or else commits White to sacrificing the a4-pawn (if the bishop retreats to a2). In return, White can hope to develop a dangerous initiative.

b3) Another fighting move is 7...c5 (D).

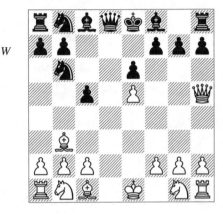

W

Black again harasses the bishop, while increasing his presence in the centre, but it is not combined with the development of the rook and takes away the c5-square from his own pieces. Here 8 c3 is best, as 8...♕d3 then poses no threat. The following game illustrates a possible course of events: 8...♘c6 9 ♕e2 g5 (sharp, yet typical of positions where the main target of attack is the e5-pawn) 10 ♗c2 ♗d7 11 ♘d2 ♗e7 12 ♘e4 ♘d5 13 ♘h3 h6 14 ♘d6+ ♗xd6 15 exd6 ♕b8 16 f4 with double-edged play, Thorhallsson-Mamedyarov, Reykjavik 2006.

The text-move (5...♗f5) sends the bishop to operate outside the fortress walls. So far all attempts to demonstrate a flaw in this method of play have failed.

**6 ♕f3 (D)**

Continuing to develop quietly by 6 ♘f3 allows Black after 6...e6 to consider most of his opening problems to be solved. Events take a sharper turn after the typical pawn sacrifice 6 e6. Both captures have been played but 6...♗xe6 7 ♗xe6 fxe6 seems the more logical choice as the exchange of bishops probably helps Black. White no doubt has some compensation, and it appears sufficient to evaluate the chances as roughly even; e.g., 8 ♘f3 ♘c6 9 0-0 g6 10 ♘g5 ♕d7 11 ♖e1 ♘d8 12 ♕d3 ♗h6 with unclear play, Ji.Nun-Konopka, Zdar nad Sazavou 2008.

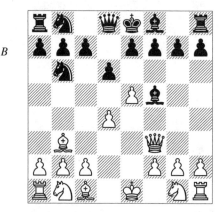

B

The queen move aims to disrupt the harmonious development of the enemy army, and should Black castle kingside, the queen will personally lead the offensive.

**6...♕c8**

The pawn sacrifice 6...e6 7 ♕xb7 d5 leads to an interesting and little-studied struggle. The queen is under arrest but its capture is not a simple affair; this process followed a curious course in the game Ristić-Shabalov, Geneva 1992: 8 ♘c3 (8 ♗a4+!?, 8 ♗d2 and 8 ♘e2 are all possible alternatives) 8...♗b4 9 ♘e2 0-0 10 0-0 a5 11 ♘b5 ♕d7 12 a4 ♖c8 13 ♘a7 ♖e8 14 ♘b5 ♘a6 15 ♘a7 ♖xa7 (note that 15...♘b8 repeats the position) 16 ♕xa7 ♕c8 (for the moment Black plays the part of the aggressor and it seems that he is about to complete the encirclement) 17 ♘c3 ♖e7 18 ♘b5 ♘a8 19 ♘d6 ♗xd6 20 exd6 ♖d7 21 ♗d2 c5 22 ♕xa6 ♕xa6 23 dxc5 (D), with an original position.

White has only a rook for the queen, but the a8-knight has no moves, and it is not clear just how strong White's pawns are. Nevertheless, the material advantage should tell in the end.

**7 ♘e2**

White can radically free himself from the possible worries about the e5-pawn by exchanging on d6, but this frees Black's game just as much. The development of the knight to h3 has its advantages – the access to the g5-square,

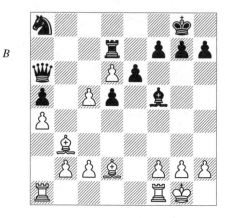

B

and its drawbacks – the d4-pawn is left unprotected.

**7...♘c6**

Attacking the pawn and inviting White to clarify the situation in the centre. 7...e6 is more common, when the centre can subsequently be closed with ...d5, while the advance of the c-pawn against the b3-bishop doesn't look bad either; for example, 8 0-0 c5 9 dxc5 dxc5 10 c3 c4 11 ♗d1 ♘c6 with comfortable development.

**8 ♕g3**

White decides to maintain the bridgehead on e5, in order to prepare under its cover a kingside offensive. The exchange on d6 would create a formation that, with other things equal, is more pleasant for Black, though at the moment the white pieces are more active. It would be interesting to include the preliminary 8 a4, when after 8...a5 the exchange 9 exd6 cxd6 weakens the b5- and b6-squares in Black's camp.

**8...g6 9 ♗f4 ♗g7 10 ♘d2 a5 11 a4 ♘b4 12 0-0** *(D)*

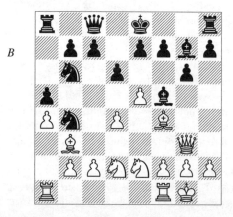

B

**12...0-0**

Black has several methods of deploying his forces of roughly similar value. For the time being, White is not afraid of 12...♗xc2?! in view of 13 ♗xc2 ♘xc2 14 ♖ac1 ♕f5 15 ♕f3, when the threat of winning a piece gives Black no time to defend c7.

**13 ♕h4?**

But this is a mistake that immediately leads to a difficult position. Strategically everything is correct, as White is implementing a standard attacking plan, with ♗h6 and ♘g5 the intended follow-up, taking aim at h7. However, White should have started by moving the knight to f3, since now the e5-pawn's lack of protection presents Black with an unexpected tactical opportunity.

**13...♗xc2 14 ♗xc2 ♘xc2 15 ♖ac1 ♘xd4!**

Not only sweeping off the board all White's centre pawns but also putting an end to his hopes for a kingside initiative.

**16 ♘xd4 dxe5 17 ♘b5 exf4 18 ♘xc7 ♖b8 19 ♘a6 ♕d8**

Winning the exchange is mandatory but it fails to restore material parity, to say nothing about the positional balance.

**20 ♘xb8 ♕xd2 21 ♖fd1 (D)**

21 ♖cd1 is a little more stubborn, when Black all the same should retreat to b4, as unnecessary complications ensue after 21...♕xb2 22 ♕xe7 ♖xb8 23 ♖b1 ♘d5 (23...♕d4 24 ♕c7) 24 ♕d6 ♕e5 25 ♕xe5 ♗xe5 26 ♖b5.

**21...♕b4 22 ♘d7 ♘xd7 23 ♖xd7 ♗xb2 24 ♖b1 ♕e4 25 ♖bd1 ♗f6 26 ♕g4 ♕xa4?!**

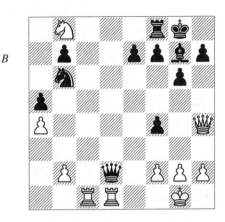

It is simpler to keep the pawn by 26...b6, as the a4-pawn cannot be defended anyway.

**27 ♖xb7 ♔g7 28 h3 ♖c8 29 ♕d7?!**

The exchange of queens eases Black's task, since now even the nebulous threats to his king are not a concern any more.

**29...♕xd7 30 ♖bxd7 ♖a8 31 ♖d8 ♖a6 32 ♖c8 a4 33 ♖dd8 ♖e6?!**

But this is unnecessary. 33...a3 is simpler, with the same endgame that appears in a dozen moves.

**34 ♔f1 a3 35 ♖a8 ♗b2 36 ♖d1 ♖c6 37 ♔e2 ♖c7 38 ♖d3 g5 39 ♖d5 h6 40 ♖a6 e6 41 ♖d3 e5 42 f3 ♖c2+ 43 ♖d2 ♖xd2+ 44 ♔xd2 f5**

Since one of the white pieces has to guard the passed a3-pawn, two extra pawns easily break through on the kingside.

**45 ♔d3 h5 46 ♖a5 ♔f6 47 ♖a6+ ♔e7 48 ♔c2 g4 49 ♖h6 e4 50 ♖xh5 g3 51 ♖xf5 exf3 52 gxf3 ♗f6 0-1**

# Game 18
# Sergei Kariakin – Rafael Vaganian
## *Pamplona 2004*

**1 e4 ♘f6 2 e5 ♘d5 3 d4 d6 4 ♘f3 (D)**
**4...g6**

The cutting-edge 4...dxe5 is the subject of the next three games; meanwhile we shall survey a variety of minor alternatives:

a) 4...♗f5 is rarely played. The g4-square looks such a natural destination that one might think Black's hand faltered and accidentally dropped the piece on this square. Still, there are a couple of points to this development of the

bishop: besides taking the game off the beaten and well-studied track, the bishop takes aim at the c2-square; for example, 5 c4 ♘b4 confines the white knight to the unprepossessing post on a3. White usually offers an exchange of bishops at once with 5 ♗d3, but there is plenty of scope for creativity; we can also mention 5 c3 and 5 ♘h4.

b) 4...c6 is more popular, and indeed was the prototype for the 4...dxe5 5 ♘xe5 c6 line –

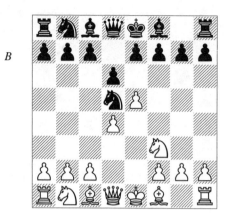

Tony Miles was a notable pioneer in both cases. In reply to 5 ♗e2, Black can return to a main line with 5...♗g4 (Game 13) or choose 5...dxe5, having restricted White's options somewhat with the change in move-order (then 6 ♘xe5 brings us to Game 19). However, after 5 c4 and the retreat to b6 it is hard to call the tempo spent on ...c6 an achievement, so 5...♘c7 is more consistent. There are no tried-and-proven lines here, and freestyle improvisation is par for the course. We can list 6 exd6, 6 ♘c3, 6 h3 and 6 ♗e2 as logical continuations for White, but he can give free rein to his fantasy; here is an example of daring play: 6 ♗e3 dxe5 7 ♘xe5 g6 8 ♘c3 ♗g7 9 h4 c5 10 ♕f3 f6 11 0-0-0 fxe5 12 dxe5, Murariu-M.Grünberg, Romanian Ch, Baile Tusnad 2005.

c) 4...♘c6 (D) is considered a risky approach, but it leads to tense, concrete play that appeals to quite a number of Alekhine players.

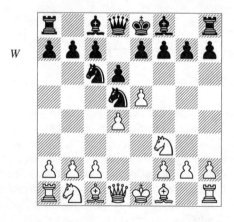

The fact that it has been played quite a lot in high-level correspondence games over many years shows that it needs to be taken seriously. White normally follows the standard prescriptions: after 5 c4 ♘b6 he chooses between the pawn sacrifice 6 e6 and the exchange by 6 exd6. The former is quite dangerous: after 6 e6 fxe6 the knight sortie 7 ♘g5 e5 8 d5 ♘d4 9 ♗d3 g6 10 ♘xh7 ♗f5 leads to unclear play, but White can also choose between 7 ♘c3 e5 8 d5 ♘d4 9 ♘xd4 exd4 10 ♕xd4 e5 11 ♕d1, with a small and lasting advantage thanks to the e4-square, and the sharp play and serious initiative after 7 ♗e3 g6 8 h4. Instead 6 exd6 exd6 (the knight has appeared on c6 too early for 6...cxd6, as after 7 d5 ♘e5 both 8 ♘xe5 and 8 ♘d4 promise White the advantage) gives us a line of the Exchange Variation where the early appearance of the knights on f3 and c6 gives both sides some extra options (most notably, White can play a quick d5), though it is also quite feasible for standard positions to be reached. One possibility is 7 h3 ♗e7 8 ♗e2 ♗f5 9 0-0 0-0 10 ♘c3 ♗f6 11 ♗f4 ♖e8 12 ♖c1 h6 13 b3, when White is seeking by a restrictive strategy to make it difficult for Black to obtain counterplay.

d) 4...♘b6 is an interesting move, quite often used by those seeking to avoid theory. By removing the knight in advance from the possible attack, Black invites his opponent to declare his intentions first. In the case of the exchange on d6 he now recaptures with the c-pawn, while in reply to most of the other natural continuations – 5 ♗e2, 5 ♗d3, 5 ♘c3 – he plays ...g6, with a position like an Alburt Variation where White has been denied the possibility of putting his bishop on the a2-g8 diagonal, but has not had to spend time evicting the black knight from the centre. White can attempt to demonstrate the drawbacks of the knight retreat by means of 5 a4, practically forcing 5...a5 (D).

In this particular situation, the main effect of the inclusion of these moves is the weakening of Black's queenside; this process can be developed further by continuing 6 ♗b5+ c6, and after withdrawing the bishop White can hope to profit from the dark-square holes in the enemy camp. 6 ♘c3 is also not bad, aiming for active operations in the centre; e.g., 6...dxe5 7 ♘xe5 ♘8d7 8 ♗f4 e6 9 ♕h5 ♘xe5 10 ♗xe5 ♗d7 11 0-0-0 ♗b4 (agreeing to 12 ♗xg7 ♖g8, to be followed by the capture on c3; naturally, 13

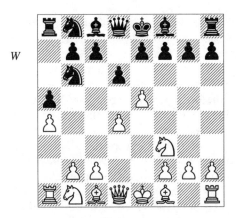

*W*

♕xh7? fails to 13...♕g5+) 12 d5 and Black's position started to fall apart in Guseinov-Yanev, Istanbul 2007.

We now return to 4...g6 *(D)*:

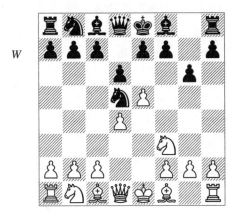

*W*

The text-move gives the game some features similar to the Pirc Defence and attempts to expose the drawbacks of the early appearance of a pawn on e5. On the other hand, the g7-bishop can find itself looking rather silly if White manages to solidify his grip on e5. In honour of the great efforts of Lev Alburt to raise 4...g6 from an obscure sideline to main-line status, it is often referred to as the Alburt Variation.

**5 ♗c4**

The transposition to the Exchange Variation with 5 c4 ♘b6 6 exd6 will be considered in the next chapter. White cannot maintain the pawn on e5 with modest development, since Black can quickly bring pressure to bear on e5 with natural moves, which will require White to show his hand, and this normally comes down to that same exchange on d6. The knight sortie 5 ♘g5

with an unequivocal threat to f7 hasn't stood the test of time; Black can choose between 5...c6, 5...dxe5 and even 5...f6, when the resulting weakening is compensated by the two tempi lost by White.

The text-move lays the strongest claim to the advantage.

**5...c6**

5...dxe5?! attempts to steer the game (via 6 ♘xe5?!) into another system that will be examined in the notes to Game 19, but 6 dxe5! renders this idea extremely dubious: 6...c6 7 ♘c3! ♗e6 (7...♘xc3?? 8 ♗xf7+) 8 ♘g5, and there is no way out for Black; for example, 8...♗g7 9 f4 ♘d7 10 ♗xd5! cxd5 11 ♗e3 ♘b6 12 ♘xe6 fxe6 13 ♗d4 left Black's bishop a 'dead' piece in P.Cramling-Alburt, Reykjavik 1984.

The main line of the Alburt Variation runs 5...♘b6 6 ♗b3 ♗g7 *(D)* (after 6...♘c6, 7 e6 leads to unclear play, but the choice between 7 exd6, 7 ♕e2 and 7 a4 is more promising; closing the centre with 6...d5 doesn't blend well with the kingside pawn-structure, weakened as it is by the fianchetto).

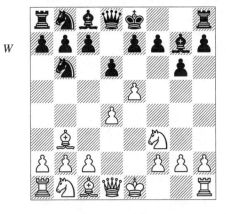

*W*

White has two main plans at his disposal, but several possible moves, as the plans can be implemented in various ways.

The first plan is to initiate an immediate attack on f7 by 7 ♘g5. Then 7...0-0?! is dubious in view of 8 ♕f3, with a subsequent h4-h5, while White also has a strong initiative after 8 e6. Black can also close the position with 7...d5; here this advance is more warranted now that White will be spending two tempi on the sortie and the return of the knight, and Black succeeds in covering the dark squares in time (e.g., 8

♗e3 f6 9 ♘f3 ♘c6 10 exf6 exf6 11 0-0 0-0, Milman-Nakamura, World Open, Philadelphia 2006). This was the main move in the early days of this line until Karpov in particular showed that 8 f4 f6 9 ♘f3 ♘c6 10 c3 gives White rather the better of a game of trench warfare. Consequently Alburt's 7...e6 became the main line in the 1980s. By now this has been analysed extensively, and the critical tests are considered to be 8 ♕f3 ♕e7 9 ♘e4 dxe5 10 ♗g5 ♕b4+ 11 c3 ♕a5 12 ♗f6 ♗xf6 13 ♕xf6 0-0 14 ♕xe5, with a small advantage (if Black wishes to dispute this, then 14...♘c6 15 ♕xc7 ♘xd4 16 0-0 ♘xb3 17 axb3 ♕xa1!? may not be fully resolved), or 8 f4 dxe5 9 fxe5 c5 10 c3 cxd4 11 0-0 0-0 12 cxd4 ♘c6 13 ♘f3, aiming for more.

The second plan begins with 7 0-0 or 7 ♕e2, reinforcing the threat of e6 and safeguarding the queen from a possible exchange, though weakening the d4-pawn's protection. After 7 ♕e2 ♘c6 8 0-0 0-0 White has to make a concession somewhere: 9 h3 prevents a pin on the knight but allows the exchange of the bishop by 9...♘a5, while if he preserves the bishop by 9 c3, then in the line 9...♗g4 10 ♗f4 a5 11 ♘a3 a4 12 ♗c2 dxe5 13 dxe5 ♖a5 the tension over the e5-pawn is mounting, Shanava-Vallejo Pons, European Ch, Dresden 2007.

There are attempts to improve both plans with the inclusion of 7 a4 (D).

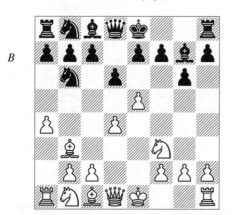

The reply 7...a5 in some lines deprives the black pieces of that square, while in others it leaves the knight on b6 unprotected; for example, 8 ♘g5 e6 (8...d5 is relatively better here than without the a-pawns' moves, but still not particularly appetizing) 9 f4 dxe5 10 fxe5 c5 11

0-0 0-0 12 c3 cxd4 13 cxd4 ♘c6 14 ♘f3 f6 15 ♘c3 fxe5 16 ♗g5 ♕d7 17 dxe5 ♘xe5 18 ♘xe5 ♖xf1+ 19 ♕xf1 ♕d4+ 20 ♔h1 ♕xe5 and here 21 ♗d8 gave White an important tempo in Kuijf-Blees, Dutch Ch, Hilversum 1990.

Therefore it is very tempting for Black to try to insert the move 7...dxe5. Black has to take into account 8 a5 ♘6d7 9 ♗xf7+ (Nunn's recommendation 9 ♕e2 keeps the position more rational) 9...♔xf7 10 ♘g5+ ♔g8 11 ♘e6 ♕e8 12 ♘xc7 with sharp, unclear play after both 12...♕d8 13 ♘xa8 (13 ♘e6 repeats) 13...exd4 14 c3 (14 0-0 ♘c6 15 ♕f3 {15 c3 ♘c5 16 b4 dxc3!; e.g., 17 ♕xd8+ ♘xd8 18 ♖a3 ♘e4 19 ♖e1 c2 20 ♘d2 ♘xd2 21 ♗xd2 ♔f7!, Cerqueira-Rain, corr. 2004} 15...♘de5 16 ♕b3+ ♘f7 17 ♖e1 is also far from clear, Limayo-Rain, corr. 2003) 14...♘f6 (14...♘c5 is more natural) 15 0-0 (15 ♕xd4 ♕xd4 16 cxd4 ♘a6 keeps the knight trapped) 15...♘a6 16 ♖a4!? and 12...♕f7!? 13 d5!?. There is still a lot of virgin territory in these lines.

**6 0-0**

We can also mention 6 h3, which restricts Black's light-squared bishop and correspondingly strengthens e5, but it costs a tempo that could be spent on development.

**6...dxe5**

Let's examine another set-up – 6...♗g7 7 exd6 ♕xd6 (D).

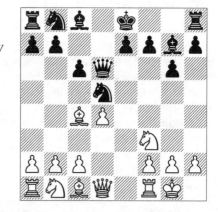

White stands a little more actively in the centre, but this achievement is natural for the side that holds the right of the first move. Such a pawn configuration occurs in many openings and is considered acceptable; Black has no incurable weaknesses and retains the possibility of preparing to undermine the d4-pawn from either side. Now White can prevent the development of the bishop to g4 or, on the contrary, allow it to reach this square and then attack it to obtain the bishop-pair. The main continuations are thus 8 h3, 8 ♖e1 and 8 ♘bd2. Here is a fresh example: 8 h3 0-0 9 ♖e1 ♗f5 10 ♗b3 a5 11 a4 ♘a6 12 ♗g5 ♗f6, Venkatesh-Rozentalis, Canadian Open, Montreal 2008.

**7 dxe5**

The position after 7 ♘xe5 is well-known; generally it is reached via another move-order (4...dxe5 5 ♘xe5 g6 6 ♗c4 c6 7 0-0), which we shall look at later. The attempt to maintain a pawn on e5 has rarely occurred in practice and was not considered dangerous.

**7...♗g7** *(D)*

After the immediate 7...♗g4 Black has to reckon with 8 ♕d4 ♗xf3 9 e6.

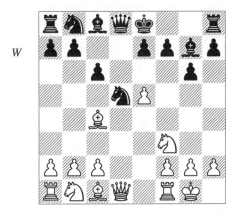

Now White can forestall the appearance of the bishop on g4 with 8 h3, but he prefers to secure the bishop-pair. For his part, Black can plan a different future for his bishop, connected with the e6-square, where it can also be exchanged; Black can even allow his pawn-chain to be broken as long as he gets real counterplay against the e5-pawn, as in the following game: 8 ♗b3 0-0 9 ♖e1 ♗e6 10 ♘bd2 ♘d7 11 ♘d4 ♘c7 ½-½ Dautov-Kengis, Baden-Baden 1990. After 12 ♘xe6 ♘xe6 13 ♗xe6 fxe6 the e5-pawn is indefensible; were it not for that, the g7-bishop may find itself imprisoned for life, as in the Cramling-Alburt example we saw at the start of the note to Black's 5th move above.

**8 ♖e1 ♗g4 9 ♘bd2 ♘d7 10 h3 ♗xf3 11 ♘xf3 e6 12 ♗f1**

White's achievements are as follows:
- The d6-square is weak, although it is unlikely that he will be able to take advantage of this any time soon.
- The dark squares on Black's kingside are vulnerable; if the black king takes up residence there, White can hope to build an attack according to the well-known plan: the queen on h4, the bishop on h6 and the knight on g5.
- He has the bishop-pair. If the light-squared bishop (and it is the one that has no adversary) remains on the queenside, it will become a target for Black's counterplay. Black is ready to attack e5 a third time, and ♕e2 is the natural defence. That's why White, while the diagonal is still open, tucks the bishop away on f1, postponing its more active redeployment to the future.

**12...♕c7 13 ♕e2 h6 14 ♗d2** *(D)*

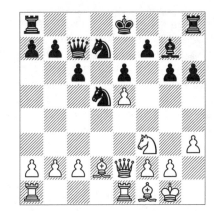

**14...0-0-0?!**

A critical decision. In such set-ups, queenside castling may not be bad; its assessment depends on the piece-set each side has at his disposal. In this case White has a clear-cut plan of attack that is hard to neutralize. A counterattack is out of the question as Black doesn't have enough space; neither can he manage to increase the pressure on the e5-pawn or simplify the game with mass exchanges along the d-file, as White has all the squares covered.

14...0-0 appears to be a more sensible idea, with definite defensive chances and freedom of action on the queenside, even though White's weaknesses there still have to be created.

**15 ♖ad1 g5 16 c4 ♘e7 17 b4 ♘f8**

Black could have swapped his g-pawn for the one on e5 by 17...♘g6 18 ♗c3 h5 19 ♘xg5 ♗xe5 20 ♗xe5 ♘dxe5, but after 21 ♕e3 White has a clear superiority in the centre and dangerous threats.

**18 ♖b1 ♘fg6 19 ♗c3 ♔b8 20 g3** *(D)*

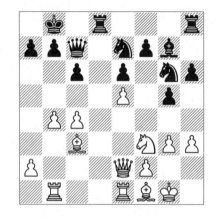

B

Defining the outlines of the impending attack: b5 and a4-a5-a6. Black can avoid opening the files, but he has nothing with which to parry the threats of the queen and bishop on the cleared long light-squared diagonal. Black attempts to thwart White's plan with tactical tricks, but White is in no hurry and meticulously prepares the offensive.

**20...♖d7 21 ♕e4 ♘f5 22 a4 ♖c8 23 a5 ♕d8 24 ♗g2 a6 25 ♖b3 ♖d1 26 b5** *(D)*

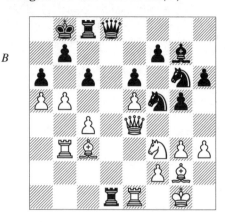

B

**26...axb5**

After 26...cxb5, 27 ♘d2 ♖xe1+ 28 ♕xe1 allows Black to retain some defensive resources, but the piece sacrifice 27 cxb5! ♕d3 28 ♕xd3 ♖xd3 29 bxa6 decides the game quickly.

**27 cxb5 ♕d3 28 ♕a4 ♘ge7 29 a6 b6 30 a7+ ♔a8 31 bxc6 ♘d5 32 c7**

With the bishop's entrance into the fray, the game swiftly concludes. Black is unable to set up even a semblance of a defence.

**32...♘fe7 33 ♗b4 ♖xe1+ 34 ♘xe1 ♕c4 35 ♖c3 ♕e2 36 ♖c2 ♕xe5 37 ♗xe7 1-0**

## Game 19

# Michailo Oleksienko – Evgeny Prokopchuk

## *Moscow 2008*

**1 e4 ♘f6 2 e5 ♘d5 3 d4 d6 4 ♘f3 dxe5 5 ♘xe5** *(D)*

Naturally, Black is happy for White to recapture with the pawn, as 5 dxe5 ♗g4 (but not 5...g6?! 6 ♗c4!, transposing to 4...g6 5 ♗c4 dxe5?! 6 dxe5! – see the previous game) makes a favourable comparison with the lines seen in the previous chapter.

This is the most common Alekhine position nowadays. It has some similarities with lines of the Caro-Kann and the Rubinstein French, and also the Scandinavian Defence. Black will generally be looking to challenge the e5-knight by ...♘d7, but the question is when, and what move(s) he should play to prepare this.

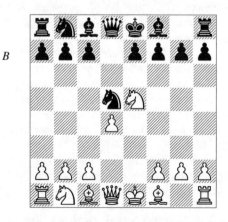

B

**5...c6**

This is by far the most popular move in modern practice. Of the two other main continuations, first let's have a look at the provocative 5...♘d7?!. It was made famous by its use by Larsen in his 1965 Candidates match against Tal. The 'Magician from Riga' displayed uncharacteristic caution and declined the challenge, but the debate in the chess press focused on the obvious sacrifice 6 ♘xf7 *(D)*.

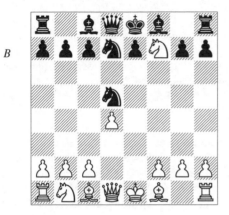

B

By analogy with the notorious Fried Liver Attack in the Two Knights Defence, White has sought (and periodically claimed to have found) a forced win, but this line is nevertheless still played today, and not just at club level. After 6...♔xf7 7 ♕h5+ ♔e6 there are two paths (if White wants more than perpetual check).

8 g3 suggests itself, with 8...b5 deemed to be the strongest reply, with the idea of securing the knight's position, while also preparing to develop the bishop and giving the king an escape route. The main continuation is 9 a4 c6 (9...b4 is an alternative) 10 ♗h3+ (10 axb5 doesn't look bad either, when Black usually secures a retreat for the king in the opposite direction by 10...g6, but after 11 ♕e2+ ♔f7 12 bxc6 ♘7b6 White already has three centre pawns for the piece, and after 13 ♗g2 ♗g7 can choose between 14 ♘c3!? and 14 0-0!?, both of them rather dangerous for Black) 10...♔d6 11 ♘c3 (11 axb5 cxb5 12 0-0 ♘7f6 13 ♕e5+ ♔c6 14 ♗g2 e6 15 b3 is also a potent attacking option). Now 11...b4 can be met with the curious-looking 12 ♗f4+ ♘xf4 13 ♘e4+ ♔c7 14 ♕a5+ ♘b6 15 ♕e5+ ♔d6 (alas, 15...♔b7?? runs into the economical mate 16 ♘c5#) 16 ♘xd6 exd6 17 ♕xf4 ♗xh3, when the material

compensation for the queen can be considered adequate, but nevertheless, Black's problems with development, his flabby pawn-structure and exposed king lead us to assess his position as difficult.

The other avenue of attack is at least as ferocious: 8 c4 ♘5f6 9 d5+ ♔d6 10 ♕f7 ♘e5 (10...♘b8 11 c5+ ♔d7 12 ♗b5+ c6 13 dxc6+ bxc6 14 0-0 ♕a5 15 ♗e2 ♕xc5 16 ♖d1+ ♔c7 17 ♗f4+ ♔b7 18 ♘a3!? and it is not clear how Black can survive) 11 ♗f4 with the threat of c5+, which means that Black's next two are forced: 11...c5 12 ♘c3 a6 *(D)*.

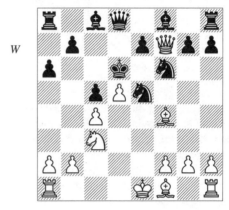

W

The white queen, attacked by the pinned knight, has no moves, which gives Black some tactical counterchances. There have been attempts to prove that White wins after 13 b4 (not 13 0-0-0?? g6!, a well-known opening trap) and perhaps that is so. After 13...♕b6 the threat of exchanging queens on e8 has been eliminated, and White can muster additional forces for the attack; e.g., 14 ♖c1 g5 15 ♗g3 h5 16 bxc5+ ♕xc5 17 ♕g6 ♕d4 18 ♕c2! h4 19 c5+ ♔d7 20 ♖d1 ♘f3+ 21 gxf3 1-0 Sakai-Rebaudo, theme e-mail 2001.

Even if one can demonstrate a clear-cut win for White in these lines (and the above-quoted analysis may well do so, at least in terms of a summary of the key variations), it is a lot of chaotic analysis to memorize in order to be ready to face a rare line. Over the board, players tend to prefer a less drastic strategy, reckoning that by playing quietly White also has fair prospects of obtaining an advantage, with 6 ♘f3 and 6 ♗c4 gaining precedence. Here is a recent example: 6 ♘f3 e6 7 c4 ♘5f6 8 ♘c3 c5 9 d5 ♘b6?! 10 ♗f4

♗d6 11 ♗xd6 ♕xd6 12 ♘b5 ♕d8 13 dxe6 ♗xe6 14 ♕d6 with a plus for White, Yakovenko-Nikolenko, Moscow Ch 2006.

The most common continuation used to be 5...g6 (D), often called the Kengis Variation.

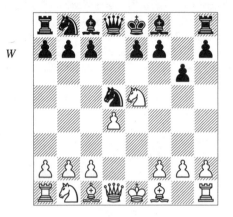

The resulting positions remind one of a system in the Scandinavian Defence, the main difference being the position of the knight on e5. The main continuation is the natural 6 ♗c4. The attempt to utilize the bishop along another diagonal by 6 g3 has also been seen in practice and has a solid reputation. After 6 c4 both 6...♘b6 and 6...♘f6 are playable, followed by preparations for the ...c5 thrust. In his turn, Black demonstrates his willingness to enter the sharp line 6 ♕f3 ♗e6 7 c4 ♘b4 8 ♕xb7; e.g., 8...♕xd4 (8...♘c2+?! 9 ♔d1 ♘xa1 10 ♕xa8 ♗g7 11 ♘d2!? – Nunn) 9 ♕xa8 ♘c2+ (9...♕xe5+?! 10 ♗e2!? favours White) 10 ♔e2 ♕xe5+ 11 ♔d1 and now 11...♕d4+! looks OK for Black, since 12 ♗d2 ♕xb2! 13 ♗c3 ♗g4+! 14 f3 ♘e3+ 15 ♔e1 ♘c2+ gives White no good way to avoid a repetition, since after 16 ♔e2 ♘d4++ 17 ♔d1 ♕c2+ 18 ♔e1 ♕c1+ 19 ♔f2 ♕c2+ 20 ♔g3?! ♗g7 it is only White who is in danger.

Let's go back to 6 ♗c4. The knight can be reinforced by two methods. The first, 6...♗e6, presents White with a pleasant choice:

a) 7 ♗b3 secures the bishop's position. White cuts out tactical tricks and hinders Black's efforts to undermine his positions in the centre; for that purpose the knight is often transferred to d3; e.g., 7...c6 8 0-0 ♗g7 9 c3 ♘d7 10 ♘d3 0-0 11 ♘d2 ♗f5 12 ♘f3 a5 13 ♖e1 a4 14 ♗xd5 cxd5 15 a3, halting Black's counterplay on the queenside and hoping to develop an initiative on the opposite flank, Hermansson-Andreasson, Swedish Ch, Gothenburg 2005.

b) 7 ♘c3 is not, of course, an offer to exchange pieces (since 7...♘xc3? allows the zwischenzug 8 ♗xe6); instead, the knight sets out to attack the enemy bishop. After 7...c6 8 ♘e4 Black usually invites simplifications by 8...♘c7 (the sharper 8...f6!? is interesting: after 9 ♘d3 White plans to gain the bishop-pair as compensation for the weakening that follows 9...♘c3, while after 9 ♘c5 ♗c8 Black can base his counterplay on the loose position of the c5-knight). After 7...♗g7 8 ♘e4 Larsen's idea, 8...♗xe5 with strategically original play, has found few supporters, but there is an alternative in 8...f6 9 ♘c5 ♗g8, when 10 ♘ed3 b6 11 ♘b3 ♘c3 12 ♕f3 ♗xc4 13 ♕xa8 ♘d5 14 ♘d2 ♗xd3 15 cxd3 a5 led to a sharp struggle in Godena-Motylev, European Ch, Budva 2009.

c) With 7 0-0 White aims for the line 7...♗g7 8 ♖e1 0-0 9 ♘d2 c6 (the attempt to simplify at once with 9...♘f4? fails after 10 ♕f3) 10 c3 ♘d7 11 ♘ef3, avoiding exchanges to keep Black cramped, or securing the bishop-pair after 11...♗g4 12 h3.

6...c6 (D) is more natural, retaining the light-squared bishop's freedom of choice.

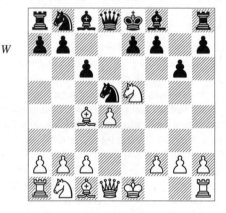

Both sides' plans remain essentially the same, and this move-order often leads to the possibilities examined above, but in some lines the bishop comes out to f5 or g4 without stopping at e6 first: 7 0-0 ♗g7 8 ♘d2 0-0 9 ♘df3 ♘d7 10 ♘d3 ♘7b6 11 ♗b3 ♗g4 (11...a5 12 a4 ♗f5 was favoured by Kengis, one of the leading experts in the 5...g6 line; the point is that exchanging the bishop for the d3-knight rather than its colleague on f3 is more disruptive to White's position) 12 c3 a5 (the pawn advance aims to seize space on the queenside or, as played in the game, to secure the b4-square for the knight should it be driven away from its centralized position) 13 a4 e6 14 h3 ♗xf3 15 ♕xf3 ♘c8, Zapata-Nogueiras, Aguascalientes 2008. White is a little better thanks to the bishop-pair, but Black's position is fairly solid and free from chronic weaknesses.

We now return to the position after 5...c6 *(D)*:

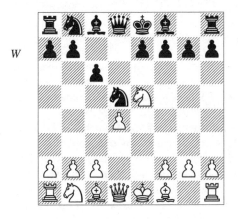

The continuation chosen by Black in the present game, 5...c6, became dominant in the past few years. If this move has to be played eventually, why not play it at once, and then choose whether to play a set-up based on either ...g6 or ...e6?

It looks somewhat passive, which may be why it has taken a long time for its merits to become appreciated. It is useful prophylaxis that reinforces the black knight and intends to offer the exchange of its aggressive white rival with ...♘d7. Sometimes it makes a lot of sense to invite the opponent to declare his intentions first and determine the set-up of one's own pieces according to his choice.

**6 ♗e2**

The development of the light-squared bishop seems the most natural choice. Although White picks the most modest square available, the bishop is not exposed to attack here and this move can also serve as preparation for an aggressive advance of the g-pawn. In current practice it is the most popular reply to 5...c6. Two other major lines also feature a move by this

bishop: 6 ♗c4 is the subject of Game 20, while 6 ♗d3 is dealt with in Game 21.

There are plenty of other moves, as one would expect given the non-forcing nature of Black's play.

The crude assault 6 ♕f3 does not force Black to acquiesce to the weakening of his pawn-structure, as the reply 6...♗e6 is now fully justified, since on f3 the queen takes away an important square from the knight: 7 ♗c4 g6 8 ♗b3 ♘d7 9 0-0 ♗g7 10 ♖e1 0-0 11 c3 ♘xe5 12 dxe5 ♕c7 and it is White who has problems to solve, Karasev-Bogdanov, Seniors World Ch, Bad Zwischenahn 2008.

After 6 c4 the knight does not have to retreat, since 6...♘b4 (possible due to the move ...c6!), with the tactical threat of ...♕xd4, once again forces the white knight's displacement to the side: 7 ♗e3 ♗f5 8 ♘a3 ♘d7 with a comfortable game for Black, while mass exchanges on d3 also promise no advantage.

With 6 ♘d2 the knight heads for f3 in order to retreat the other knight to d3, thus hindering counter-thrusts directed at the d4-pawn. Black has many ways to respond, of which we can note 6...♘d7 7 ♘d3 e6 8 ♗e2 c5, which equalized rather easily in Lakos-Luther, Oberwart 2003.

6 g3 ♘d7 7 ♘f3 g6 8 ♗g2 ♗g7 9 0-0 0-0 10 ♖e1 is another viable set-up. After 10...♖e8 11 ♘bd2 c5 12 dxc5 ♘xc5 13 ♘b3 ♘a4 Black had healthy play in Tkachev-Grishchuk, Almaty blitz 2008.

We now return to 6 ♗e2 *(D)*:

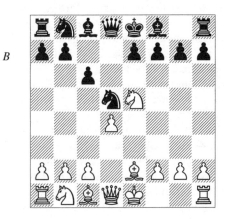

**6...♗f5**

Here too, Black can enquire about the e5-knight's intentions by 6...♘d7. Now White has more reason to avoid the exchange with 7 ♘f3. As a rule, White will subsequently play c4, evicting the knight from its central home and increasing his space advantage. Black must play carefully in order to equalize; e.g., 7...♕c7 (7...♘7f6 8 0-0 ♗f5 9 ♘h4 ♗g6 10 c4 ♘b6 11 ♘c3 e6 12 g3 with an edge for White, Anand-Carlsen, Amber Blindfold, Nice 2008) 8 0-0 e6 9 c4 ♘f4 10 ♘c3 ♗e7 11 ♖e1 ♘xe2+ 12 ♕xe2 0-0 13 ♗g5 ♗xg5 14 ♘xg5 h6 15 ♘f3 b6 16 ♕e3 ♗a6 17 b3 ♖ad8 18 ♘e4 c5, Anand-Mamedyarov, Amber Blindfold, Nice 2008.

The fianchetto by 6...g6 7 0-0 ♗g7 encourages White to reinforce his knight's position on e5 and under its cover demonstrate the drawbacks of Black's pawn-formation: 8 c4 ♘c7 9 ♗e3 0-0 10 f4 ♘d7 11 ♘c3, and Black failed to attain an acceptable game in either Nevednichy-M.Grünberg, Timisoara 2006 or Svidler-Baburin, Bunratty 2009.

**7 g4**

The motivation for this sharp move is that White wants to drive the knight out of the centre, but after the immediate 7 c4 it will go to b4, where it will feel secure since its white counterpart will be forced to occupy the a3-square. Spending a tempo on prophylaxis with 7 a3 is undesirable, while 7 0-0 allows Black to implement his main idea by 7...♘d7. In reply, all the possible knight moves have been tried, and the most natural, 8 ♘f3, leads to familiar play after 8...e6 9 c4 ♘5f6 (9...♘b4 is ineffective here as White can reply 10 a3 ♘c2 11 ♖a2), with White having the freer game, though neither side's position provides very clear targets to attack; an attempt to force matters by 10 ♘c3 ♗d6 11 ♘h4 ♗g6 12 f4 allowed Black counterplay after 12...♘e4 in Sutovsky-Miroshnichenko, Serbian Team Ch, Kragujevac 2009. 8 c4 can still be met by 8...♘b4, but another idea is 8 ♗g4 ♗xg4 9 ♕xg4, when 9...e6 (9...♘xe5 10 dxe5 e6 leads to a more standard type of Alekhine position) 10 ♖d1 ♘5f6 11 ♕e2 ♗e7 12 c4 0-0 13 ♘c3 ♖e8 14 ♖d3 ♘f8 15 ♗f4 ♕b6 16 ♖ad1 gave White a pleasant advantage in Adams-Zhao Xue, Edmonton 2009.

We now return to 7 g4 (D):

**7...♗c8**

7...♗g6?! is clearly dubious due to 8 h4, but 7...♗e6!? leads to interesting and little-studied positions after both 8 f4 f6 9 ♘d3 ♗f7 10 0-0

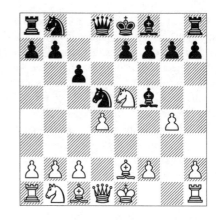

B

♘a6, when White seems over-committed (e.g., 11 ♘c3 e6 and in Navara-Short, Wijk aan Zee 2009, Black gradually brought his pieces to bear on the f4-pawn), and 8 c4 ♘b6 9 b3 f6, when White had to sacrifice a pawn in Kasparov-Short, Moscow rapid 2002. It is perhaps noteworthy that this was also chosen by Topalov's second Cheparinov in a game played after Topalov's loss to Carlsen (Game 21). However, the compensation seems unclear at best after 10 ♘d3 ♕xd4 11 ♗b2 ♕d8 12 ♘c3 ♘a6 13 ♕d2 ♕c7 14 ♕e3 (Kasparov chose 14 0-0-0) 14...♗f7 15 ♖c1 ♘d7 16 ♘e4 e5 17 g5 f5 18 g6 ♗xg6 19 ♘g5 ♗a3 20 ♘e6 ♕a5+ 21 ♗c3 ♗xc1 22 ♕xc1 ♕xa2 23 c5 ♕xb3 24 ♘xg7+ ♔d8 25 ♘xe5 ♘xe5 26 ♗xe5 ♕d5 27 ♗f6+ ♔c8 28 0-0 (Cheparinov-Narciso Dublan, Spanish Team Ch, Montcada 2009) 28...♕f7.

**8 c4 ♘b6**

The c7-square seems to offer better prospects as a transit point, but Black's actual choice indirectly attacks the c4-pawn.

**9 ♘c3 (D)**

We trust that White was reluctant to spend a tempo on 9 ♖g1 and that this was a sacrifice, not an oversight!

**9...f6 10 ♘f3 ♗xg4 11 ♕b3 ♗e6**

One obvious argument in favour of accepting a sacrifice is the possibility of returning the extra material should favourable circumstances arise. Now Black had the opportunity to do just that and, by playing 11...e5!?, call into question White's play, as 12 dxe5 ♘8d7 highlights the drawbacks of the enemy queen's development to b3. However, the desire to keep the loot has its logic as well.

**12 a4**

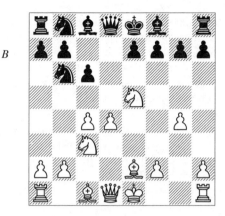

B

White wants to force ...a5 in order to weaken the b6-square. Completing his mobilization by 12 ♗e3 intending 0-0-0 also deserved consideration.

**12...a5**

There were also other ways to protect the b7-pawn; for instance, 12...♕c7, when the exchange sacrifice 13 a5 ♘6d7 14 ♗f4 ♕xf4 15 ♕xb7 ♗g4 leads to very sharp play: while the white queen takes the rook and returns, Black has time to complete his development and create serious threats.

**13 ♗e3 ♘8d7 14 ♖d1**

The king decides against the trip to the queenside. Of course, taking up residence there doesn't look as attractive after the a4 advance, but sitting in the centre, getting in the way of the traffic and disconnecting the rooks, is not the best solution either.

**14...♗f7 15 d5** *(D)*

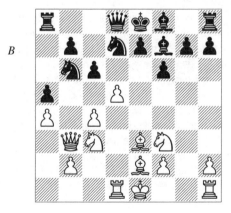

B

White initiates forcing play, and perhaps it is his best option. It's hard to see a good way to increase the pressure, whereas the resulting position looks quite enticing from afar, and it was not easy to calculate that Black could survive.

**15...♕c7 16 ♘d4**

Neither player can side-step the following line.

**16...♘c5 17 ♘e6 ♗xe6 18 ♗xc5 ♘d7 19 ♗b6 ♕xb6 20 ♕xb6 ♘xb6 21 dxe6**

We have reached the end position of the forced complications. It looks promising for White, but Black manages to hold out.

**21...♖d8 22 0-0**

White removes his king from the centre in order to detain the enemy king there for the time being and retain control of the d-file. Another plan involved the advance of the h-pawn, developing the rook via the flank and, should the opportunity arise, opening hostilities there, although no decisive manoeuvre is apparent in these lines either.

**22...f5**

Black could also consider 22...g6.

**23 c5 ♘a8 24 ♘b5** *(D)*

Despite the pitiful state of the black pieces, it is not easy to find a way through the pawn barricades. White gains nothing with 24 ♖xd8+ ♔xd8 25 ♖d1+ ♔c8 26 ♖d7 ♘c7 27 ♗c4 ♘e8, followed by the transfer to f6.

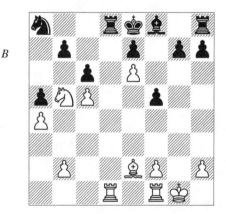

B

White has placed the knight *en prise* in order to hobble its counterpart on a8; its capture is clearly out of the question, but there's nothing to reinforce the attack with. Black is only left with moves on the kingside, but that's also a viable road to freedom.

**24...g6 25 ♖xd8+ ♔xd8 26 ♖d1+ ♔c8 27 ♖d7 cxb5?**

Black must have missed something. After 27...♗h6 White does have a draw by 28 ♗f3 ♗g5 (here too, 28...cxb5? is bad: 29 ♗xb7+ ♔b8 30 axb5 ♘c7 31 ♗c6 ♘xe6 32 b6 ♘d8 33 ♗f3 ♗f4 34 ♖xe7 ♔c8 35 c6) 29 ♗xc6 bxc6 30 ♘a7+ ♔b8 31 ♘xc6+ with perpetual check, but an attempt to play for more would be too risky.

**28 axb5 ♘c7 29 ♗c4 ♘e8?!**

This accelerates the process. It was possible to prolong the game, though not by much, by returning the surplus with 29...♘xb5 30 ♗xb5, but Black has no time to mobilize the rest of his pieces and, despite the limited material remaining, the bishop transfer to d5 with the attack on the b7-pawn is impossible to parry and would decide the game quickly enough.

**30 b6 ♘f6 31 c6**

The *coup de grâce*. The remaining small white force manages to finish off the black king, cut off from the rest of his army.

**31...bxc6 32 ♗a6+ 1-0**

# Game 20
# Milos Perunović – Kiril Georgiev
## *European Ch, Plovdiv 2008*

**1 e4 ♘f6 2 e5 ♘d5 3 d4 d6 4 ♘f3 dxe5 5 ♘xe5 c6 6 ♗c4 (D)**

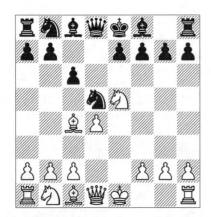

White tries another square for the bishop, offering Black a transposition to the older lines with ...g6. At the moment the bishop's working diagonal is blocked but he hopes for a brighter future.

**6...♘d7**

With the present move-order this is the most popular and principled continuation, and it is also the one with the best record in practice. Now White has to decide: to retreat, keeping the pieces on the board, allow the exchange on e5 or carry out the exchange of knights himself.

The position after 6...g6 is more common, especially in older games, but it is usually reached in a different way, viz. 4...dxe5 5 ♘xe5 g6 6 ♗c4 c6, and we examined it in the previous game.

**7 ♘xd7**

One alternative is 7 0-0 ♘xe5 8 dxe5. By relocating to e5, the d-pawn hopes to assist White's attacking aims, but often becomes a target for a counterattack. As a rule, exchanges serve to decrease the value of a pawn on e5 and amplify its potential weakness. 8...♗f5 9 ♘d2 e6 is not particularly promising for White, as he must resort to the prophylactic 10 a3 or 10 ♗b3 to secure the safety of c2, since after 10 ♘f3 ♘b4 Black seizes the initiative.

7 ♘d3 is an interesting idea, seeking to deny Black the ...♗g4 option, and with possibilities of transposing to good lines against the older 5...g6 system if Black fianchettoes. However, 7...♘7b6 8 ♗b3 ♗f5 gives Black comfortable development.

7 ♘f3 is more reasonable. Generally this formation promises White a small but lasting advantage, but in this version Black can expect to use the two tempi spent by the knight to develop and carry out a freeing advance in the centre; e.g., 7...♘7f6 (intending ...♗g4 and ...e6; in contrast to the lines with ...g6 already played, this does not commit Black to exchanging off this bishop for a knight, as it can drop back to h5 here if need be) 8 h3 ♗f5 9 0-0 e6 10 ♗g5 ♗e7 11 ♘bd2 h6 12 ♗xf6 ♘xf6 13 c3 0-0 14 ♗b3 c5, Shirov-Carlsen, World Blitz, Moscow 2007.

By choosing the move in the game, White makes the exchange of knights in a way that keeps the current pawn-structure intact.

**7...♗xd7 8 0-0**

White can temporarily restrict the enemy bishop by 8 ♕f3, but this merely delays its activation following ...c5: 8...e6 9 0-0 ♕f6 10 ♕xf6 ♘xf6 11 ♘d2 c5, Haba-Carlsen, European Clubs Cup, Kemer 2007.

**8...♗f5 9 ♗g5 (D)**

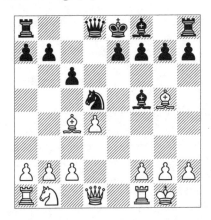

Black's centralized knight restricts the options for this bishop. It has no better square, for now it pins the e7-pawn and prepares to retreat to g3, if necessary, in order to forestall the possible attack on the h2-pawn by Black's queen and bishop without weakening the king's cover.

**9...h6 10 ♗h4 g5!?**

Black is in a belligerent mood and chooses the sharpest plan with castling on opposite sides. Moving the queen and then playing ...e6 leads to a quieter game.

**11 ♗g3 ♗g7 12 c3**

Prophylaxis: White has to reckon with ...♕b6 or ...♘b4.

**12...h5 13 h3 ♕d7 14 ♗e2**

There are two reasons for this move. First of all, White prevents the opening of lines that was threatened after ...h4 followed by ...g4. Secondly, the bishop leaves the c4-square, where it was getting in the way of White's queenside pawn-storm, and is ready to switch to the long diagonal, where it will be most useful for the planned attack.

**14...♘f4?!**

Black reckons that in the case of the exchange on f4, his bishop-pair and the half-open g-file should be significant gains, but the pawns lose their mobility and cannot help to force open the white king's cover. Although he was

reluctant to relinquish control of the g4-square, it would have been interesting to continue the preparations for the thematic advance by 14...h4 15 ♗h2 ♘f6 16 ♗e5 ♖g8. Even after mass exchanges on g4, Black would have kept the initiative, while his king would have been completely secure.

**15 ♗xf4 gxf4 16 ♗f3 0-0-0 17 ♘a3 (D)**

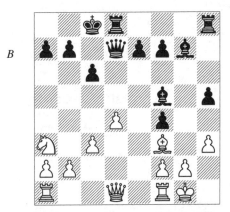

**17...e5?!**

For the moment the sacrifice on h3 doesn't work, and in reply to the preparatory 17...♗f6 or 17...♖hg8 White has 18 ♔h2; thus a frontal assault fails to reach its objective.

The move played is a highly critical decision. It is founded on strategic considerations: it widens the g7-bishop's scope and opens the d-file with the possible occupation of the weak d3-square to follow. However, in return for losing control of the d-file, White acquires pressure along the neighbouring e-file. Another factor is that while Black's kingside pawn-structure had some defects, they were not catastrophic, whereas now it is reduced to rubble. Sometimes that is an acceptable price to pay for the widening of the bishop-pair's scope, but sometimes it is not. Even if this advance were the only plan, it would have been appropriate to take some useful prophylactic measures first, such as starting with 17...♔b8!?.

**18 dxe5 ♕e6?!**

After 18...♗xe5 and the exchange of queens, Black's position is defensible, but White will dictate the course of events.

**19 ♕a4 ♗xe5**

Although 19...♗g4 or 19...♖d3 may have looked tempting several moves ago, when faced with the choice Black didn't have the heart to play them. However, his actual choice is no better.

**20 ♖fe1**

20 ♕xa7 is also good, but White decided to include a useful move for the time being, reckoning that 20...♔b8 is met with 21 ♘b5 a6 22 ♘d4 and the sacrifice on c6 yields even higher gains.

**20...a6 21 ♗xc6** *(D)*

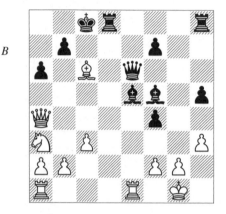

An obvious sacrifice that Black was unable to prevent.

**21...bxc6?**

But this capture already amounts to suicide. After 21...♗xh3 Black has real hopes for salvation. Even in the endgame a pawn down after 21...♕xc6 22 ♕xc6+ bxc6 23 ♖xe5 ♗e6, his active pieces ensure some counterplay.

**22 ♕xa6+ ♔d7 23 ♘c4?**

This prolongs the struggle and presents Black with some chances. The game could have been concluded much more quickly with 23 ♘b5, when the knight joins the attack with decisive effect.

**23...f6 24 ♖ad1+ ♔e7 25 ♕a7+ ♖d7**

After the retreat to the back rank everything is simpler: 25...♔e8? 26 ♖xd8+ ♔xd8 27 ♘xe5 fxe5 28 ♕a5+ and 29 ♖xe5.

**26 ♕c5+ ♔f7 27 ♖xd7+ ♕xd7 28 ♖xe5!** *(D)*

Forcing a transition to an endgame where White has enough pawns for the piece, while Black's remaining pawns are weak and his king is exposed.

**28...♕d1+ 29 ♔h2 fxe5 30 ♕xe5 ♕d5**

Thanks to this move, Black is able to spend a little more time at the board.

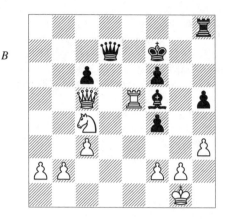

**31 ♕xh8 ♕xc4 32 ♕xh5+ ♔f6?!**

Trying to stay close to the f4-pawn. Nevertheless, 32...♗g6 offered better chances; then after 33 ♕e5 Black can sharpen the play with 33...f3, whereas on g4 the queen is not as active.

**33 ♕h8+ ♔g6 34 ♕e5**

The queen occupies a commanding height.

**34...♗b1**

After 34...♕xa2 35 ♕e8+ ♔g7 36 ♕xc6 ♕xb2 37 ♕c7+ ♔g6 38 ♕d6+ White retains four pawns for the piece, which with precise play should be sufficient for victory.

**35 b3 ♕e4**

Black himself offers the exchange of queens, but the bishop is unable to defend against the pawns on both flanks.

**36 ♕xe4+**

The presence of the queens favours White on general grounds, but a professional player usually does not avoid simplifications if he is confident that he can most easily reach his objective that way.

**36...♗xe4 37 a4** *(D)*

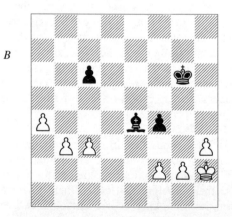

White doesn't cling to material and sends the distant soldier on a raid, aiming to reach the a7-square. This will tie the bishop to guarding the a8-square, while the black king has to watch over the passed pawns on the kingside, which frees his white counterpart for duty elsewhere.

**37...♗c2 38 a5 ♗xb3 39 a6 c5 40 a7 ♗d5 41 g4 ♔g5 42 ♔g1 ♔h4 43 ♔f1 ♗f3 44 ♔e1 c4 45 ♔d2 ♗e4 46 ♔c1 ♗d5 47 ♔c2**

A little zugzwang. Instead of racking his brain trying to determine if his position is won after 47 ♔b2 f3 48 ♔a3 ♔xh3 (there is no other counterplay) 49 g5 ♔g2 50 g6 ♔xf2 51 g7, when White has to part with one of the queening candidates, he achieves the same goal with an extra tempo, as either the bishop relinquishes control of one of the promotion squares or the enemy king has to return. Nor can Black's f-pawn advance yet, as this would allow the white king into e3.

**47...♗e4+ 48 ♔b2 f3 49 ♔a3 ♔xh3 50 g5 ♔g2 51 g6 ♔xf2 52 g7 ♗d5**

Black has to spend time to return. Much simpler is 52...♔e1 53 g8♕ f2 54 ♕e6 or 52...♔e3 53 g8♕ f2 54 ♕xc4.

**53 ♔b4**

White also wins easily after 53 a8♕ ♗xa8 54 g8♕ ♗e4 55 ♕xc4, but if you have the time, why not calculate the line that appears the most convincing?

**53...♔e3 54 ♔c5 f2 55 ♔xd5 f1♕ 56 g8♕ ♕f3+ 57 ♔d6 ♕f4+ 58 ♔d7 1-0**

The checks come to an end, and Black is not tempted by the coming triple-queen endgame.

## Game 21

# Veselin Topalov – Magnus Carlsen
### Morelia/Linares 2008

**1 e4 ♘f6 2 e5 ♘d5 3 d4 d6 4 ♘f3 dxe5 5 ♘xe5 c6**

As we see from the names of the players and the event, the 5...c6 line has boosted the Alekhine's reputation to the extent that it has made a return to top-level events. While no world-class players have been willing to put their trust in it as their principal reply to 1 e4, a number use the Alekhine as an occasional weapon. In the current game, Black scores a remarkable success against one of the best-prepared and most aggressive players in the world.

**6 ♗d3** (D)

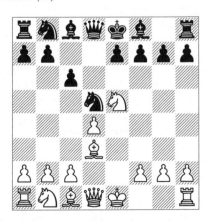

B

With this move, White's bishop denies its black counterpart the natural square f5.

**6...♘d7**

Black carries out his main idea: seeking to remove the centralized knight by offering an exchange of knights.

**7 ♘xd7**

White accepts the offer, in the hope that the bishop will prove ineffective on d7, while White will smoothly develop the rest of his pieces.

White can retain his knight by 7 ♘f3 – he has more space and on general grounds he should avoid simplifications. Then after 7...♘7f6 the bishop is ready to settle on g4, and if White denies it that square as well by 8 h3, there follows 8...♘b4 and in order to save his own bishop from exchange, White is forced to allow its rival to reach f5 after all. Then 9 ♗c4 (9 ♗e2 ♗f5 10 ♘a3 e6 offers White little) 9...♗f5 10 ♘a3 e6 11 c3 ♘bd5 12 ♘c2 ♗e7 led to a draw in Adams-Carlsen, Moscow blitz 2007.

White can choose 7 0-0 ♘xe5 8 dxe5, but this change in structure is generally speaking not in his favour. 8...♗e6 9 ♘d2 g6 10 ♘f3 ♗g7 11 h3 ♘b4 12 ♗e4 ♗c4 turned out to be satisfactory for Black in Adams-Short, London 2008.

**7...♗xd7**

White now has more room for operations, but Black has no chronic defects and he can solve the problem of the light-squared bishop by deploying it to g4 (after ♘f3, although Black then has to agree to its exchange, leaving White with the bishop-pair) or postpone a decision until his development is complete.

**8 0-0 g6** *(D)*

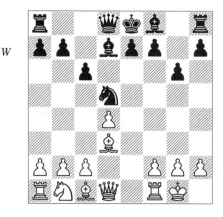

**9 ♘d2**

9 ♖e1 ♗g7 10 c3 0-0 11 ♗g5 is another way to play the position, adopting a fairly active stance. Then 11...♖e8 12 ♘d2 ♕c7 13 ♘c4 c5 is one possibility, as played in Muzychuk-Zhao Xue, Krasnoturinsk 2007.

9 c4 ♘f6 10 h3 ♗g7 11 ♘d2 0-0 12 ♘f3 ♕c7 13 ♖e1 ♗f5 14 ♗xf5 gxf5 15 ♗e3 ♖ad8 16 ♕c2 e6 17 ♖ad1 ♘e4 18 ♕c1 ♔h8 19 ♗f4 ♕e7 20 ♕e3 ♖g8 gave Black good play in Zhigalko-Rozentalis, Cappelle la Grande 2006.

**9...♗g7 10 ♘f3 0-0 11 ♖e1?!**

11 c3 can again be met by 11...♕c7 12 ♖e1 c5, but this at least side-steps the tactical coup that occurs later in the main game.

**11...♗g4! 12 c3?!**

A careless move, allowing a nice tactic, which Magnus of course notices.

**12...c5!** *(D)*
**13 ♗e4?!**

Lars Bo Hansen indicates in *Improve Your Chess* that White's best idea is to fall into the main line of Black's tactical idea by 13 dxc5 ♘xc3! 14 bxc3 ♗xc3, since he can then bail out by 15 ♗h6! ♗xe1 16 ♗xf8 ♔xf8 17 ♗e4!, leading to equality.

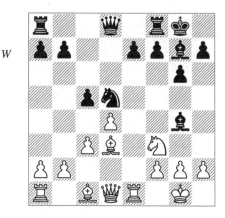

**13...cxd4 14 cxd4 e6**

Black enjoys a clear positional advantage, and real chances of winning White's d-pawn. If Topalov believed that his activity would compensate for this defect, he was in for a rude awakening.

**15 ♕b3?! ♗xf3 16 ♗xf3 ♗xd4 17 ♗xd5 ♕xd5 18 ♕xd5 exd5 19 ♖d1 ♗g7 20 ♔f1**

The critical line is 20 ♖xd5 ♖fd8 21 ♖xd8+ ♖xd8 22 ♗e3 ♗xb2 23 ♖b1 b6!, when White's weak back rank means that Black stays a pawn up.

**20...♖fd8 21 ♗g5 ♖d7 22 ♖d2 h6 23 ♗e3 d4 24 ♖d3 ♖c8 25 ♗d2 ♖c2 26 ♖b1 ♖e7 27 a4 f5 28 b3 ♖ec7 29 ♗e1 ♔f7 30 ♖d2 ♖c1 31 ♖xc1 ♖xc1 32 ♔e2 ♖b1 33 ♖d3 ♔e6 34 h4 ♔d5 35 ♗d2 ♔e4 36 ♖g3 f4! 37 ♖d3**

The white rook must move along the rank because 37 ♖xg6? is met by the neat mate 37...d3#.

**37...♗e5 38 f3+ ♔d5 39 ♗e1 ♗d6 40 ♗d2 g5 41 hxg5 hxg5 42 ♗e1 g4! 43 fxg4 ♔e4! 44 g5 0-1**

Black would have continued 44...♖xe1+! 45 ♔xe1 ♔xd3.

Concluding the chapter, I would like to mention once again that the system examined in Games 19, 20 and 21 is considered today to be the most correct in this difficult opening. So far, White has been unable to get to grips with this line in any way that questions the fundamental viability of Black's approach. But you can be sure that some of the best chess minds in the world are working hard on that problem.

# 6 Exchange Variation

This system arises after the moves 1 e4 ♘f6 2 e5 ♘d5 3 d4 d6 4 c4 ♘b6 5 exd6 *(D)*.

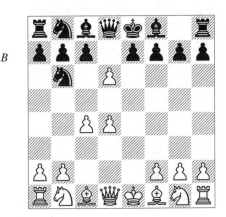

B

This is a fully viable way to fight for the advantage, and its popularity is on the rise. The outpost on e5, despite all its merits, presents one of the main targets for Black's counterplay, and here White radically solves this problem. He retains, albeit in reduced form, an advantage in space and gives himself a great freedom of choice in development, and can hope to achieve

better centralization; although the black knight on b6 fulfils new, non-standard functions, it would still look better on f6.

We should note that the increased interest in the Exchange Variation is not solely as a result of its intrinsic merits; it is also partly in response to Black's achievements in the variations with 4 ♘f3 dxe5, examined in the previous chapter, that has led to some players seeking a different pattern of play as White.

In some lines of the Alekhine, the capture on d6 also can be played at a later stage of the opening, transposing into the same or similar variations, but then it is Black who along the way acquires opportunities to turn off the main road.

The recapture can be made by either c- or e-pawn; each method has its pros and cons and its adherents. The popularity of the symmetrical recapture with the e-pawn has risen in recent years, partly due to White's successes with some subtle new set-ups against the more unbalancing recapture with the c-pawn. Games 22 (Volokitin-Ivanchuk) and 23 (Caruana-Agdestein) examine the lines after 5...exd6, while Game 24 (Nakamura-Shabalov) is devoted to 5...cxd6.

## Game 22
## Andrei Volokitin – Vasily Ivanchuk
### *Foros 2006*

**1 e4 ♘f6 2 e5 ♘d5 3 d4 d6 4 c4 ♘b6 5 exd6 exd6** *(D)*

Recapturing with this pawn keeps the pawn-structure symmetrical. Generally this leads to positions that are more solid but offer less scope for hostilities.

**6 ♘c3**

Black's main problem is his lack of space, leading to a slight traffic-jam for his minor pieces, with the light-squared bishop the main problem. (However, White cannot completely deny this piece any living space; for instance, 6

♗d3 leaves the d4-pawn weak, which Black can probe immediately with 6...♘c6. Then supporting the pawn with 7 ♘f3 allows 7...♗g4, while 7 ♗e3 invites 7...♘b4.) Even when this bishop has found a posting on the kingside, Black must take care that White cannot advantageously target it with a space-grabbing pawn advance on this wing. In many cases, Black is in no rush to develop this bishop, and may wish to clarify the central structure first.

All the same, White needs to develop his king's knight, and only the h-pawn can provide

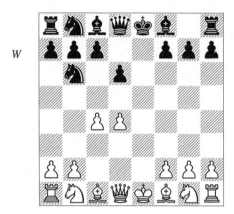

W

secure control of the g4-square, which it some-times does at once – 6 h3. We shall illustrate the further typical development of events with the game B.Socko-Baburin, Turin Olympiad 2006: 6...♗e7 7 ♘f3 ♗f5 8 ♗e2 0-0 9 ♘c3 ♗f6 10 0-0 h6 *(D)*.

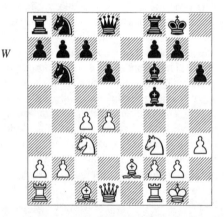

W

The traditional defender of the castled position, the king's knight, is on the opposite flank, and the bishops have pitched camp here instead. For now, White sticks to the strategy of restriction while keeping in mind the possibility of a pawn offensive on either flank. Hence Black's prophylactic move ...h6, slowing down such an offensive and providing the h7-square for the queen's bishop, is quite appropriate. 11 b3 ♘c6 12 ♗e3 d5 (this method of clarifying the situation in the centre and the subsequent knight route are standard and already familiar to us) 13 c5 ♘c8 14 ♖c1 ♘8e7 15 ♕d2 ♗e4 16 ♘h2 with complex double-edged play.

If White resents spending a tempo on pro-phylaxis and sees no big problem in the enemy

bishop's appearance on g4, he can choose 6 ♘f3. The following energetic plan of deploy-ment is interesting: 6...♗e7 7 ♗d3 ♗g4 8 h3 ♗h5 9 0-0 ♘c6 10 ♗e3 0-0 11 ♘c3 ♗f6 12 g4 ♗g6 13 ♗xg6 hxg6 14 g5 ♗e7 15 d5 ♘e5 16 ♘xe5 dxe5 17 ♕g4, Shirov-Macieja, Byd-goszcz rapid (1) 2001. Nevertheless, in this line Black more often than not is OK.

The text-move is the most natural continua-tion that retains the option of choosing any method of development.

**6...♗e7** *(D)*

This move is also hard to find fault with. The other route to the long diagonal – with 6...g6 – further restricts the other bishop's normal posi-tion on f5 and, as standard with a fianchetto, weakens a complex of squares.

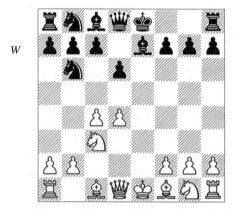

W

**7 h3**

White decides to rule out ...♗g4 after all. We shall examine the currently most popular set-up – with the bishop on d3 and the other knight on e2 – in the next game; for now we should men-tion another aggressive plan of development that begins with 7 ♕f3 (or 7 ♗e3) 7...0-0 8 ♗e3. By developing the queenside first, White aims to castle on that side, subsequently intend-ing to combine the pawn offensive on the enemy king's position with operations in the centre. The aim is to cramp Black's pieces, while the possible opening of the d-file will expose a dan-gerous opposition of the white rook and the black queen. Black may play 8...c6, preparing ...d5, to neutralize the threats in the centre, and the king's intact cover allows him to hope for a successful defence against a kingside attack. Another continuation leads to sharp play:

8...♘c6 9 0-0-0 ♗e6 (9...f5 and 9...♗g5 are also played), when White either starts a war in the centre by 10 c5 ♘d7 or continues with his policy of restriction by 10 b3. Of course, his king becomes more vulnerable as well, which is common with opposite-side castling.

An old line, considered to lead to balanced play, runs 7 ♗e2 0-0 8 ♘f3 ♗g4 9 b3 ♘c6 10 0-0 ♗f6 11 ♗e3 d5 12 c5 ♘c8 13 h3 ♗e6 14 ♕d2 ♘8e7.

We now return to 7 h3 *(D)*:

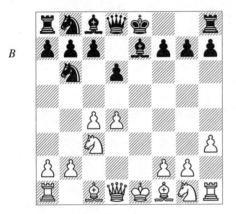

**7...0-0 8 ♘f3**

For now, neither side is in a hurry to secure the f5-square. Black could have occupied it instead of castling, and the subsequent play would most likely have developed along lines similar to Socko-Baburin above. White could now have taken it under control with 8 ♗d3, but after 8...♖e8 his knight would need to occupy a more modest square by 9 ♘ge2; in this set-up the inclusion of h3 is not at all mandatory, and Black would prepare the deployment of the queen's bishop with ...♗f6, ...g6 and ...♘c6-e7.

**8...♗f6 *(D)***

After 8...♗f5, 8...♖e8 and the text-move, the play usually proceeds along similar lines to Socko-Baburin above. There is also an attempt to clarify the situation in the centre at once by 8...c5. After the exchange on d4, Black is ready to push ...d5, completely freeing himself. Therefore White usually chooses 9 d5. This formation often occurs in King's Indian Benoni set-ups, but in this version the differences don't favour Black, most pertinently because his knight is posted less well on b6.

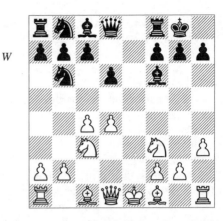

Ivanchuk attempts to provoke White to fix the centre without Black having to weaken the d6-pawn or deny his pieces use of the c5-square.

**9 ♗e2 ♗e6**

This rare but interesting move was played for the first time by Ivanchuk in this game. 9...♘c6 and 9...♖e8 are the standard moves, normally leading to positions we have already examined.

**10 d5**

White accepts the challenge. Traditional play with 10 b3 d5 11 c5 allows Black, thanks to the d5-pawn being protected, to choose the other retreat and start to chip away at the enemy pawn-chain at once by 11...♘6d7 12 ♗b2 b6.

**10...♗xc3+ 11 bxc3 *(D)***

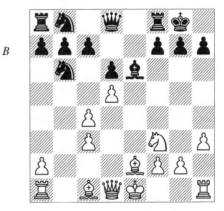

**11...♗d7**

Black doesn't want to place the bishop on f5, inviting the attack by ♘d4 with gain of time, and much less to transfer it to g6 and provoke the advance of White's kingside pawns. One gets the immediate impression that White can count on an initiative on the kingside, which the bishops are ready to target and where there are few defenders. However, it is not easy to find an efficient way of regrouping, as the c4-pawn demands constant attention, while trying to drive away its attacker, the b6-knight, with the advance of the a-pawn is risky: the pawn will be fixed in place on a4, which Black can quickly attack with three pieces.

**12 0-0 ♞a6 13 ♗g5 f6**

Black concludes that White cannot profit from the weakening of the e6-square – the weakness on c4 again gets in his way. Black's next few moves are obvious, whereas White is faced with making important choices.

**14 ♗e3 ♞c5 15 ♖e1 ♖e8 16 ♗f1**

If White has settled for the knight route to b5, then why not 16 ♞d4 at once? He probably doesn't risk anything with 16 ♗d3 either, but just considers parting with the bishop-pair to be premature.

**16...♖e7 17 ♞d4 ♛f8 18 ♞b5**

Interesting play could ensue after 18 ♞b3. If Black avoids the exchange, then the knight would find an original post on a5, at the same time relieving the bishop from the task of defending the c4-pawn.

**18...♗xb5 19 cxb5 ♖ae8** *(D)*

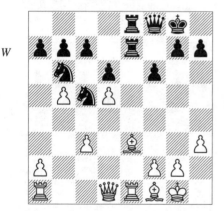

Here we have a textbook case of the bishop-pair battling the knight-pair. If the position is relatively open, the side with the bishops usually has the better claim to the advantage. A lot depends on the availability of strong points for the knights. The c5-knight is on one such point, and the queenside pawn-structure is partially fixed, with limited chances of opening it. Moreover,

Black has pressure down the e-file that White would like to neutralize without compromising the placement of his pieces too much.

**20 a4**

The advance of this pawn eventually provides White with an open a-file, but the counter-advance of the enemy f-pawn at the very least secures a second outpost on e5. 20 ♖e2, freeing the dark-squared bishop, deserved consideration. The loss of control over c4 is only temporary, and the immediate 20...♞c4?? is not possible because of 21 ♗xc5.

**20...f5**

20...♛f7, aiming to provoke White to play c4 and restrict the light-squared bishop still further, fails to achieve its objective, since the complications after 21 a5 ♞xd5 22 ♗c4 c6 23 a6 clearly favour White.

**21 a5 f4 22 ♗d2 ♖xe1 23 ♗xe1 ♞bd7 24 f3** *(D)*

A critical decision. On the one hand, this way White activates one of the bishops without having to reckon with ...f3, but on the other hand, he restricts the other bishop and allows the kingside to be fixed. A possible alternative is 24 c4 (while the threat of b6 is on, White would prefer not to deprive the bishop of the b5-square, but this advance will be forced anyway) 24...♞e5 25 ♖a3 (or 25 ♗c3) 25...f3 26 g3, when his position looks precarious, but the question of whether the f3-pawn will prove to be a force or a weakness remains open.

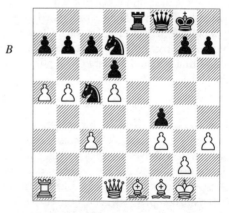

**24...♛f6 25 ♖c1 b6**

Before starting the transfer of the d7-knight, Black decides to let White open the a-file but to forestall b6, at the same time reinforcing the c5-knight. This completely blocks the queenside, and the focus of the struggle moves to the opposite side of the board.

**26 axb6 axb6 27 ♗f2 h6**

On e5 the knight's position looks pretty, but it is insufficiently active. Therefore Black plans to transfer it to g3. If it is carried out at once by 27...♕g5 28 ♖a1 ♘f6, then after 29 ♖a7 there is no convenient way to defend the c7-pawn. The move in the game weakens the light squares still further, but Black comes to the conclusion that there is no way around it, while it is useful to remove the pawn from a possible attack, and the square can be covered. The advance of its neighbour – 27...g6 – weakens the squares of the opposite colour and precludes the use of that square as a transit point by the knights.

**28 ♗d4**

Allowing Black to carry out the planned knight transfer. Should a waiting move have been made instead? First, no useful waiting move is apparent; second, what's wrong with placing the bishop on d4?

**28...♕g5 29 c4 ♘f6 30 ♖a1 ♘h5 31 ♖a7 ♕e7**

At the moment Black doesn't want to weaken the back rank. After 31...♖e7 32 ♖a8+ ♔f7 33 ♕c2 the threat of ♕h7 seemed to him unpleasant.

**32 ♕c2 ♘g3 33 ♖a1**

With the knight on g3, White cannot allow an invasion of his back rank. The other way of covering the e1-square – 33 ♗f2?! – decentralizes the bishop and presents Black with more freedom in carrying out the regrouping.

**33...♕g5 34 ♔h2 ♔f7 (D)**

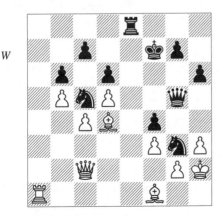

The king personally covers the g6-square, through which the knight's planned route lies, while also avoiding a possible tempo-gaining check on the back rank. Black turns his attention to the search for an improved version of the invasion on e3 by one of his stallions.

**35 ♔g1 ♘d7 36 ♔h2 ♘e5 37 ♗f2**

White doesn't mind a draw, but cannot see a convincing way of forcing it, and doesn't think he is obliged to simplify the position and find himself the defending side. Exchanging the dark-squared bishop with all his pawns fixed on light squares may spell a hopeless endgame. He is ready to part with the light-squared one, but only in exchange for the g3-knight; if it is exchanged for the other knight, White will have to reckon with an invasion on e2.

**37...♘g6 38 ♗d3 ♘h4 (D)**

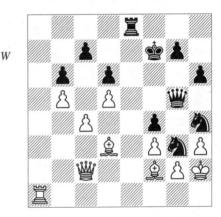

**39 ♖a7?!**

White has no grounds for initiating active operations. While he can meet the regrouping of the black knights, the most important thing is not to stumble into a discovered check after a sacrifice on g2. Therefore it is prudent to hold the position with 39 ♕b2. Weakening the back rank is perilous.

**39...♖e7?**

In the last moves before the time-control, Black didn't want to risk giving up the pawn to carry out the prepared manoeuvre, but his fears were ungrounded. After 39...♘gf5! 40 ♖xc7+ ♔g8 41 ♗f1 ♘e3, in the case of the exchanges, events would develop similarly to the game, so White has to give up the g2-pawn, when his king will be in greater danger.

**40 ♖a8? (D)**

The rook had to return at once, when no decisive regrouping is apparent.

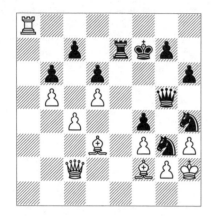

Now Black's knight can transfer to e3 with decisive threats.

**40...♘gf5 41 ♗f1**

It is already too late to cover the back rank: 41 ♗xh4 ♕xh4 42 ♖a1 ♕g3+ 43 ♔g1 ♖e1+ 44 ♖xe1 ♕xe1+ 45 ♔h2 ♘g3 46 ♕b1, and now the simplest continuation is 46...♕xb1 and the king enters the enemy camp with decisive effect. After the text-move, White has no time to blockade the passed e3-pawn. There is more than one path to victory, and Black picks one that is the smoothest.

**41...♘e3 42 ♗xe3 fxe3 43 ♕e2 ♘f5 44 ♖a2 ♕f4+ 45 ♔g1 ♕d4 46 ♔h2 ♕e5+ 47 f4 ♕xf4+ 48 ♔g1 ♘g3 49 ♕d3 ♖e4 50 ♗e2 ♖d4 51 ♕b1 ♖d2 0-1**

# Game 23
# Fabiano Caruana – Simen Agdestein
## *Amsterdam 2008*

**1 e4 ♘f6 2 e5 ♘d5 3 d4 d6 4 c4 ♘b6 5 exd6 exd6 6 ♘c3** *(D)*

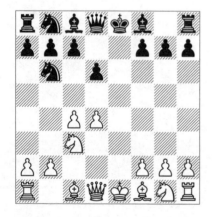

**6...♗e7**

A possible move-order subtlety for Black is 6...♘c6, when the pressure on d4 forces White to play an early ♗e3 if he wishes to adopt the line with ♗d3 and ♘ge2. After 7 ♗e3 ♗e7 8 ♗d3 0-0 9 ♘ge2, Black can play 9...♘b4 10 b3 (10 ♗b1? ♘xc4 hits the e3-bishop) 10...♘xd3+ 11 ♕xd3 c6 12 d5 ♖e8, when his bishop-pair compensates for the structural defects, Hou Yifan-Short, Wijk aan Zee 2009.

**7 ♗d3**

Today this is the most common plan of development. Now that the knight has moved from b1, the bishop has the option of retreating to b1 and so White doesn't have to fear the ...♘b4 leap (if the c4-pawn is directly or indirectly defended, of course). However, White doesn't always cling to this bishop and is often ready to use the time spent by Black exchanging it to gain an advantage in development.

The restriction of the c8-bishop is not a dominant idea either; White's control of the g4-square is of a temporary nature and can only be solidified by spending a tempo on a pawn move, as the g1-knight has to be brought out anyway. If White lets the bishop out, he plans to force its exchange on g6, which will reduce the mobility of Black's kingside pawn-formation, which may tell in both the middlegame and the endgame. Many players find the resulting position for White to be comfortable – the advantage is minimal but Black has no counterplay.

**7...0-0**

Generally, Black prefers a more forcing continuation: 7...♘c6 8 ♘ge2 ♗g4 9 f3 ♗h5 10 0-0 ♗g6 *(D)*.

White can fight for the advantage by continuing the restriction strategy with 11 b3 (or 11 ♗xg6 hxg6 12 b3), intending to meet the

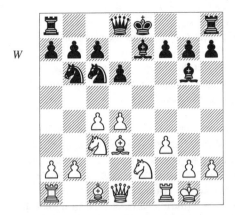

traditional ...d5 under favourable conditions (the e2-knight is ready to take part in the attack on the d5-pawn from the f4-square). However, crossing the demarcation line by 11 ♗xg6 hxg6 12 d5 is an enticing option as well. White temporarily cedes e5 but secures central posts for his knights; e.g., 12...♘e5 13 b3 0-0 14 f4 ♘ed7 15 ♘d4 ♗f6 16 ♘e4, Langrock-Sergeev, Rakovnik 2008.

**8 ♘ge2 (D)**

8 h3 and 8 ♘f3 are not impossible either. However, we have already examined better versions of these ideas.

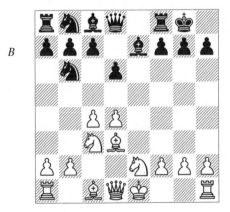

**8...c6**

A rare move, rarity possibly being its main merit. Usually this move serves to prepare ...d5, so that the pawn will be overprotected and after White replies c5 the knight can drop back to d7. In the present game, Black assumes a defensive stance and hopes to find counterchances by provoking White into advancing without adequate preparation. 8...♘c6 would transpose to

positions considered above, but the tempo Black has spent on castling slightly widens White's choice; for example, 9 0-0 ♗f6 (now 9...♘b4 is pointless in view of 10 ♗b1, when 10...♘xc4? loses to 11 a3!) 10 b3 ♗g4 11 ♗e3 ♖e8 (by 11...♗xd4 12 ♗xh7+ ♔xh7 13 ♕d3+ and 14 ♘xd4 Black swaps a flank pawn for one in the centre, but the weakening of the black king's cover is the more important factor) 12 ♕d2 ♗h5 13 ♘f4 ♗g6 14 ♘xg6 hxg6 15 ♗e4 with a very pleasant game for White, Cicak-Solozhenkin, European Clubs Cup, Rethymnon 2003.

**9 ♕c2**

White takes the opportunity to force the advance of one of the black kingside pawns.

**9...f5**

The least obliging reply seems to be 9...h6, whereas in the not-so-distant past the adherents of the classical style wouldn't have seriously considered the text-move on general grounds. But computer chess has lowered the importance of general considerations (of the 'hole on e6' type) in favour of a greater focus on specifics. Indeed, the move played by Black is not devoid of certain merits, such as the control of the e4-square.

**10 0-0 ♘a6 11 a3 ♘c7 (D)**

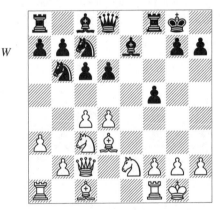

**12 b3**

The insufficient protection of the f5-pawn doesn't allow Black to obstruct the c8-bishop's diagonal, so Black must remain inactive in the centre for the time being. White does not need to force ...g6 by means of 12 ♘g3 as Black will play this move of his own accord. He has several attractive continuations, such as 12 a4, but he plays at an emphatically deliberate pace.

The point of White's last move is to deny the c4-square to the enemy knight before deploying the bishop to e3.

**12...g6 13 ♗e3 ♗f6**

Now that the preparations for the advance in the centre are complete, 13...d5 suggests itself. In reply White can advance with 14 c5, to be followed by the traditional queenside offensive, or he can maintain the pawn tension, for instance with that same 14 a4. Black decides not to alter the pawn-structure for now but to focus on improving the position of his pieces. Naturally, the bishop is more useful on the long diagonal.

**14 ♖ad1 ♗g7 15 ♘f4**

Having set up a masked opposition of the rook and the black queen and taking advantage of the fact that 15...d5 cannot be played because of the weakness of the e6-square, White threatens a favourable opening of the centre with c5.

**15...♕f6 16 a4**

The line 16 c5 ♘d7 17 cxd6 ♕xd6 18 d5 ♘e5 didn't appear to be convincing enough, so White plans a regrouping of his pieces, striving to occupy the best post before opening the position.

**16...♘d7 17 ♘ce2**

Vacating the square for the bishop transfer, in order to oppose its counterpart on the long diagonal. The exchange of these bishops will make the weakness of the dark squares in Black's camp more palpable.

**17...♕e7 18 ♖fe1 ♘f6 19 ♗d2 ♕f7 20 ♗c3 ♖e8 21 d5** *(D)*

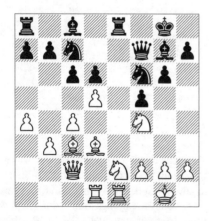

White decides that his position has been strengthened to the maximum and commences active operations.

**21...c5**

Capturing on d5 opens the diagonal on which Black's queen and king both stand and allows a pin with fatal consequences. Allowing the knight onto d4 is also unpleasant, so this move can be considered forced.

**22 b4**

Continuing the offensive. Taking on b4 now looks altogether bad – an avenue of attack on d6 is opened, and Black's control of the d4-square is lost. Black has three methods of reinforcing c5. The least impressive of these involves the plan to recapture symmetrically and allow the opening of the b-file: 22...b6 23 bxc5 bxc5 presents White with several additional opportunities for an invasion. The second, and evidently the best is to support the c5-pawn with a knight. After the exchange White gains the d4-square but cedes Black the no less attractive c5-square. The pawn can be supported with either knight: in the case of 22...♘a6 23 b5 ♘c7 (after 23...♘b4 Black's compensation for the pawn will be insufficient) White has advanced the pawn to b5 without loss of time, but the value of this change is not great; or 22...♘d7 23 b5 ♘e5, when the knight has traded his post for one that is more active. In both cases Black is cramped, but the position remains closed, which complicates White's task.

**22...♗d7**

The third method. A pawn is preserved on c5, but it arrives there from d6. If only a blockading knight could be transferred to the square it vacates...

**23 bxc5 dxc5 24 ♕b2 ♖ab8 25 ♗c2**

Not only protecting the pawn but also vacating the square for subsequent manoeuvres.

**25...♘e4** *(D)*

There were no specific threats, but Black decided that it was time to simplify the position before White cramped him still further by taking away this possibility with f3, followed by the further activation of his pieces, for instance by the knight transfer to e5.

**26 ♗xe4**

Exchanging only the bishops for now by 26 ♗xg7 ♕xg7 27 ♕a3 b6 28 d6 deserved consideration. White can then pursue another simplifying plan; e.g., 28...♘e6 29 ♗xe4 ♘xf4 30 ♘xf4 ♖xe4 31 ♖xe4 fxe4 32 ♘d5. White is taken up with another idea.

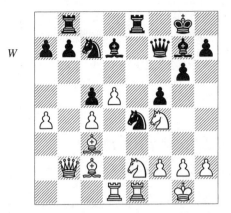

**26...♖xe4 27 ♗xg7 ♕xg7 28 ♕xg7+?!**

It appears that White overestimated his prospects in the resulting complex ending. He could have retained a small advantage with the queens on the board: 28 ♕b3 b6 29 f3.

**28...♔xg7 29 ♘c3 ♖xf4**

Black has difficulties in the minor-piece endgame that arises after 29...♖xe1+ 30 ♖xe1 ♖e8 31 ♖xe8 ♘xe8 32 ♘d3 b6 33 ♘e5.

**30 ♖e7+ ♔f6?!**

Moving toward the centre, in accordance with general endgame principles, but in this particular situation the king finds itself under the threat of a possible check from d5. Facing such a menacing passed pawn, Black is naturally wary of retreating to the back rank by 30...♔g8, but in that case Black's counterplay is more substantial; e.g., 31 ♖xd7 ♘e8 32 ♔f1 ♖xc4 33 ♖d3 ♘f6, and wherever the rook goes, Black takes on c3, followed by a knight fork.

**31 d6 ♗e6?!**

And now the knight cannot move because of the check mentioned above, and the passed pawn relocates to c7. Black retains control over the c8-square, but another one proves more important – b5. After 31...♗c6 32 dxc7 ♖c8 33 ♖xh7 ♖xc4 34 ♘b5 ♗xb5 35 axb5 ♖d4 Black obtains an improved version of the rook endgame considered in the next note (35...♖e4?! is worse because of 36 f4 ♖e7? 37 ♖d6+ ♖e6 38 ♖dd7).

**32 dxc7 ♖c8 33 ♖xh7 ♖xc4?** (D)

The ending is sharp and not easy to calculate, especially with the time-control approaching, but the move played by Black loses. The struggle would continue after 33...♖d4 34 ♖xd4

cxd4, when 35 ♘d5+?! ♗xd5 36 cxd5 d3 37 ♔f1 ♖e8 is insufficient for White, who has to part with the pride of his position by 38 c8♕ with a likely draw. Winning chances remain after 35 ♘b5 d3 36 ♔f1 ♗xc4 37 ♔e1 ♗xb5 38 axb5 ♔e5 39 ♔d2.

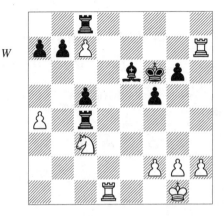

**34 ♘b5 ♖xa4 35 h4 c4**

Striving to advance his own passed pawns as far as possible. It is clear that the c7-pawn will cost Black a piece, and White will not allow it to be the bishop unless he can destroy or devalue Black's pretty queenside pawn-chain first; e.g., 35...♖f8 36 ♖d8 ♖f7 37 ♖xf7+ ♔xf7 38 ♘d6+ and 39 ♘xb7.

**36 ♖d8 ♖a6**

36...a6 would be met by 37 ♖hh8; for example, 37...axb5 38 ♖xc8 c3 39 ♖ce8 ♖c4 40 ♖xe6+ ♔xe6 41 c8♕+ ♖xc8 42 ♖xc8 b4 43 ♔f1 or 37...c3 38 ♖xc8 c2 39 ♖cf8+ ♔e5 40 c8♕ ♗xc8 41 ♖xc8 ♖a1+ 42 ♔h2 c1♕ 43 ♖he8+ ♔f6 44 ♖xc1 ♖xc1 45 ♘d6.

**37 ♖hh8?**

This unexpectedly throws away the win, falling into a cunning trap that Black apparently didn't know he had set. 37 ♘d6?? is even worse, as 37...c3 then wins. The correct path is 37 ♘c3! ♖c6 38 ♘d5+ ♔e5 39 f4+ ♔d4 40 ♘e7+ ♔c5 41 ♘xc6 ♔xc6 42 ♖e7.

**37...♖c6?**

37...c3! draws: 38 ♖xc8 (38 ♘xc3? ♖xc7 leaves White worse) 38...c2 39 ♖cf8+ ♔g7! (not 39...♔e5? 40 c8♕ ♗xc8 41 ♖xc8, when 41...♖c6 is ineffective because 42 ♖he8+ enables White to stop the pawn) 40 c8♕ ♗xc8 41 ♖xc8 and now the key idea is 41...♖c6!, when White has no way to prevent the pawn from promoting apart from giving perpetual check on f8, g8 and h8 (as we have seen, the king may not dare step onto the e-file).

**38 Xxc8 Bxc8 39 Xxc8 ♔e7 40 Xh8 a6 41 Xh7+**

41 c8♕ Xxc8 42 Xxc8 axb5 43 ♔f1 is more than sufficient, but this is already a question of taste.

**41...♔f6 42 ♘a7 c3 43 c8♕ Xxc8 44 ♘xc8 b5 45 Xc7 b4 46 Xc4 a5 47 ♘a7 1-0**

## Game 24
## Hikaru Nakamura – Alexander Shabalov
### USA Ch, Stillwater (Oklahoma) 2007

**1 e4 ♘f6 2 e5 ♘d5 3 c4 ♘b6 4 d4 d6 5 exd6 cxd6** *(D)*

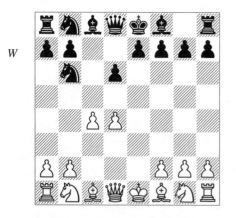

The recapture with this pawn is the most natural continuation, if we base the assessment on such factors as presence in the centre. In a sense it is the recapture that screams out to be played, and the one most in harmony with the unbalancing, counterattacking spirit of the Alekhine as a whole. Its loss of popularity in the last decade in comparison with the relatively sterile recapture with the e-pawn can be attributed to White's successes with certain specific move-orders that severely restrict Black's counterplay, most notably the Voronezh Variation, in which White plays ♘c3, ♗e3, Xc1 and b3, presenting Black with very little to bite on.

So why might this natural move not be so ideal for Black? First of all, he will need to spend an extra tempo developing his king's bishop, which is generally accomplished by a fianchetto. This in turn may leave the e-pawn a little sensitive on e7, and like in the Dragon Sicilian, if this pawn advances, then it leaves a possible sore point in a backward pawn on d6.

White has plenty of logical continuations from the position after 5...cxd6, many of them with detailed theory that hasn't changed a great deal in recent years. Here we shall focus on the most commonly employed and promising setups that are topical today. Note that the line 6 ♘f3 ♗g4 with a subsequent ...e6 and ...♗e7 was examined in Game 14; it occurs much more often via the 4 ♘f3 ♗g4 move-order and has every right to be listed there.

There is another set-up where the f8-bishop develops into the centre; it occurs when White attempts to crystallize his space advantage and fix the e7-pawn immediately by 6 d5 *(D)*.

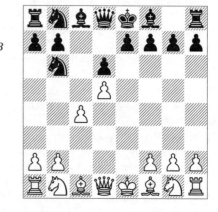

Now the idea of 7 ♕d4 hinders the standard fianchetto plan with 6...g6. On the other hand, Black can solve the problem of the e7-pawn at once by choosing between 6...e6 and 6...e5. Since so far White has played only pawn moves, he is not developed enough to exchange on e6 and take advantage of the d6-pawn's weakness, and one of the typical opening formations appears: 6...e6 7 ♘c3 (7 a4 exd5 8 cxd5 ♗e7 9 a5 ♘6d7 10 ♘f3 was an interesting new approach in Shirov-Degraeve, Bundesliga 2009/10) 7...♗e7 8 ♗d3 0-0 9 ♘ge2 ♘a6 10 a3 ♘c5 11 ♗c2 a5 12 ♗e3 exd5 13 cxd5, Dobosz-Zelčić, Austrian Team Ch 2006/7 or 6...e5 7 ♘c3 ♗e7 8 ♗d3 0-0 9 ♘ge2 f5 10 b3. In both lines White's chances are marginally preferable, yet Black's counterplay is also real.

However, as noted, a dominant feature of the Exchange Variation is the fianchetto of Black's dark-squared bishop. Thus a basic position arises after 6 ♘c3 g6 *(D)*.

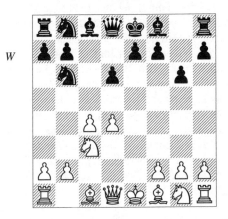

The set-ups that involve kingside development with h3 and ♘f3 or ♗d3 and ♘ge2 have gone out of fashion, and recent practice confirms that in these variations Black's chances are fully adequate:

a) 7 ♗d3 ♗g7 8 ♘ge2 0-0 9 ♗e3 (after 9 0-0, Black is well advised to avoid 9...♘c6?! 10 d5, and should choose between 9...e5 and 9...d5) 9...d5 10 c5 ♘6d7 11 0-0 ♘c6 12 ♕a4 e5 with plenty of counterplay, Abergel-Mirallès, French Team Ch 2006.

b) 7 h3 ♗g7 8 ♘f3 0-0 (a line of particular importance since it can arise by transposition from the Alburt Variation, 4 ♘f3 g6) and now:

b1) 9 ♗e3 ♘c6 10 ♖c1 e5 11 dxe5 dxe5 12 c5 ♘d7 13 ♗c4 and rather than the standard 13...♘d4, Black may have a better option in 13...♕a5!?; e.g., 14 a3 e4 15 ♘d2 ♘xc5 16 b4 ♕xa3 17 ♗xc5 ♗xc3 18 ♗xf8 ♔xf8 19 b5 ♘e5 20 0-0 ♗b2 (Chekhov).

b2) 9 ♗e2 ♘c6 10 0-0 ♗f5 11 ♗g5 (the even older line 11 ♗e3 d5 12 c5 ♘c4 13 ♗xc4 dxc4 14 ♕a4 e5! has not seen any major developments since Alburt's games in the 1980s) 11...h6 12 ♗e3 d5 13 c5 ♘c4 14 ♗c1 b6 15 b3 bxc5 16

bxc4 cxd4 17 ♘xd5 e6 18 ♗a3 ♖e8 19 ♘f4 e5 20 ♘d5 d3 21 ♗xd3 ♗xd3 22 ♕xd3 e4 23 ♕e3 exf3 24 ♕xf3 ♘e5 25 ♕b3 ♖b8 26 ♕a4 and now the new move 26...♘f3+! forced an immediate draw in Lukez-Gather, corr. 1999.

Today most games continue with 7 ♗e3 ♗g7 8 ♖c1 0-0. The rook overprotects the c3-knight and, indirectly, the c4-pawn, grants mobility to the pawns on b2 and d4, and itself is ready for various operations. The line 9 ♗e2 d5 10 c5 ♘c4 11 ♗xc4 dxc4 12 ♘ge2 ♗f5 is regarded as acceptable for Black, so the most accurate continuation is 9 b3 *(D)*, denying the knight the c4-square and impeding ...d5, which now simply loses a pawn.

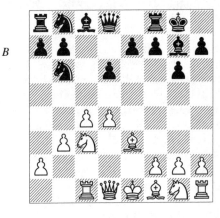

Black faces a major decision here. It is not easy to continue to aim for ...d5 – for that the bishop has to be brought out to f5, where it is more vulnerable, given the fianchetto structure, and where in the best scenario he will move with the loss of a tempo to g4 (if White permits) after the appearance of the knight on f3. Alternatively, Black can prepare the advance of the d-pawn with ...e6, but then the light-squared bishop's fate is even more depressing.

Black's main plans involve play in the centre, but there are also ideas based on making some initial moves on the flanks, seeking to strike in the centre later on with greater effect.

a) 9...a5 is the first of the 'side' plans. Black seeks to open the a-file and develop the a8-rook without moving it. After 10 ♘f3 ♘a6 11 ♗e2 a4 12 0-0 axb3 13 axb3 ♘b4 14 ♕d2, Black managed to carry out 14...d5 after all in Baklan-Varga, Romanian Team Ch, Tusnad 2005.

b) 9...f5 intends to make progress on the kingside: besides creating a direct threat to the d4-pawn it serves as an introduction to ...e5. Now 10 ♕d2 and 10 ♘ge2 look like concessions on White's part, so generally he chooses between 10 d5, 10 g3 and 10 ♘h3. The move 10 d5 defines a clear superiority in pawn-structure, but Black hopes to make up for this with his development advantage after 10...e5 11 dxe6 ♘c6 or even 10...f4 11 ♗d4 e5 12 dxe6 ♗xd4 13 ♕xd4 ♘c6. After the other two continuations the play develops similarly to the lines examined below; here is a fresh example: 10 ♘h3 ♘c6 11 d5 ♘e5 12 ♗e2 ♘bd7 13 0-0 ♘f6 14 f4 ♘f7, and strategically the position resembles the Leningrad Dutch, Fedorowicz-Shabalov, USA Ch, Tulsa 2008.

c) The developing 9...♘c6?! is the reply most in accordance with Black's traditional treatment of the Exchange Variation: Black first develops and will then decide whether to strike White's pawn-centre with either ...e5 or ...d5. However, it is exactly here where White's idea is shown to greatest effect. White does not play the pedestrian 10 ♘f3, which permits the development by 10...♗g4 in one move and ...d5 again appears on the agenda. White instead takes the opportunity to combine the deployment of his pieces with chasing Black's by 10 d5! ♘e5 11 ♗e2 (D).

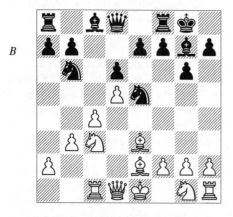

Here we see the benefit of White's overprotection of the c4-pawn and the c3-knight: Black has no meaningful counterplay against these standard targets, and the focus is immediately on the possibility of White kicking around the e5-knight.

However, the pawn-structure itself is known from other openings and quite often suits Black. His weakness – the e7-pawn – can be defended easily, whereas White's queenside pawns may turn out to be the more vulnerable if Black manages to carry out ...b5 advantageously. However, in this specific situation the inferior positions of Black's minor pieces spoil his chances; first, there are too many of them getting in each other's way: the transit square d7 is overloaded and the threat of f4 has to be constantly kept in mind; second, the knights' relocation is desirable but takes time. Let's get down to specifics:

c1) 11...♖e8 appears logical. If White now advances his f-pawn, Black will open the e-file, and his pressure along this file should counterbalance the resulting weaknesses. However, if White simply proceeds with his development, the rook move may remain 'mysterious', and in S.Petrosian-Degraeve, Cappelle la Grande 2007 an immediate counterattack failed to achieve anything: 12 ♘f3 ♘g4 13 ♗d4 ♗h6 14 ♘d2 ♘e5 15 0-0 f5 16 f4 ♘f7, with a general retreat.

c2) 11...f5 is another option. After 12 f4 ♘g4 13 ♗xg4 fxg4 14 ♘ge2 e5 15 dxe6 Black's bishop-pair and the g4-pawn that denies White the important f3-square serve as a consolation of sorts for the new weaknesses. However, Black's score in practice from this position has been somewhat depressing.

c3) Black can also try immediate manoeuvres by the knights with 11...♘ed7, followed by the transfer to f6, but, as has already been mentioned, this takes a lot of time, and simply 12 ♘f3 ♘f6 13 ♘d4 leaves White well on top.

d) 9...e5 is left as Black's most natural move. By 10 dxe5 dxe5 11 ♕xd8 ♖xd8 12 c5 ♘6d7 (D) (naturally not 12...♘d5? 13 ♖d1) White seeks the advantage in a queenless middlegame, where he has a mobile queenside majority.

This is a very important position from a theoretical perspective, because both sides have played the most natural and consistent moves available to them, and the position occurs virtually by force if Black chooses 9...e5. If Black is OK here, then the whole line isn't much of a threat, and the other options can be regarded as 'interesting ways to create imbalance'. If White is better here, then Black needs to make something else work. It seems that while great

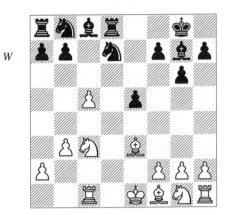

accuracy is demanded of Black, he can hope to equalize gradually, and the fact that he has been holding the position in top-level correspondence games augurs well. The following excerpts give a taste of the typical play: 13 ♗c4 ♘c6 14 ♘f3 (14 ♘e4 ♘a5 15 ♗b5 a6 16 ♗e2 h6 17 ♘f3 ♘c6 18 0-0 f5 19 ♘d6 e4 20 ♘d2 ♘d4 21 ♗c4+ ♔h7 22 b4 ♘c6 23 f3 ♘de5 24 fxe4 ♘g4 gave Black counterplay in T.Murray-Machycek, corr. World Ch 2007-9) 14...h6!? (or 14...♘a5 15 ♗e2 b6 16 ♘a4 bxc5 17 ♘xc5 ♘xc5 18 ♖xc5 e4, Pavasović-Shabalov, FIDE World Cup, Khanty-Mansiisk 2007) 15 ♘e4 (Black has little to complain about after 15 0-0 ♘f8 16 ♘e4 ♗e6 or 15 ♖d1 ♘f6 16 ♖xd8+ ♘xd8 17 0-0 ♘e8 18 ♘d2 ♗e6 19 f3 f5 20 ♖d1 ♔f7, Firnhaber-Machycek, corr. World Ch 2007-9) 15...♘a5 (15...♘f8?! 16 ♘d6 is considered good for White) 16 ♗d5 ♘f6 17 ♘xf6+ ♗xf6 and Black survived both 18 ♗e4 ♗g7 19 b4 ♘c6 20 b5 ♘b4 (de Almeida-Rain, corr. 2003) and 18 ♖d1 ♔g7 19 0-0 ♗d7 20 b4 ♗c6 (Stephan-Rain, corr. 2004).

**6 ♗e3**

Usually this amounts to a mere transposition of moves after 7 ♘c3.

**6...g6 7 d5 (D)**

However, this is another line of play altogether. Postponing d5 for one move (compared to the 6 d5 line examined above), White waited until Black played ...g6, after which an advance of the e-pawn became dubious because of the exchange on e6 followed by ♕d4, and is ready to offer the exchange of bishops immediately. If such a plan had only pluses, it would be everybody's choice. However, its minuses are evident as well: White falls behind in development

and the early queen sortie provides Black with extra tempi.

**7...♗g7**

7...♘8d7 is also possible, when Black can prevent the exchange by blocking the long diagonal. This had already occurred in a game featuring one of the same players, although there he had Black: 8 ♕d2 ♘f6 9 ♘c3 ♗d7 10 ♗d3 ♗g7 11 ♗d4 (in the new situation this is a questionable place for the bishop, since sooner or later it will come under attack; the exchange on h6 would also require a lot of time) 11...0-0 12 ♘ge2 e5 with double-edged play, Hess-Nakamura, Foxwoods 2007.

**8 ♗d4 ♗xd4 9 ♕xd4 0-0 10 h4 (D)**

This advance may look terrifying if one is not aware that Black had a great predecessor: 10 ♘c3 e5 11 ♕d2 f5 12 ♘f3 ♘8d7 13 0-0-0 ♕f6 14 ♕h6 ♕e7 15 ♖e1 e4 16 ♘d2 ♘e5, Suttles-Fischer, Palma de Mallorca Interzonal 1970. If the h4-pawn is not destined to advance further, it will only make castling kingside problematic.

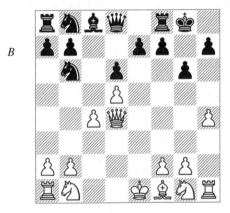

**10...e5 11 ♕d2**

Opening the centre while behind in development is, naturally, imprudent.

**11...f5 12 ♘f3 ♕f6 13 ♘c3 ♘a6 14 ♕h6**

White is not tempted by the prospect of changing the structure with 14 h5 e4 15 ♘d4 (there are insufficient grounds for a piece sacrifice) 15...g5.

**14...♕g7 15 ♕d2**

It's hard to tell whether White is testing Black's mood or is somewhat disappointed in his set-up and already doesn't mind a peaceful conclusion.

**15...h6 16 ♘b5 ♖f6 17 ♕a5** *(D)*

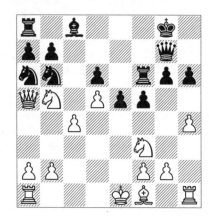

White attempts to create a diversion with a small force, but its outcome is doubtful. For the moment he keeps the knight away from c5 with the threat of the capture on d6 and menaces the a7-pawn.

**17...♘d7**

Here Black could try an interesting pawn sacrifice: 17...♗d7 18 ♘xa7 ♘a4 (definitely not 18...♘xc4? 19 ♗xc4 ♖xa7 20 ♕b6 ♖a8 21 ♕xb7). The text-move is logical though: the advantages of the e5-square for the knight are clear.

**18 ♕a3 ♕e7 19 ♗e2 e4 20 ♘d2**

It's debatable which square is preferable – this one or d4. White's choice is based on two considerations: in some lines it is useful to keep the e4-pawn under attack in order to hamper ...f4, while d4 is reserved for the other knight.

**20...♘e5 21 0-0-0**

There is no point in waiting for ...♘d3+, so it is time to decide which side is safer. After 21 0-0 ♗d7 22 ♘d4 ♖f7, as in the game, the initiative is with Black.

**21...♘c5 22 ♔b1 ♘cd3 23 ♗xd3 ♘xd3 24 ♖hf1 ♗d7 25 ♘d4 ♕e5 26 ♕c3 b5** *(D)*

Black opens lines on the queenside while undermining the d5-pawn's support.

**27 cxb5**

27 ♘xb5? is no good; after 27...♖b8 Black either gets through to the b2-pawn or ends up with an extra pawn in general or two in the active combat sector: 28 ♕xe5 dxe5 29 ♘b3 (the reply to 29 b3 is the same) 29...♗xb5 30 cxb5

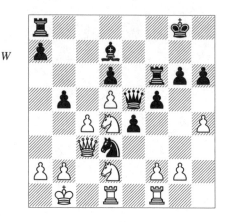

♖xb5. The flashy 27 ♘2f3 doesn't look tempting either, as the appearance of a black pawn on g2 doesn't improve White's mood.

**27...♖f7**

This mysterious move removes the rook from the line of possible attack by the queen, freeing Black's own queen, and covers the e7-square in advance, so as not to have to reckon with a knight fork on that square in some lines.

**28 f3 ♖c8 29 ♘c4?**

The variations arising after 29 ♘c6 ♕xc3 (or 29...♗xc6) 30 bxc3 e3 31 ♘c4 e2 32 ♘xd6 are complex, unclear and not easy to calculate with little time remaining before the control. The move actually played is simply bad and fails rather trivially.

**29...♕xd5 30 fxe4?! ♕xc4 31 ♕xd3 ♕xd3+ 32 ♖xd3 fxe4 33 ♖xf7 exd3 34 ♖f1?!**

34 ♖f2, intending to blockade the passed pawn on the d2-square, is more stubborn. Nevertheless, even then after 34...♖c4 35 ♘f3 d2 (or 35...♗xb5) 36 ♘xd2 ♖xh4 Black's extra pawn should bring him victory.

**34...♖c4 35 ♘c6 d2 36 ♘e7+ ♔g7 37 ♖d1 ♔f7 38 b3 ♖c1+ 0-1**

White's choice of the Exchange Variation noticeably restricts Black's aggressive ambitions. Even though the main lines are currently experiencing no crisis, the pattern of the struggle itself is changing, and Black has to spend some time defending accurately.

The recapture with the c-pawn leads to a more interesting game, but, as is often the case, at the cost of a greater strategic risk.

# 7 2 e5 ♘d5: 3 ♘c3 and Other Moves

In the position that arises after 1 e4 ♘f6 2 e5 ♘d5 we have so far considered variations that begin with 3 c4 or 3 d4. Of course, there are other continuations besides these two, and they are the topic of this short final chapter. Of the remaining moves, the most notable continuation is 3 ♘c3, allowing a weakening of White's pawn-structure in pursuit of other strategic aims.

After 3...♘xc3 4 bxc3 White aims to build a powerful pawn-centre. Game 25 (Zviagintsev-B.Savchenko) is devoted to this line.

4 dxc3 (the subject of Game 26, Sedlak-Spraggett) pursues different objectives. It opens a diagonal for the c1-bishop and the d-file for the queen, and White will strive to put his advantage in development and mobility to use to create an enduring initiative.

## Game 25
## Vadim Zviagintsev – Boris Savchenko
### *Russia Cup, Serpukhov 2007*

**1 e4 ♘f6 2 e5 ♘d5** *(D)*

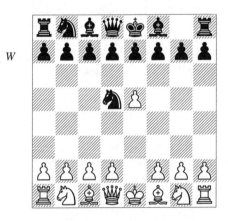

W

**3 ♘c3**

If White avoids moving the c- and d-pawns, this is his most common choice. Of the alternatives we shall mention the following:

a) 3 ♕f3 is not a move that will keep Alekhine players awake at night, but it is comforting to know that after 3...e6 4 ♗c4 ♘c6 5 ♗xd5 exd5 6 ♕xd5, Black has a choice between 6...♕g5, winning the pawn back, and 6...d6 with promising gambit play.

b) 3 b3 is mostly a curiosity, because then 3...g6 4 ♗b2 ♗g7 transposes to a line of the Nimzowitsch-Larsen Attack: 1 b3 g6 2 ♗b2 ♘f6 3 e4 ♗g7 4 e5 ♘d5. 3...c5 is also logical, and transposes to a sideline of the Sicilian.

c) 3 g3 cannot claim to refute the Alekhine, of course, but the bishop on the long diagonal is not a bad piece, though the price is a loss of time and White's ambitions in the centre. Much will depend on which player is more familiar with the subtleties of the resulting formation. Similar set-ups frequently arise in other openings as well, and there are more than a few fans of this restrained strategy. After 3...d6 4 exd6 all three methods of recapture are equally playable; e.g., 4...♕xd6 5 ♗g2 ♘c6 6 ♘c3 ♘xc3 7 bxc3 e5 8 d3 ♗e7 9 ♘e2 ♗e6 10 c4 ♕d7 11 ♖b1 0-0-0 12 0-0 ♗h3, T.L.Petrosian-Nakamura, Gibraltar 2008.

d) After 3 ♘f3, White can seek independent play only in the case of 3...d6 4 ♗c4, but normally it is only Black who gains useful extra options after 4...♘b6, if we don't count the trappy 5 ♗xf7+? ♔xf7 6 ♘g5+ ♔g8 7 ♕f3 ♕e8 8 e6, when 8...g6! is the only defence against the checkmate, but more than sufficient. After 5 ♗b3, Black can choose between 5...♗f5 (compare the 3 d4 d6 4 ♗c4 line), 5...d5 and 5...c5!?. Both 4...c6 and 4...dxe5 are also solid, and aim for set-ups that are already familiar to us, with transpositions to the New Main Line quite likely.

e) 3 ♗c4 is normally met by 3...♘b6. After 4 ♗b3 besides the traditional 4...d6 keeping to normal Alekhine plans, Black can close the position by 4...d5, but open the discussion as to whose bishop is worse in this case. There is also 4...c5 *(D)*:

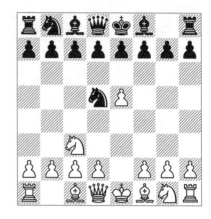

*B*

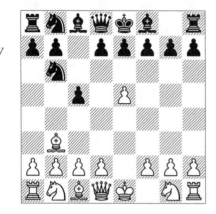

*W*

e1) 5 d3 (this modest advance is the theory-avoider's choice) 5...d5 6 exd6 e6 7 ♕g4 h5 8 ♕e2 ♘c6 9 ♘f3 ♗xd6 10 ♘c3 ♗d7 11 ♗e3 ♘a5 12 ♘e4 ♕c7 13 ♘xd6+ ♕xd6 14 ♘g5 (quite a trip to create a threat against the c5-pawn) 14...♗c6 and in Dzhumaev-Mamedyarov, Dubai 2004, the position of the knight on a5 provoked White into curious but unclear complications following 15 ♗xe6 fxe6 16 ♗d2.

e2) It is important to note that 5 c3 transposes to a rare line of the c3 Sicilian, viz. 1 e4 c5 2 c3 ♘f6 3 e5 ♘d5 4 ♗c4 ♘b6 5 ♗b3, but that this often moves into the heavily analysed modern main lines of that opening via 5...c4 6 ♗c2 ♘c6 7 ♘f3 or 5...♘c6 6 ♘f3.

We now return to 3 ♘c3 *(D)*:

In choosing the text-move, White hopes to prove that the exchange on c3 is rather to his advantage, despite the spoiling of his pawn-structure.

**3...♘xc3**

Again there are three traditional methods to decline the exchange:

a) 3...♘b6 retreats along the familiar route. White can credit himself with the centralization of the knight achieved by economical means: he has developed a piece and kept the f1-a6 diagonal open for the bishop and will fight for the

advantage by d4, ♘f3 and ♗f4, maintaining a presence on e5. White can continue the chase with 4 a4, though after 4...a5 it is not clear whose position is weakened more, while a gambler may be enticed with yet another version of the standard pawn sacrifice: 4...d6 5 a5 ♘6d7 6 e6. We should note that transpositions to the line 3 d4 d6 4 ♘f3 ♘b6 are very possible.

b) 3...c6 is a relatively rare method of supporting the knight. We shall note two reasons that explain this continuation's lack of popularity: after 4 ♘xd5 cxd5 5 d4 d6 6 f4 the absence of the c-pawn deprives Black of the traditional counterplay against the d4-pawn; alternatively, White can implement the same plan of building the centre without exchanging on d5, when if Black wishes to play the typical counter-thrust ...c5, it will come with loss of tempo.

c) 3...e6 is the continuation that Alekhine himself used to employ. This move has retained a reliable reputation; e.g., 4 ♘xd5 exd5 5 d4 d6 6 f4 dxe5 7 dxe5 ♗c5 8 ♘f3 ♘c6 9 ♗d3 0-0 10 ♕e2 f6 with fully-fledged counterplay, Macak-Baburin, British League (4NCL) 2005/6. However, 4 d4 may give White better chances, as the pawn on e6 gets in the way of the c8-bishop's development.

**4 bxc3** *(D)*

White recaptures 'by the rules' – toward the centre. He hopes to build an imposing pawn-wedge.

**4...d6**

An attractive alternative is 4...d5 (or first 4...c5). Black aims to reach a set-up well known from the French Winawer, but there are two substantial differences:

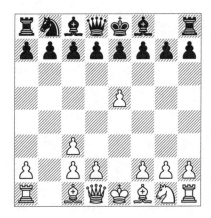

- A black knight (not the dark-squared bishop) was used in the exchange, and the g7-pawn (and, quite likely, later the dark squares as well) is not a chronic weakness. However, in closed positions the knight's value is also high.
- Black's light-squared bishop can still be developed outside the pawn-chain, thus relieving Black of the problem of finding gainful employment for it. However, in his new field of work he is destined either to be exchanged for the knight, leaving White with the bishop-pair, or to be a target for the advance of White's kingside pawns.

In practice, White normally seeks to disrupt Black's position before he can complete his development; e.g., 5 d4 c5 6 ♘f3 ♘c6 7 ♗e2 ♗g4 8 ♖b1!? (after 8 0-0 e6 9 ♖b1 both 9...♖b8 and 9...♕d7 are considered solid for Black) 8...♕d7 (8...♖b8?! 9 e6 ♗xe6 10 ♗f4 ♖c8 11 ♖xb7 c4 12 ♘g5 gave White the initiative in Baklan-Miroshnichenko, Alushta 1999) 9 c4 (White opens the centre without wasting time on h3 and all the same secures the bishop-pair) 9...dxc4 (9...cxd4 10 cxd5 ♕xd5 11 ♖xb7 a6 could be tried, while 9...e6 10 cxd5 exd5 is not out of the question either) 10 d5 ♗xf3 11 ♗xf3 ♘xe5 12 ♗e2, and the sacrifice of two pawns (one of them clearly temporary) allowed White to seize the initiative in Baklan-Almeida, Solsonès 2004. In the game, Black sought safety by 12...0-0-0 13 f4 ♘g6 14 0-0 e6 15 dxe6 ♕xd1 16 ♖xd1 ♖xd1+ 17 ♗xd1 fxe6, and a draw later resulted.

**5 f4** *(D)*

This is the move the centre-building project is founded upon. Both 5 ♘f3 and 5 exd6 are played sometimes, but the choice of these continuations is based on practical considerations as opposed to the search for an objective advantage. In the case of the exchange, the most logical recapture appears to be 5...cxd6, opening the c-file against the doubled pawns.

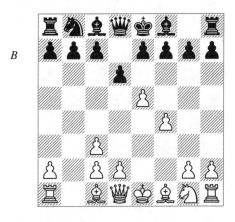

**5...♘c6?!**

Blocking the c-pawn does not fit into any development scheme that has been shown to be effective in this line.

Black has to decide on the order of the blockading and undermining actions. The most popular line is 5...g6. After the logical sequence 6 d4 ♗g7 7 ♘f3 0-0 8 ♗d3 c5 9 0-0 dxe5 10 fxe5 (Keres advocated 10 dxe5, seeking to reduce Black's counterplay at the cost of structure) 10...♘c6 11 ♗e3 ♗g4 12 ♗e4 ♕a5 13 ♕e1 ♖ad8 14 ♖d1 Black steals up to the base of the enemy fortification, but White's kingside attack may turn out to be dangerous.

With the play focused on the centre, Black would like to involve the c-pawn in upcoming operations at once (5...c5 or 5...dxe5 6 fxe5 c5), in order to undermine the d4-pawn's confidence and have the option of acquiring another half-open line. However, this takes time at a sensitive stage in the opening battle, which White can put to good use; e.g., 5...c5 6 d4 dxe5 7 fxe5 ♘c6 8 ♘f3 ♗g4 9 d5! ♗xf3 10 ♕xf3 ♘xe5 11 ♗b5+ ♘d7 12 0-0 f6 with a treacherous position for Black.

**6 d4 ♗f5?!** *(D)*

Inviting the d4-pawn to advance with gain of a tempo and hoping to take advantage of the weakening of its neighbour on e5. However, the whole plan of development with an early ...♗f5 is ineffective, as Keres indicated when he wrote

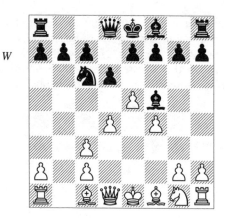

about the 3 ♘c3 line in his final theoretical article before his death in 1975.

**7 ♖b1**

White isn't tempted by the invitation and sticks to his development plan; as a result of Black's last move, the rook occupies its intended square and at the same time creates a threat.

**7...dxe5 8 fxe5 e6 9 ♘f3 ♘a5**

The threat to the b7-pawn has become serious, and Black chooses this way of defending it, counting on the knight's help in setting up a blockade on the c4-square. However, the position of the knight on a5 proves to be vulnerable. The line 9...♕d5 10 ♖b5 ♕xa2 11 ♖xb7 0-0-0 hardly looks better.

**10 ♗d3 ♕d5**

With the knight on a5, it is even riskier to exchange on d3, opening a path to a4 for the white queen.

**11 0-0 ♗e7**

To grab the a2-pawn, one must be either very brave or reckless.

**12 ♗g5 (D)**

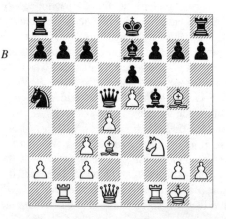

The exchange on f5 also leaves White with a solid advantage, but it won't run away, whereas the bishop maintains the threat of ♖b5. For now White prepares to use the half-open f-file.

**12...♗xd3**

Black picks the least of the evils and tries to cover the centre squares. After 12...♗xg5 13 ♘xg5 h6 14 ♗xf5 he has nothing better than 14...exf5, since 14...hxg5? 15 ♗d3 leaves the black queen overloaded trying to cover a5, g5 and f7. In case of the immediate 12...f6? 13 ♖b5 ♕xa2 14 exf6 gxf6 15 ♗xf5 exf5 (or 15...fxg5 16 ♕e2 followed by ♕e5) 16 ♕e1 Black cannot hold out for long.

**13 cxd3 f6 14 exf6 gxf6 15 ♕a4+ c6**

Naturally, 15...♘c6 16 ♖xb7 is no better.

**16 c4 ♕d7 17 ♗d2**

Here White had to decide which continuation simplified the realization of his advantage better: the one that occurred in the game or 17 ♕xa5 fxg5.

**17...b6 18 ♗xa5 bxa5 19 ♕xa5 0-0 (D)**

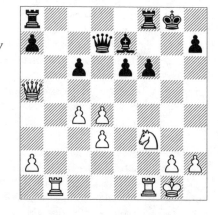

White has settled for an extra pawn, even though it seemed that he could lay claim to more. Of course, his advantage suffices for victory, and in such situations the main priority is to find a reliable way to win. His next target is the e6-pawn; in return Black has some slight chances of creating counterplay against White's unstable cluster of pawns in the centre.

**20 ♖b2 ♖ab8**

The immediate 20...c5 promises little: 21 ♖e2 cxd4 22 ♕e1 and now 22...e5? fails to 23 ♘xe5 fxe5 24 ♕g3+.

**21 ♖e2**

White simultaneously covers the second rank and prepares the queen transfer to g4 or h3.

**21...e5**

Black initiates complications, as another chance may never materialize.

**22 ♕e1 ♗b4 23 ♕g3+ ♔h8 24 dxe5 ♖g8?!**

Objectively, 24...♕xd3 25 exf6 ♖b7 is preferable, but Black will still be a solid pawn down after he captures White's f-pawn.

**25 ♕f2 ♕xd3 26 exf6!** *(D)*

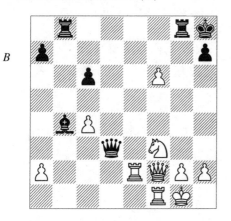

This is no blunder, of course; an experienced player doesn't need to calculate far ahead to see that the team of g5-knight and f6-pawn is in no way inferior to a rook. Moreover, having the initiative is more pleasant than defending.

**26...♗c5 27 ♖xc5 ♕xe2 28 ⟐g5 ♕h5 29 h4**

The choice of this continuation rather than 29 f7 ♕xg5 30 fxg8♕+ ♖xg8 31 ♕xc6 (which, of course, wins as well) is based on the desire to expose the enemy king still further.

**29...h6 30 f7 hxg5 31 ♕e5+ ♔h7 32 fxg8♕+ ♖xg8 33 c5**

It is clear that White has an easy win, not so much because of his extra pawn as thanks to the continuing attack, and there are several paths that lead to the goal.

**33...♕e8 34 ♕f5+ ♔h6 35 ♖d1 gxh4 36 ♖d6+ ♖g6 37 ♔h2**

A queen ending with a strong passed pawn on d6 suits White; after 37...♖xd6 38 cxd6 ♔g7 39 d7 ♕b8+ 40 ♔h1 ♕d8 41 ♕e6 ♔f8 42 ♕xc6 he achieves what he was striving for.

**37...♔g7 38 ♖d7+ ♔g8 39 ♖c7 ♕e6 40 ♖c8+ ♔h7 41 ♕h5+ ♖h6 42 ♖c7+ ♔h8 43 ♕g5 ♖h7 44 ♕d8+ ♕g8 45 ♖xh7+ 1-0**

## Game 26
# Nikola Sedlak – Kevin Spraggett
### *Vršac 2008*

**1 e4 ⟐f6 2 e5 ⟐d5 3 ⟐c3 ⟐xc3 4 dxc3** *(D)*

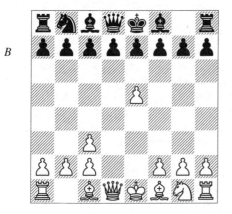

Recapturing away from the centre runs counter to general principles, and needs to be justified by concrete considerations. A glance at the position tells us that White is relying on rapid development to compensate for the structural defects. Although for the moment the opposing armies still occupy their back ranks, White already has three combat units ready to come into play, whereas their black counterparts need some preparatory work to be carried out first.

**4...d6** *(D)*

This is the most popular continuation, but not the only one; the pawn can pass by its rival with 4...d5. By avoiding conflict in the centre, Black stabilizes the position, and rather than seeking to seize the initiative in the short term, hopes in due course to exploit White's weaknesses on the c-file, although this may constitute no more than a slightly backward pawn by that stage. White will try to force Black to give up his dark-squared bishop for a white knight, and maybe straighten out his pawns by playing c4, and thanks to his bishop-pair hope to acquire an edge in the subsequent play.

4...g6 is also played sometimes, but it is not as soundly based. A standard attack according to the plan ♗f4, ♕d2, 0-0-0, ♗h6 and h4 (the order may vary), based on the advantage in development, promises to be more dangerous than usual.

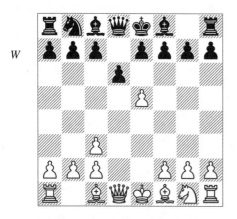

W

By playing his pawn to d6, Black formulates the main strategic idea: if this pawn and the white one on e5 are removed, Black's kingside pawn-majority will be superior to White's queenside majority. A similar idea serves as the basis of certain systems in the Ruy Lopez, except that there the plaintiff gets the bishop-pair as compensation, whereas here White is pinning his hopes solely on his advantage in development.

**5 ♘f3**

It is possible to delay the exchange by one move with 5 ♗c4, but after 5...♘c6 6 ♘f3 dxe5 7 ♕xd8+ ♘xd8 8 ♘xe5 the bishop's position aids Black in his quest for simplifications; e.g., 8...f6 9 ♘d3 ♗e6 10 ♗xe6 ♘xe6 11 ♗e3 g6 12 0-0-0 ♔f7, and after defending accurately Black may produce trumps of his own, Charbonneau-Nogueiras, North Bay 1999.

The other method of supporting the e5-pawn, 5 ♗f4, retains a strategic outline of the struggle that is similar to that of the continuation in the game, while adding certain lines and excluding others.

**5...dxe5**

The most straightforward continuation, allowing the loss of the right to castle. Instead, Black can increase the pressure on the e5-pawn by two obvious methods. The pin of the knight by 5...♗g4 may lead to the exchange of this bishop, or it may serve as an introduction to complications, as in the following game: 6 h3 ♗h5 7 e6 fxe6 8 ♗c4 ♕d7 9 ♕e2 ♗xf3 10 gxf3 d5 11 ♗d3 ♘c6 12 f4, Dzhumaev-Hoang Canh Huan, Vietnam 2008.

5...♘c6 (D), increasing the pressure and providing the queen with extra protection, is more natural and popular (Black's last two moves can also be played in reverse order).

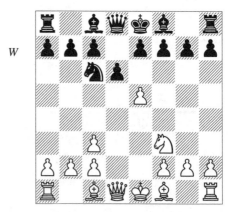

W

White has three options:

a) 6 ♗c4 is an indirect defence that we examined above via the move-order 5 ♗c4 ♘c6 6 ♘f3.

b) 6 ♗b5 pins the attacking knight. Then playing for simplification by 6...♗d7 7 ♕e2 dxe5 8 ♘xe5 ♘xe5 9 ♕xe5 f6 10 ♕e2 e5 offers good prospects of equalizing, while 6...a6 is also possible, going for a complex position with chances for both sides after 7 ♗xc6+ bxc6.

c) 6 ♗f4 supports the e5-pawn directly. In the lines where the tension is maintained after 6...♗g4 7 ♗b5 (it is possible to drive the bishop away to h5 at once with 7 h3, as 7...♗xf3 8 ♕xf3 dxe5 9 ♗a6 is bad for Black) 7...a6 8 ♗xc6+ bxc6 each side has his trumps: White has pressure along the centre files and prospects of a kingside attack, while Black has the bishop-pair plus the more compact pawn-formation. After the immediate capture by 6...dxe5 7 ♕xd8+ ♘xd8 8 ♗xe5 c6 9 0-0-0 f6 10 ♗g3 e5 11 ♗c4 Black, having lost the support of d6, experiences some difficulties with development and consolidation, although they don't appear to be insurmountable.

**6 ♛xd8+ ♚xd8 7 ᗌxe5** *(D)*

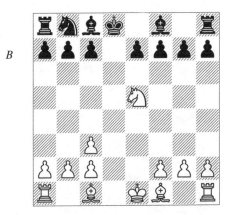

By choosing this line, Black agrees to suffer a little, hoping that with the queens off the board, White's initiative will gradually peter out and the kingside pawn-majority will remain. There are two ways to defend f7, but in practice placing the bishop on e6 occurs very rarely.

**7...♚e8**

Now that the king is back on e8, it is important for both players to bear in mind that Black has lost his castling rights, and to avoid analysing lines based on him escaping from the centre by castling. This sounds obvious, but there have been cases of well-known grandmasters citing variations that involve Black subsequently castling!

**8 ♝e3**

Black is behind in development but has no weaknesses. White has a little time to decide how to develop his initiative. It is not mandatory that this should be done by means of tempo-gaining threats; the most important factor is to make sure the initiative can be sustained. The obvious and most common continuation is 8 ♝c4, forcing 8...e6, but Black cannot complain about the results. For the moment, the text-move keeps the c4-square available to the knight as well; from that square it may attack the enemy bishop's post on d6. The outwardly more active 8 ♝f4 presents Black with a tempo for ...f6 and ...e5.

**8...e6**

8...ᗌd7 looks more logical, intending after 9 ᗌc4 to continue chasing the knight by offering to exchange with 9...ᗌb6. Erecting a barrier with 8...f6 and a subsequent ...e5 presents

White with an opportunity to play f4, in order to open the centre and initiate play against the black king that is stuck there.

**9 0-0-0 ᗌd7 10 ♝b5** *(D)*

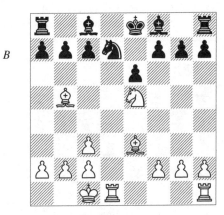

White attempts to force 10...c6, in order to deprive Black's dark-squared bishop of the d6-square and to restrict its light-squared colleague for a while. However, it is not clear how serious his achievements are after 11 ᗌxd7 (11 ᗌxc6 a6 12 ♝a4 bxc6 13 ♝xc6 ♖b8 favours Black) 11...♝xd7, when 12 ♝c4 halts the e6-pawn but allows 12...c5 and a subsequent ...♝c6, while 12 ♝e2 is met by 12...e5.

**10...♝d6 11 ᗌc4 ♚e7**

After 11...a6 12 ♝xd7+ ♚xd7 13 ᗌxd6+ cxd6 14 ♖xd6 ♝c6 15 f3 ♖d8 Black's drawing chances are considerable, but for now he has no reason to go for such lines. After 11...♝e7 the knight moves to another attractive post: 12 ᗌa5. The text-move offers another target for attack – a pawn on d6.

**12 ♖d2 ᗌf6 13 ♖hd1** *(D)*

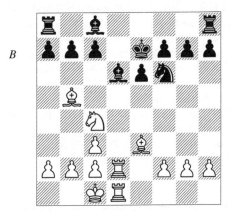

**13...♘d5**

13...♖d8 is not prudent as it ties the rook down to the defence of the squares on the d-file. After 14 ♘xd6 cxd6 15 ♗f4 White has real prospects of exploiting the pinned state of the d6-pawn, while if it advances then c4 rids White of the defects in his pawn-structure while the bishop-pair remains.

**14 ♘xd6 cxd6** *(D)*

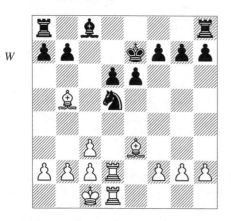

**15 c4?!**

White overestimates the outcome of his chosen line. The bishop-pair deserves a more careful treatment: 15 ♗d4! retains the possibility of strengthening the position further; e.g., 15...f6 16 c4 ♘c7 17 ♗a4 ♗d7 18 ♗xd7 ♔xd7 19 ♗e3 ♘e8 20 ♗c5 or 15...♘c7 16 ♗e2 ♘e8 (after 16...e5 17 ♗e3 d5 the prospects of maintaining the pawn-centre are slim, given White's options of c4 and f4) 17 ♗f3, and it is hard for Black to complete his development.

**15...♘xe3 16 fxe3 a6 17 ♗a4 b5 18 cxb5 axb5 19 ♗xb5 ♖xa2 20 ♔b1 ♖a5**

Among other changes, the long forced sequence helped Black develop a rook and prepare the deployment of the rest of his pieces. White's remaining assets – the passed b-pawn and Black's weakness on d6 – promise no advantage.

**21 c4 ♗b7** *(D)*

If Black wished, he could have rid himself of the weakness by playing 21...d5. In the line 22 b4 ♖a7 (riskier is 22...♖a3?! 23 ♔b2 ♖xe3 24 ♖a1, with a dangerous initiative to White) 23 cxd5 exd5 24 ♖xd5 ♗b7 25 ♖c5 ♗e6 26 ♖dc1 ♖hb8 27 ♖c7+ ♖xc7 28 ♖xc7+ ♔d6 White's most prudent course is to keep checking on c6

and c7. However, Black need not force a draw, as his chances are not worse.

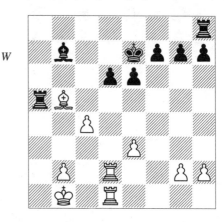

**22 ♔c2**

Clearly, the d6-pawn is taboo: 22 ♖xd6?? ♗e4+ 23 ♔c1? ♖a1+.

**22...♖c8 23 ♔b3**

The king sortie helps Black's counterplay more than it helps the passed pawn.

**23...d5?**

This is a poor choice that allows White not only to get rid of a potential weakness on e3 but even to use it in the fight for the initiative. 23...♖d8 is preferable, allowing the bishop through to e4 before advancing the d-pawn, and meanwhile spending a move on the defence.

**24 ♔b4 ♖aa8 25 e4 ♖ab8 26 exd5 exd5** *(D)*

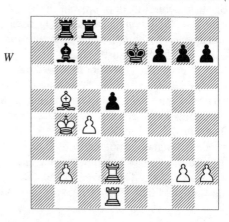

**27 b3**

27 cxd5 ♗a6 28 d6+ ♔d8 29 ♖d5 ♗xb5 30 ♖xb5 ♖xb5+ 31 ♔xb5 ♖b8+ leads to a draw, while a sharp and unclear endgame arises after

27 ♖xd5 ♝xd5 28 ♖xd5; the passed pawn duo may become a decisive factor, but here it is not easy to restore its mobility.

**27...dxc4?!**

Black could have done without this exchange, which grants the white rooks more freedom; perhaps he didn't want to have to watch out constantly for the exchange sacrifice on d5.

**28 bxc4 ♝c6 29 ♖e1+ ♔f8 30 ♖e5 g6** *(D)*

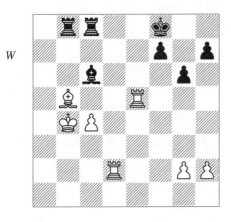

**31 ♖c5**

The white pieces have got bogged down, and to strengthen the position he needs to apply enough pressure on c6 to force Black to make a decision. Black understands that the passed pawn will sooner or later cost him the bishop and pins his hopes on the limited material remaining.

**31...h5 32 h4 ♔e7 33 g3 ♔f8?!**

A strange decision. Black could have held his ground by playing one of the rooks to his second rank.

**34 ♖d6 ♝g2 35 ♖xc8+ ♖xc8 36 c5 ♖b8?**

And this loses. 36...♔e7 was the obvious move.

**37 ♖b6 ♖d8 38 c6 ♖d4+** *(D)*

**39 ♔c5?**

A move in the wrong direction and one that presents Black with the opportunity to give up the bishop for the passed pawn and the time to latch on to g3. 39 ♔a5 was correct, when after the immediate capture on c6 White succeeds in

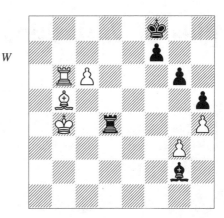

defending his kingside in time, while if the pawn is allowed to make a step forward, then in lines like 39...♔g7 40 c7 ♝h3 41 ♖b8 ♖d1 42 ♖d8 the future queen will no longer acquiesce to giving up its life for the bishop.

**39...♖d5+ 40 ♔c4?** *(D)*

There was still time to return to the correct path by 40 ♔b4.

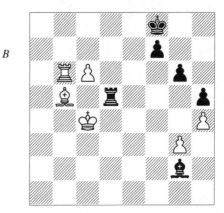

**40...♖d1 41 ♖b8+ ♔g7 42 ♔c5 ♖c1+ 43 ♔b6 ♝xc6 44 ♝xc6 ½-½**

Sidelines such as these cannot challenge our opening's right to exist, but because they are less well-studied, they present a fertile field in the search for new possibilities, while close familiarity with their ideas and subtleties promises pleasant returns in the tournament table.

# Index of Variations

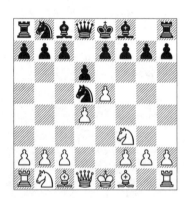
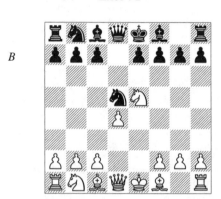

4 f4 *83*
4 ♗c4 *83*

| **4** | **...** | **♘b6** |
|---|---|---|
| **5** | **f4** *42* | |

Or **5 exd6** *103*:

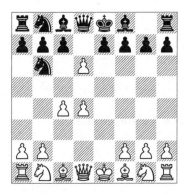

*B*

a) 5...exd6 *104* 6 ♘c3 ♗e7 *103* (6...♘c6 *108*):
a1) 7 ♕f3 *104*
a2) 7 ♗e2 *105*
a3) 7 h3 *104*
a4) 7 ♗d3 *108*
b) 5...cxd6 *112*

| **5** | **...** | **dxe5** |
|---|---|---|

5...♗f5 *43*
5...g6 *43*
5...c5?! *43*
5...g5?! *43*

| **6** | **fxe5** | |
|---|---|---|

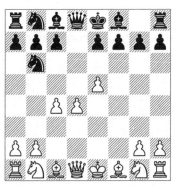

*B*

| **6** | **...** | **♘c6** *52* |
|---|---|---|

6...c5 *43*
6...♗f5 *48*

| **7** | **♗e3** | **♗f5** |
|---|---|---|
| **8** | **♘c3** | **e6** |
| **9** | **♘f3** | |

9 ♗e2 *53* 9...♗e7 10 ♘f3 *57*

Now (after 9 ♘f3):
9...♗b4 *53*
9...♘b4 *53*
9...♕d7 *54*
9...♗g4 *53*
9...♗e7 *57*

## C)

| **1** | **e4** | **♘f6** *7* |
|---|---|---|

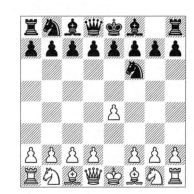

*W*

| **2** | **e5** | |
|---|---|---|

2 d3 *7*
**2 ♘c3** *11* 2...d5 *11*:
a) 3 exd5 *12*
b) 3 e5 *15*:
b1) 3...d4 *15*
b2) 3...♘e4 *19*
b3) 3...♘fd7 *23*

| **2** | **...** | **♘d5** *117* |
|---|---|---|

2...♘e4?! *28*

| **3** | **c4** *28* | |
|---|---|---|

3 ♕f3 *117*
3 b3 *117*
3 g3 *117*
3 ♘f3 *117*
3 ♗c4 *118*
**3 ♘c3** *117* 3...♘xc3 *118*:
a) 4 bxc3 *118*
b) 4 dxc3 *121*

| **3** | **...** | **♘b6** *28* |
|---|---|---|
| **4** | **c5** | |

4 d4 d6 – *see 3 d4 d6 4 c4 ♘b6*

| **4** | **...** | **♘d5** *29* |
|---|---|---|
| **5** | **♗c4** *33* | |

5 ♘c3 *29* (5...e6 6 ♗c4 *33*; 5...c6 6 ♗c4 *37*)
Now (after 5 ♗c4):
5...e6 *33*
5...c6 *37*

# Other Books from Gambit Publications

## Understanding Chess Endgames
*John Nunn*
"Each two-page spread has four to six diagrams so it is suitable for reading without recourse to a board. It is admirably clear and attractively presented." – John Saunders, BRITISH CHESS MAGAZINE
*232 pages, 248 x 172 mm; $24.95 / £15.99*

## Instructive Modern Chess Masterpieces – new enlarged edition
*Igor Stohl*
"The first printing won the United States award for Best Chess Book, and this new expanded edition maintains the same standards ... there are more than 400 pages, with 62 games analyzed in detail" – Bab Wilders, NEDERLANDS DAGBLAD
*448 pages, 248 x 172 mm; $34.95 / £17.99*

## Grandmaster Secrets: Counterattack!
*Zenon Franco*
"...consists of much more than just classic games. It's a guide to all possible ways of countering an attack, such as simplification and prophylaxis, logically ordered by theme, each followed by lots of good exercises" – Arne Moll, CHESSVIBES
*240 pages, 248 x 172 mm; $29.95 / £14.99*

## Mastering the Chess Openings Volume 2
*John Watson*
"The book has convinced me entirely! Watson has managed to present the most important openings after 1 d4 and analyses them in detail as well as explaining the backgrounds. It may sound exaggerated, but I believe Watson is a sort of modern Aron Nimzowitsch" – Martin Rieger, FREECHESS
*320 pages, 248 x 172 mm; $29.95 / £19.99*

## Understanding the King's Indian
*Mikhail Golubev*
"Golubev has not written often, but his contributions to sharp opening theory have not been overlooked ... his lifelong account of his King's Indian practice is well-worth the small investment. A great opening book..." – Lou Mercuri, CHESS HORIZONS
*208 pages, 248 x 172 mm; $27.50 / £15.99*

## Win with the Stonewall Dutch
*Sverre Johnsen, Ivar Bern, Simen Agdestein*
"...won me over with its flowing, enjoyable prose, its detailed descriptions of the plans for both sides, its historic discussions, its simple but logical layout which makes it easy to find anything and everything, and its lesson overviews and summaries, which make sure you understand the ideas it's trying to impart" – IM Jeremy Silman, JEREMYSILMAN.COM
*224 pages, 248 x 172 mm; $29.95 / £14.99*

## Secrets of Positional Chess
*Dražen Marović*
"A feast of instructive examples, including demonstrations of power and co-ordination among pieces and pawns" – GM Paul Motwani, THE SCOTSMAN
*224 pages, 248 x 172 mm; $23.95 / £16.99*

## Understanding the Chess Openings
*Sam Collins*
"To create an overview of all the main openings and their ideas is not an easy task ... it seems to me that Collins has achieved it splendidly. The explanations are clear and lucid with just enough variations to give readers a reasonable base..." – Jean Hébert, AU NOM DU ROI
*224 pages, 248 x 172 mm; $28.95 / £16.99*

**About the Publisher:** Gambit is a specialist publishing company, owned and run exclusively by chess masters and grandmasters. Chess is our subject, and we work with our authors to produce books of the highest quality. We are passionate about producing innovative and instructive chess books, suitable for all levels of player.

www.gambitbooks.com